S0-ACM-072

Bloom's Modern Critical Views

Bloom's Modern Critical Views

RALPH ELLISON
New Edition

Edited and with an introduction by
Harold Bloom
Sterling Professor of the Humanities
Yale University

BLOOM'S
LITERARY CRITICISM
An imprint of Infobase Publishing

Bloom's Modern Critical Views: Ralph Ellison—New Edition

Copyright © 2010 by Infobase Publishing
Introduction © 2010 by Harold Bloom

All rights reserved. No part of this publication may be reproduced or utilized in any form or by any means, electronic or mechanical, including photocopying, recording, or by any information storage or retrieval systems, without permission in writing from the publisher. For more information contact:

Bloom's Literary Criticism
An imprint of Infobase Publishing
132 West 31st Street
New York NY 10001

Library of Congress Cataloging-in-Publication Data
Ralph Ellison / edited and with an introduction by Harold Bloom.—New ed.
   p. cm.—(Bloom's Modern Critical Views)
   Includes bibliographical references and index.
   ISBN 978-1-60413-578-7 (hardcover: alk. paper)
   1. Ralph Ellison—Criticism and interpretation.   2. African Americans in literature.
   I. Bloom, Harold.
   PS3555.L625Z872 2009
   813'.54—dc22   2009008055

Bloom's Literary Criticism books are available at special discounts when purchased in bulk quantities for businesses, associations, institutions, or sales promotions. Please call our Special Sales Department in New York at (212)967-8800 or (800)322-8755.

You can find Chelsea House on the World Wide Web at
http://www.chelseahouse.com

Contributing editor: Pamela Loos
Cover designed by Takeshi Takahashi

Printed in the United States of America
IBT IBT 10 9 8 7 6 5 4 3 2 1

This book is printed on acid-free paper.

All links and Web addresses were checked and verified to be correct at the time of publication. Because of the dynamic nature of the Web, some addresses and links may have changed since publication and may no longer be valid.

Contents

Editor's Note

My Introduction, written in 1997, emphasizes both the uniqueness of Ellison's great novel, and his immense conviction, decades later, that its eminence had isolated him from other African American writers.

Alan Nadel sees Tod Clifton as a contradictory Christ figure, since violence is crucial to him, while Andrew Hoeberek contextualizes *Invisible Man* in American economic history.

The learned Morris Dickstein (the first Ph.D. I ever supervised) rightly praises Ellison for representing "the triumph of the center, the victory of moderation". One could say that Ellison prophesied the triumph of Barack Obama, who would have fascinated him.

Ellison, named for Emerson and a close friend of Kenneth Burke, is compared to them as apostles of an individualistic ethos by James M. Albrecht, whose essay seems to me illuminating and comprehensive.

The Trueblood blues-singing interlude is set within the novel's frame by Bertram D. Ashe, who demonstrates anew *Invisible Man*'s intricate design.

The invisible man himself is judged to be a sermon-influenced narrator by H. William Rice, after which Christopher Hanlon accurately assesses the relation between the eloquence of the two Ralph Waldo's—Emerson and Ellison.

Invisible Man's revisions of African American desires for "home" are analyzed by Valerie Sweeney Prince, after which Tuire Valkeakari brings together Ellison's false Messiahs: the Founder, Norton, Ras, Rinehart, Clifton, all of them variants of the way not to go.

The final three essays turn to Ellison's other writings. Robert Penn Warren reviews the essay collection *Shadow and Act*; Joseph F. Trimmer explicates the short story "Flying Home"; and Sanford Pinsker discusses the posthumously published *Juneteenth*.

HAROLD BLOOM

Introduction

Invisible Man reads as freshly and strongly today as it ever did. Most American novels of the last 50 or 60 years are already period pieces; very few have joined the major works of Dreiser, Faulkner, Hemingway, Fitzgerald, and Cather as classic American fictions. *Invisible Man* is indisputably one of those few, together with Thomas Pynchon's *The Crying of Lot 49* and *Gravity's Rainbow*, Cormac McCarthy's *Blood Meridian*, Don DeLillo's massive *Underworld*, Vladimir Nabokov's *Pale Fire*, Philip Roth's *Zuckerman Bound*, and one or two others. There is an intensity and vividness throughout *Invisible Man* that allies it to Faulkner's *As I Lay Dying* and Nathanael West's *Miss Lonelyhearts*. Faulkner in particular is Ellison's prime American precursor, as he is also for Toni Morrison, the principal African-American novelist since Ellison. Like Faulkner, Ellison had a stylistic debt to Joyce. There is also a Kafkan strand to *Invisible Man*, particularly evident in the novel's irrealistic elements, including its curious comic effects. For all this, *Invisible Man* remains a refreshingly original work, carefully controlling its Biblical allusions (particularly to the Book of Jonah) and its stance in relation to previous American fiction, from Melville through Mark Twain to Faulkner.

Invisible Man is astonishingly rich in its textures, overtones, and undersongs; in a profound sense it is akin to jazz, the African-American art in which Ellison was profoundly immersed. Berndt Ostendorf, a German scholar both of jazz history and of African-American literature, subtly finds Ellison's structural and thematic reliance upon jazz to be the novelist's attempt to reconcile his high aesthetic modernism with African-American folk culture. The greatest figures in jazz tradition—Louis Armstrong and Charlie Parker—mediate

1

T.S. Eliot, Joyce, Faulkner, and Kafka for Ellison. A novelist born in Oklahoma City in 1914 necessarily became aware of American literature from Emerson through Eliot, and as an African American similarly developed an early awareness that jazz was the uniquely American art form, blending an African base with European influences much as Walt Whitman fused the American language with Western poetic and prophetic tradition. Ostendorf, in my judgment, joins the late Kenneth Burke as Ellison's most useful critic to date. Burke, the finest American critic since Emerson, emphasized that *Invisible Man* constantly *remade its epoch*, and never merely reflected the age. The truth of Burke's insight is reaffirmed by Ostendorf's tactful account of African-American nationalist resistance to Ellison's achievement. No one who knew Ellison could fail to be aware of his scorn for mindlessness, whether it emanated from whites or blacks, past or present. The aesthetic eminence of *Invisible Man* isolated Ellison, who nevertheless refused Richard Wright's and James Baldwin's self-exiles, and remained in a country where he suffered the experience of having many more white than African-American admirers. He once told me that he sadly agreed with my melancholy conclusion that the poetry of Langston Hughes was overesteemed, but also chided me for admiring Zora Neale Hurston's *Their Eyes Were Watching God*, which he judged to be more improvised than written. A critical stance as uncompromising as Ellison's cost him a great deal, and certainly was one of the factors that kept him from publishing a second major novel in his lifetime. Ellison was highly conscious that he had joined Armstrong and Parker as an artist of the highest order, and he refused to descend below that extraordinary eminence.

It is difficult, only three years after Ellison's death, to reread *Invisible Man* without experiencing a sadness that in one sense is wholly external to the novel's exuberance, since the nameless narrator prophesies for himself a world of "infinite possibilities:"

> Yes, but what *is* the next phase? How often have I tried to find it! Over and over again I've gone up above to seek it out. For, like almost everyone else in our country, I started out with my share of optimism. I believed in hard work and progress and action, but now, after first being "for" society and then "against" it, I assign myself no rank or any limit, and such an attitude is very much against the trend of the times. But my world has become one of infinite possibilities. What a phrase—still it's a good phrase and a good view of life, and a man shouldn't accept any other; that much I've learned underground. Until some gang succeeds in putting the world in a strait-jacket, its definition is possibility. Step outside the narrow borders of what men call reality and you step into chaos—

ask Rinehart, he's a master of it—or imagination. That too I've learned in the cellar, and not by deadening my sense of perception; I'm invisible, not blind.

The choice of stepping into chaos *or* imagination is Emersonian, even if, as an African American, Ellison sometimes was rueful about bearing Emerson's name (though I dispute the critic Kun Jong Lee's contention that Emerson was racist, that being unfair to the Concord Abolitionist, who should be judged, in this one regard, by the unhappy standards of his own day, and not by ours.) The Invisible Man indeed is a black Emersonian, which is a difference that makes a difference, but still has more in common with Emerson, than with T.S. Eliot or with Faulkner, or any other white American precursor. Emerson, when most himself, wrote as a universalist. Since his chief work was his endless journal, he did not always refrain from self-contradiction, but Ellison had a shrewd sense of what was deepest in Emerson, as did W.E.B. DuBois, who quarried from the Sage of Concord his fecund but dark sense of "double consciousness." *The Souls of Black Folk* seems to me to have the same relation to Emerson that *Invisible Man* achieves. DuBois and Ellison transform Emerson just as Whitman and Dickinson did; they transumptively triumph by making Emerson black, even as Whitman and Dickinson extended Emerson to poetic ends that sometimes fulfilled his implicit criteria, and sometimes reversed him, Whitman by an Epicurean materialism, and Dickinson by a skepticism so nihilistic as to go beyond even the abyss-worship of "Fate" in *The Conduct of Life*. Ellison, like DuBois, became more Emersonian than Emerson himself had been, once his earliest, most antinomian phase was over. DuBois translated an Emersonian asset into a dialectical burden, and DuBois's disciples have retranslated that burden into a pained and painful opportunity. Ellison's ironies can be sublimely difficult, and they make even contradictory readings of "infinite possibilities" equally possible. What Emerson himself called "the cost of confirmation" was tragically high for Ellison, but it gave him, and anyone capable of authentic reading, a great novel.

ALAN NADEL

Tod Clifton: Spiritual and Carnal

I want to approach *Invisible Man* by asking a simple question: who is Tod Clifton? Perhaps the simplest answer is "a character in *Invisible Man.*" That answer, like any other answer, as simple as it may be, implies assumptions. The first, of course, is that I am asking a literary question. Otherwise, the answer might come from a Who's Who directory, a phone book, or the FBI files. The first assumption, then, is a necessary context, without which the question is meaningless. That context is implied by the question's appearance here, in a book of literary criticism focused on *Invisible Man*. Given that necessary context, however, the answer seems trivial. Recognizing the context thus creates expectations about the sufficiency of the answer, expectations the answer I gave leaves unfulfilled.

A more fulfilling answer might go on to say that Clifton appears in the last third of the novel. He works for the Brotherhood as Harlem director of youth and he befriends the invisible man, who has become the Brotherhood's newly appointed Harlem organizer. Together they plan a campaign against evictions which includes street-corner speeches. At one rally they are accosted by black separatists led by Ras the Exhorter. In the fighting, Ras has the opportunity to kill Clifton but instead tearfully exhorts him to abandon the Brotherhood, where, Ras feels, he functions as the puppet of white masters. Clifton, angered, knocks Ras down and leaves. Some time after this event,

From *Invisible Criticism: Ralph Ellison and the American Canon.* © 1988 by the University of Iowa.

5

the Brotherhood transfers the invisible man out of Harlem, only to recall him when Clifton disappears. Clifton reappears in midtown, selling Sambo dolls. When a policeman repeatedly pushes Clifton while arresting him for illegal peddling, Clifton punches the policeman and is gunned down. The invisible man, who has witnessed the shooting, then organizes a public funeral for Clifton which precipitates riots in Harlem.

Is this outline of Clifton's actions a more sufficient answer? If so, rendered as it has been, with the flatness of a crib sheet, comic book, or opera program synopsis, it is hardly more interesting. One reason for its dullness is that I have attempted to omit any details which might suggest interpretation. I have tried to give, in other words, what Kermode would call a "carnal" reading, by which he means one hinting no secret meaning to Clifton's presence, no meaning which would be revealed through interpretation.

Next we can try to decide whether the text requires anything more than a carnal answer to the question of his identity. The first clue that it does is the inordinate repetition of Clifton's name. Although Clifton actually only appears in two chapters (three if we count his funeral), his name is mentioned in each of the nine chapters from the point of his introduction through the epilogue; in all, it is mentioned well over 150 times.[1] Clifton's behavior, moreover, leaves much to be explained. We know almost nothing about his origins; we don't know why he disappears or why he chooses to reappear selling Sambo dolls. Like the invisible man, we can only formulate assumptions to help answer our questions and thus interpret Clifton's behavior. The invisible man's search, of course, differs from our own in that he is still a character, like Clifton, created by a text. Yet from his limited position he replicates our hermeneutic enterprise (as he suggests in the final words of the epilogue: "Who knows but that, on the lower frequencies, I speak for you?").

Many critics, from their broader vantage, have attempted to complete the narrator's inquiries by supplying interpretations of Clifton's significance in the novel. Their interpretations, like all interpretation, result from trust in some system of beliefs outside the text which explains what the text does not.

Most critics attempt to explain the puzzle of Clifton's decision to sell Sambo dolls, which precipitates his death. The simplest explanation is that Clifton, in the words of Barbara Christian, "goes nuts" ("Ralph Ellison: A Critical Study," 363). Christian supports this interpretation by citing an earlier piece of the text in which Clifton states that "a man sometimes has to plunge outside history ... otherwise he might kill somebody, go nuts." Christian's pieces clearly fail to interlock with each other or with the other parts of the narrative. Clifton equates going nuts with killing somebody, not with being killed, and he sees plunging outside of history as the alternative to going nuts, not the consequence of it. The invisible man, too, regards Tod's actions as plunging outside of history, and Tod's decision to do that structures much of the invisible man's subsequent interpretation.

Kirst tells us that Clifton's behavior indicates that the invisible man's grandfather was wrong, that "aggression through compliance is a potentially self-destructive tool. It demands that one violate his inner nature; the virtual suicide of Tod Clifton is its logical outcome" ("A Langian Analysis of Blackness," 23). This interpretation is interesting in isolation, that is, if we choose to see the entire novel as a dream fantasy meant to help the invisible man decode his grandfather's initial injunction. If, however, we expect the parts of the novel to cohere in any other way, Kirst's explanation fails because it doesn't explain why Clifton, who has not heard the injunction and does not seem implicitly to be following it, should elect to convert himself into an emblem to solve someone else's riddle.

Others view Clifton as a victim of his own conscience and/or the white manipulators. For them his peddling of dolls represents an admission of guilt, or a spiritual or psychological death with self-destructive overtones.[2] Unclear about Clifton's motives, the interpreters reach no consensus about what his relationship to the dolls signifies. Some suggest that Clifton has come to accept the inevitable dehumanization and exploitation of blacks. Another adds that the dolls also symbolize the invisible man, dancing on Brother Jack's string.[3] These critics are failing to account, in their readings, for the string's being black, or they are failing to explain what in the text allows us to convert a picture of a black man (a very black man) manipulating a black-and-orange doll with a black string into a sign of white manipulation of blacks.

Eleanor Wilner focuses on that thread "that the narrator, like the white people whose vision he shared, had been always too blind to see—that black identity that threaded its way, hidden, through all the oppressed past, the possession of those picaresque black men who manipulated the mask of the slave, but never merged with it, men who were never entirely the captives of their historical role, and who kept pride alive against a better day" ("The Invisible Black Thread," 249). Attributing this meaning to the black string effectively discounts other interpretations, but it also renders Tod's actions, for Wilner, indecipherable, and she concludes that "there is no way to resolve the various roles Tod may play in this work since they tend to work against each other" (253), yet she does suggest that Tod might

> serve as a kind of *alter ego*, a man whose integrity leaves nothing out. It is Tod, not the narrator, who opposes Ras, but at the same time admits to being tempted by his emotionally releasing rage; and it is Tod who turns, as the last act of his life, against the authority which has always opposed and oppressed him. It is Tod, then, as has been

shown, who carries the black identity, and the human dilemma; he may be the vicarious bearer of the narrator's repressed identity, placed at a distance from himself, observed in the infinite way of the dimly comprehended inner truth, and destroyed in the very way that the narrator fears his emotions would destroy him. (256)

We need, then, a spiritual reading that will reconcile Wilner's insights about Clifton to the details in the text which, nevertheless, render him indecipherable to her. Jonathan Baumbach suggests the beginnings of one by identifying Tod as martyr-saint. In hawking the Sambo dolls, he asserts, "Clifton was not so much mocking the Brotherhood's attitude toward the Negro as he was parodying himself" (*The Landscape of Nightmare*, 81). Baumbach's argument implies that he understands the crucial quality of a "parody" is not its sameness to something else but its difference. Only through its differences can we tell parody from parallel, and yet, paradoxically, only by noting parallels can we begin to suspect that we are reading a parody. Jonathan Culler notes that "in calling something a parody we are specifying how it should be read … making the curious features of the parody intelligible" (*Structuralist Poetics*, 152). One key, then, to a coherent "spiritual" reading is the recognition of a generic structure, one which asks us to interpret not by trying to extend parallels but by trying to identify the ways in which we cannot. Baumbach focuses on the difference between Clifton's play and Jack's: "Clifton makes only *paper* Negroes dance; it is Jack and Tobitt who treat flesh-and-blood Negroes as if they were puppet Sambo dolls" (*The Landscape of Nightmare*, 83).

Similarly, Clifton's plunging outside history also acquires significance through the concept of parody. Clifton's ostensibly nonhistorical act is recorded in police records and in newspapers, and it effects riots similarly recorded in historical documents. His acts thus mock the Brotherhood's "history" in which his acts go unrecorded: "Deceived by the bogus historians of the Brotherhood, Clifton has 'plunged outside history,' though in punching the white policeman he demonstrated that he had not quite 'turned' his back! [Clifton] became a heckler of the Brotherhood, of the Negro, of the white man's treatment of the Negro, of himself, of the universe" (*The Landscape of Nightmare*, 81). Understanding the significance of Clifton's final scene, Baumbach views Clifton's death not as a self-destruction but as purposeful

sacrifice to a culpability too egregious to be redeemed in any other way, and, at the same time, a final gratuitous act of heroism. In giving himself up to be murdered, Clifton takes on the whole responsibility for the Brotherhood's betrayal of the Negro. If by his sacrifice he does not redeem the hero from his own culpability, he at least through his example sets the possibility of Brother _____'s redemption. (80)

With a nod to Baumbach and homage to Hermes, I would like to suggest my "spiritual" reading of the Clifton chapters.

* * *

The first thing that we learn about Tod Clifton is that he is not on time. The invisible man arrives at a meeting of the Brotherhood at which all are present except Brother Clifton.

> "Well," Brother Jack said, "you are on time. Very good, we favor precision in our leaders."
>
> "Brother, I shall always try to be on time," I said.
>
> "Here he is, Brothers and Sisters," he said, "your new spokesman. Now to begin. Are we all present?"
>
> "All except Brother Tod Clifton," someone said.
>
> His red hair jerked with surprise. "So?"
>
> "He'll be here," a young brother said. "We were working until three this morning."
>
> "Still, he should be on time—Very well," Brother Jack said, taking out a watch, "let us begin. I have only a little time here, but a little time is all that is needed. . . ." (273–74)

The numerous references to time which differentiate Tod from the invisible man might seem trivial in a "carnal" reading, but we already know that "time" is one of the keys to the narrator's hermeneutics. As he informed us in the prologue, "invisibility, let me explain, gives one a slightly different sense of time, you're never quite on the beat. Sometimes you're ahead and sometimes you're behind. Instead of the swift and imperceptible flowing of time, you are aware of its nodes, those points where time stands still or from which it leaps ahead, and you slip into the breaks and look around" (7). In the prologue, from the vantage of his invisibility, the narrator tells us, further, of the yokel who stepped inside the scientific boxer's sense of time, and of his own stepping inside Louis Armstrong's sense of time. Under the influence of a reefer, that musical time became historical time which itself subdivided into folk history, literary history (with echoes of Melville, Hawthorne, Poe, and Faulkner), and, finally, personal history. So Tod's not being on time—on the Brotherhood's time—prepares us for his contemplation of plunging outside, of history, his decision to do so, and even his emulation of the boxing yokel as he shifts out of his role as humiliated black peddler and transforms into a graceful, dancerlike boxer to step inside the policeman's sense of time.

This accentuated difference between Tod and the invisible man at the moment of their meeting, however, is also an accentuated similarity between Tod and the narrator, twenty years later, who also has plunged outside of the Brotherhood's time. By comparing Clifton's introduction with the narrator's, in other words, we can see Clifton is set up as something the invisible man will become. Other details underscore this suggestion. Clifton was about the same age as the invisible man and "was moving with an easy Negro stride out of the shadow and into the light" (274). That motion replicates the general motion of the invisible man from his preinvisible days to the time of the narration in a room covered with lights.

Tod differs from the ginger-colored invisible man, however, in that he is "very black," even though his description shows distinct signs of miscegenation:

> ... he possessed the chiseled, black-marble features sometimes found on statues in northern museums and alive in southern towns in which the white offspring of house children and the black offspring of yard children bear names, features and character traits as identical as the rifling of bullets fired from a common barrel. And now close up, leaning tall and relaxed, his arms outstretched stiffly upon the table, I saw the broad, taut span of his knuckles upon the dark grain of wood, the muscular, sweatered arms, the curving line of the chest rising to the easy pulsing of his throat, to the square, smooth chin, and saw a small X-shaped patch of adhesive upon the subtly blended, velvet-over-stone, granite-over-bone, Afro-Anglo-Saxon contour of his cheek. (274)

Tod seems to have acquired hybrid bone structure while retaining deeply black skin. He looks like an artist's ideal not of an African but of a uniquely Afro-American black—ideal in that he had infused American traits without diluting his blackness and without any unnaturalness, a point stressed by the reminder that "his head of Persian lamb's wool had never known a straightener" (277).

The other detail that suggests a secret in the text is the "X-shaped patch of adhesive" on Clifton's face. A few paragraphs later it is called the "cross of adhesive on the black skin." Clifton bears this cross as the result of his confrontation with Ras, and it foreshadows another confrontation, one which deeply troubles Tod. Keeping in mind Baumbach's view that Clifton's death is self-willed and sacrificial, when we see that physically he suggests some natural but impossible ideal at the same time as he foreshadows the path that the invisible man will follow and the enlightenment he will achieve, the cross gains significance. Taken together with the associations with the East (Persia) and the lamb, the cross seems to suggest that Tod is a Christ figure.

This tentative hypothesis, nevertheless, has problems, the most notable at first being Tod's proclivity toward violence, of which the cross is also a sign: it covers a wound he got in an encounter with Ras. When someone at the meeting warns, furthermore, that Ras "goes wild when he sees Black and white people together," Tod responds, "'We'll take care of that,' . . . touching his cheek" (276). Tod thus associates his wound and his cross with fighting Ras, as he had earlier with being late for the Brotherhood meeting. Tod's cross, in other words, signifies his difference from both Ras and the Brotherhood, each of whom tempt him in different ways.

Although we don't know how Tod was recruited into the Brotherhood, we do know how the invisible man was, and we do know that his initial interest arose from a need for money. Guilty about accepting Mary's support after his accident compensation money ran out, he decided to call Brother Jack, who had offered him a job as spokesman. At the meeting where the offer is made, Jack, whose red hair is often noted, appears very much a mysterious stranger: "There was something mysterious in the way he spoke, as though he had everything figured out—whatever he was talking about. Look at this very most certain white man, I thought. He didn't even realize that I was afraid and yet he spoke so confidently" (221–22). And Jack's offer to the invisible man echoes traditional Satanic appeals: "'You are wise to distrust me,' he said, 'You don't know who I am and you don't trust me. That's as it should be. But don't give up hope, because some day you will look me up on your own accord and it will be different, for then you'll be ready. Just call this number and ask for Brother Jack. You needn't give your name, just mention our conversation'" (222). When the invisible man responds, he is very rapidly taken to a party at a building named "Chthonian" (an "expensive-looking building in a strange part of the city" [277]), where the elevator moves "a mile a minute" (288) but leaves the invisible man uncertain "whether we had gone up or down" (228). The woman who greets them at the apartment door has an exotic perfume and "a clip of blazing diamonds on her dress." Jack's constantly pushing the invisible man forward adds to the onerous quality of the scene, which is underscored by a nightmarishly "uncanny sense of familiarity" (227).

> Then I was past, disturbed not so much by the close contact, as by the sense that I had somehow been through it all before. I couldn't decide if it were from watching some similar scene in the movies,

from books I'd read, or from some recurrent but deeply buried dream. Whatsoever, it was like entering a scene which, because of some devious circumstances, I had hitherto watched only from a distance. How could they have such an expensive place, I wondered. (228)

His pact concluded for the sum of $300 and the promise of $60 a week, the invisible man returns to Mary's and goes to sleep, preparing to leave the next day for his new quarters and new identity. Before falling asleep, he hears the clock tick "with empty urgency, as though trying to catch up with time. In the street a siren howled" (240). The clock in Mary's house thus seems out of synchronization with the world outside where the siren beckons, the world of Jack's watch and history which Tod, three years earlier, had entered, no doubt with similar promises of power and similar monetary rewards. The recruitment scene is indeed familiar in literature, film, nightmare, and, as well, in the experience of the invisible man's black brothers.

The similarity between Tod's relationship with Jack and his relationship with Ras becomes clearer when Ras tempts Tod. Although the scene has the same motifs as the invisible man's Chthonian initiation, it emphasizes power a great deal more than money. Both scenes, however, have a Satanic red cast over them—in the Chthonian apartment created by Jack's red hair and the "Italian-red draperies that fell in rich folds from the ceiling" (228), in the street confrontation created by the red neon "CHECKS CASHED HERE" sign, which glowed mysteriously over the whole scene (279–84).

Ras has the opportunity to kill Clifton but instead asks Clifton to join him: "I saw his face gleam with red-angry tears as he stood above Clifton with the still innocent knife and the tears red in the glow of the window sign. 'You *my* brother, mahn. Brothers are the same color; how the hell can you call these white men *brother?*'" (280). The word "brother" suggests Ras is vying with Jack, in an analogous way, for Tod's loyalties, and the word "hell" along with the red glow emphasizes the Satanic similarities. This emphasis gets even stronger when Ras refers to Tod as "a chief, a black King!" (281). Ras repeats this theme (" ... you wan the kings among men! ... I will do it now, I say, but something tell me, 'No, no! You might be killing your black King!'" [282], and the scene resembles one of Christ's temptations as the speech concludes with a reiterated exhortation for Tod to join Ras:

"So why don't you recognize your black duty, mahn, and come jine us?"

His chest was heaving and a note of pleading had come into the harsh voice. He was an exhorter, all right, and I was caught in the crude, insane eloquence of his plea. He stood there, awaiting an answer. And suddenly a big transport plane came low over the buildings and I looked up to see the firing of its engine, and we were all three silent, watching.

Suddenly the Exhorter shook his fist toward the plane and yelled "Hell with him, some day we have there too! Hell with him!"

He stood there, shaking his fist as the plane rattled the buildings in its powerful flight. Then it was gone and I looked about the unreal street. They were fighting far up the block in the dark now and we were alone. I looked at the Exhorter. I didn't know if I were angry or amazed. (282–83)

At this point the invisible man intervenes and, after they argue, Ras appears similar to a fire-spitting devil: "He spat angrily into the dark street. It flew pink in the red glow" (283).

Although we could interpret this scene to affirm our hypothesis that Clifton is a Christ figure, in so doing we would have to discount specific details that confound that reading. If the scene concludes with Tod's rejection of Ras' temptation, for example, it does so with violence. Tod rejects Ras as he does the policeman later, not with articulate refutation or ascetic restraint, but rather with a swift 180-degree turn: "And before I could answer Clifton spun in the dark and there was a crack and I saw Ras go down and Clifton breathing hard and Ras lying there in the street, a thick, black man with red tears in his face that caught the reflection of the CHECKS CASHED HERE sign" (284). Another problem with casting Ras as the devil is that Ras casts the invisible man in that same role, calling him "a reg'lar little black devil" (180). The invisible man is, moreover, an agent—a paid agent—of Brother Jack's Chthonian organization, working on Brother Jack's time.

After he strikes Ras, Tod seems perplexed, but the invisible man calls him away from his self-doubting or remorse:

And again, as Clifton looked gravely down he seemed to ask a silent question.

"Let's go," I said. "Let's go!"

We started away as the screams of sirens sounded, Clifton cursing quietly to himself. (284)

Clifton's questions thus remain silent as the sounds of sirens surround his self-cursed state. The invisible man, too, heard sirens when other members of the Brotherhood first noticed him at an impromptu street rally, just as he heard them again after he decided to join the Brotherhood. Because these lures to self-destruction surround the Brotherhood's temptations, the language of the text makes it hard for us to discount Ras' charge that the invisible man is a devil.

How then are we to interpret the conversation that follows this meeting?

"Where'd he get that name?" I said.

"He gave it to himself. I guess he did. Ras is a title of respect in the East. It's a wonder he didn't say something about 'Ethiopia stretching forth her wings,'" he said, mimicking Ras. "He makes it sound like the hood of a cobra fluttering. . . . I don't know . . . I don't know . . ."

"We'll have to watch him now," I said.

"Yes, we'd better," he said. "He won't stop fighting. . . . And thanks for getting rid of his knife."

"You didn't have to worry," I said. "He wouldn't kill his king."

He turned and looked at me as though he thought I might mean it; then he smiled.

"For a while there I thought I was gone," he said. As we headed for the district office I wondered what Brother Jack would say about the fight.

"We'll have to overpower him with organization," I said.

"We'll do that, all right. But it's on the inside that Ras is strong," Clifton said. "On the inside he's dangerous."

"He won't get on the inside," I said. "He'd consider himself a traitor."

"No," Clifton said, "he won't get on the inside. Did you hear how he was talking? Did you hear what he was saying?"

"I heard him, sure," I said.

"I don't know," he said. "I suppose sometimes a man has to plunge outside history . . ."

"What?"

"Plunge outside, turn his back. . . . Otherwise he might kill somebody, go nuts."

I didn't answer. Maybe he's right, I thought, and was suddenly very glad I had found Brotherhood. (284–85)

Ras here is compared to a snake, Tod to a king, and both Tod and the invisible man regard Ras in the kind of language used to caution against the devil. Ras, furthermore, had called the invisible man a mongoose—the natural predator of snakes—which would identify the invisible man as a disciple of Tod, affirming his need to ward off Ras' serpentine subversions. Tod, nevertheless, seems to reject the Brotherhood as well.

One can see why Wilner was confused about how to interpret Tod's role. As we build an hypothesis around some details in the text, others seem to undermine it. The first point to be made, however, is that allusions, like parodies, work not through their sameness but through their differences. So the first question we can raise is not whether Tod is a Christ figure, but rather, being identified with Christ through a number of signs in the text, how does he differ from the referent of the allusions? To put it another way, how is Ellison using Christ and Satan images?

We need to remember that the invisible man is not the narrator but a person whom the narrator has renounced or distanced himself from. The crucial difference between them is that the invisible man did not know how to interpret signs, did not know that in limiting his possibilities to other people's versions of reality, he was yielding up his identity. I do not think, moreover, that it would be an inappropriate pun, in this context, to call his ethnic identity his soul. The name that Tod knows him by, after all, was not the one his grandfather knew him by, but the one given to him when he accepted Jack's offer, by a white woman who drew it from an envelope kept in her bosom. Although he has given his soul, then, for money and the promise of power, as yet unable to read the signs, he remains unaware of the terms of the exchange. When the scene above concludes with an affirmation of faith in the Brotherhood, as though it were different from Ras' black Satan idolatry, the irony emerges out of the disparity between the invisible man's carnal reading and our spiritual one.

Yet Ras is no more astute than the invisible man. His entire offer to Tod was motivated by his belief that Tod was pure African. We know, however, that, although very black, Tod has Afro-Anglo-Saxon features. If the invisible man is blind to the Brotherhood's true composition, Ras is blind to Tod's; if the invisible man fails to see he is manipulated by whites, Ras fails to see he is manipulated by blackness. Both of them lure Tod for the wrong reasons, and just as Tod turned around to hit Ras, some time earlier he had also turned on and struck a white member of the Brotherhood (298). Tod thus seems to know and manifest what the narrator will learn—that, as he tells us in the prologue: "contradiction . . . is how the world moves: Not like an arrow, but a boomerang. (Beware of those who speak of the *spiral* of history; they are preparing the boomerang. Keep a steel helmet handy.) I know; I have been boomeranged across my head so much that I now can see the darkness of lightness" (5). In his turnabouts, then, we see another way in which Tod anticipates the invisible man's motion out of darkness into light.

If there is something messianic in this movement, however, it is still marked by violence. If Tod is a Christ figure in that he seems to discover and rebuff the temptations of a Satan figure, and in that his sacrificial death points the way to the invisible man's salvation, he seems more an anti-Christ in that his life is circumscribed by violence that he precipitates. To call Tod an anti-Christ, however, seems just as inappropriate as discounting or rationalizing his violence in order to call him a Christ figure.

The text captures us in an apparent interpretive paradox, resolved, I think, by accepting the contradictions and simply saying: Ellison's Christ is violent, not nonviolent. This approach takes us to a basic understanding of Ellison's use of allusion. His allusions almost always force us to reconsider the referent; although he gives us enough clues to suggest a specific secret (spiritual) reading, in considering the implications of that reading, we constantly find that we cannot take referents for granted; Ellison's text requires reinterpretation of the constants. In this case, Ellison is making us challenge or suspend our idea of Christ by finding a context in which our reading requires a coherent but different view of the figure. In a larger sense this becomes the direction of the whole book. The alluded-to becomes a network of tradition, the standard assumptions about which are both actively and tacitly challenged to make the reader aware of possibilities. For the purposes of forming a coherent spiritual reading of the Tod Clifton episodes, therefore, we have to entertain the possibility that the black Christ may be violent, or at least ask the question: under what circumstances, is Ellison suggesting, may the black Christ be violent?

Thinking about Tod's role also takes us to some important questions about keeping the faith and about betrayal, as these, too, are themes in the Christ myth challenged directly by our reading of Clifton's story. Ras and the Brotherhood both come to regard Tod as a betrayer, but they also come to regard the invisible man as one. At the same time that the Brotherhood believes he's betrayed them for not following orders, the people of Harlem believe that he's betrayed them by letting the Brotherhood order him elsewhere. After Tod's death, moreover, the invisible man feels betrayed by Tod, but he also considers himself Tod's betrayer. Since the Christ-myth allusions seem to highlight a motif of betrayal in the novel, the invisible black thread that Wilner identifies as the thread of tradition can also be seen as a thread of betrayal. The invisible man's grandfather, whom Wilner associates with the string, was after all a betrayer, "a traitor all my born days, a spy in the enemy's country ever since I give up my gun back in the Reconstruction" (13). "Live with your head in the lion's mouth" he advised the invisible man. "I want you to overcome 'em with yeses, undermine 'em with grins, agree 'em to death and destruction . . ." (13). Having heard his grandfather's advice, the invisible man always felt "guilty and uncomfortable" (14) when things went well for him:

When I was praised for my conduct I felt guilt that in some way I was really doing something that was against the wishes of the white folks, that if they had understood they would have desired me to act just the opposite, that I should have been sulky and mean and that would have been really what they wanted, even though they were fooled and thought they wanted me to act as I did. It made me afraid that some day they would look upon me as a traitor and I would be lost. (14)

Those feelings become a self-fulfilling prophecy. At the battle royal, the black boys in the ring consider him as much a traitor, when he takes the place of one of their friends, as the white townsfolk do when he accidentally says "social equality" in his speech instead of "social responsibility." Similarly, Bledsoe considers him a betrayer for bringing the white trustee, Mr. Norton, to the Golden Day, as much as the black vet at the Golden Day considers him one for identifying with Mr. Norton. At the Liberty Paints factory, the union fears he is a scab and Lucius Brockway fears he is a union man. Yet at the same time that he is considered a betrayer, he feels betrayed, betrayed by the secret agreement among the other blacks in the ring at the battle royal as well as by the white citizens who compensated him with false coins on an elec-trified rug; betrayed by Norton and Bledsoe and Brockway and Wrestrum, before Tod's turnabout, and later by Brother Jack.

In terms of the folk motifs, this accounts for the invisible man's thinking of himself as both rabbit and bear, trickster and dupe; in Stephen Dedalus' terms, he is both kinetic and aesthetic; and in Christian mythology he is both Jesus and Judas. This doubling of possibilities, this mirroring, forces us to defer our understanding until we can reconcile the differences. The text continues to evoke Christ comparisons which not so much inform as confront us with the difficulty of affixing meaning because we cannot be sure what informing assumptions to make about the allusion. The concept of betrayal, for example, ties inextricably to the concept of faith. If one believes in the Brotherhood or in black separatist nationalism, the assumptions become clear. These alterna-tive religions, in fact, are in many ways interchangeable. The sense of proph-esy and ordination in Ras' rhetoric differs little from the Brothers' faith in the doctrines of "history" and "science." Brother Wrestrum, for example, talks of the Brotherhood in the language of a born-again Christian, stressing the good fortune of salvation and the need for unremitting vigilance:

"I'm fair. I ask myself every day, 'What are you doing against Brotherhood?' and when I find it, I root it out, I burn it out like a man cauterizing a mad-dog bite. This business of being a brother

is a full-time job. You have to be pure in heart and you have to
be disciplined in body and mind. Brother, you understand what
I mean?"

"Yes, I think I do," I said. "Some folks feel that way about
religion."

"Religion?" He blinked his eyes. "Folks like me and you is full
of distrust," he said. "We been corrupted 'til it's hard for some
of us to believe in Brotherhood. And some even want revenge!
That's what I'm talking about. We have to root it out! We have
to learn to trust our other Brothers. After all, didn't *they* start the
Brotherhood? Didn't *they* come and stretch out their hand to us
black men and say, 'We wan y'all for our brothers?' Didn't they
do it? Didn't they, now? Didn't they set out to organize us, and
help fight our battle and all like that? Sho they did, and we have
to remember it twenty-four hours a day. *Brotherhood.* That's the
word we got to keep right in front of our eyes every second. Now
this brings me to why I come to see you, Brother." (297)

Brother Jack, moreover, in his final confrontation with the invisible man,
allows his glass eye to pop from his head and roll on the table, a grotesquely
literal interpretation of Jesus' command, which he uses to intimidate the
invisible man. Even more ironically, Jack's need to "cast out the offending eye"
enacts Norton's words to Jim Trueblood. Hearing of Trueblood's act of incest,
Norton, horrified and fascinated, asks: "You feel no inner turmoil, no need to
cast out the offending eye?" (40). For Norton as for Jack (as well as the blind
Reverend Homer A. Barbee), faith comes from blindness. The casting out
of the offending eye—the failure to see the realities or possibilities of black
American experience—allows their religiouslike dedication to their respective causes. Within the realm of their assumptions, marked by the limitations
of their vision, the idea of betrayal has meaning. When the invisible man
begins, however, to see around corners, those limitations and the meanings
they provided start to dissolve, a point that becomes clear in the language of
Tod's death scene.

Tod has disappeared for about one month (forty days?). Recalled to Harlem to reorganize the deteriorated Brotherhood chapter, the invisible man,
now considered a betrayer by the people, is also betrayed by the Brotherhood,
which intentionally holds a strategy meeting without informing him.

While the meeting from which he is barred goes on, he discovers Clifton selling paper Sambo dolls on 42nd Street:

For a second our eyes met and he gave me a contemptuous smile,
then he spieled again. I felt betrayed. I looked at the doll and felt

my throat constrict. The rage welled behind the phlegm as I rocked back on my heels and crouched forward. There was a splash of whiteness and a splatter like heavy rain striking a newspaper and I saw the doll go over backwards, wilting into a dripping rag of frilled tissue, the hateful head upturned on its outstretched neck still grinning toward the sky. The crowd turned on me indignantly. The whistle came again. I saw a short, pot-bellied man look down, then up at me with amazement and explode with laughter, pointing from me to the doll, rocking. People backed away from me. (328–29)

As the invisible man describes it, Tod is the betrayer, but the crowd, applying a different set of assumptions, sees a likeness between the doll and the invisible man, a likeness further borne out by his own earlier descriptions: "It was Clifton, riding easily back and forth on his knees, flexing his legs without shifting his feet, his right shoulder raised at an angle and his arm pointing stiffly at the bouncing doll as he spieled from the corner of his mouth" (327). Being soaked in phlegm, the doll also undergoes an experience analogous to that which the invisible man imagined himself experiencing when he recognized Tod: "It was as though I had waded into a shallow pool only to have the bottom drop out and water close over my head" (327).

As a "frill of paper," the doll also resembles all the other papers in this novel, each one a sign of betrayal. Not until he burns them, of course, does the narrator realize how universally this signification holds true. Again the sign has a different meaning for the reader and narrator than for the invisible man. Yet that meaning confounds rather than clarifies when the doll is put in the same pocket "where I carried Brother Tarp's chain link" (238), a broken link which signifies freedom. Our inability to separate the betrayer from the betrayed is further exacerbated by the invisible man's reluctance to face Tod, as though the invisible man were the betrayer, not Tod.

Following this comes language which treats Tod as a fallen angel:

How on earth could he drop from Brotherhood to this in so short a time? And why if he had to fall back did he try to carry the whole structure with him? What would non-members who knew him say? It was as though he had chosen—how had he put it the night he fought with Ras?—to fall outside of *history*. I stopped in the middle of the walk with the thought. "To Plunge," he had said. But he knew that only in the Brotherhood could we make ourselves known, could we avoid being empty Sambo dolls. Such an obscene flouncing of everything human! My God! And I had been worrying about being left out of a meeting. (328)

This passage starts out treating, with a sense of Christian pity, the fallen ideal who had dropped to earth, fallen back, and was therefore in danger of subverting the system. The "God" in the passage is history, with the Brotherhood its practicing religion. In his praise of the Brotherhood, the invisible man echoes Brother Wrestrum's blind dicta; yet at this point in the text we can also identify Wrestrum with the Sambo dolls, for, as the invisible man noted about him earlier, "Clifton would know how to handle this clown" (304). Wrestrum had betrayed the invisible man by encouraging him to accept a magazine interview and, subsequently, accusing him of disloyalty to the Brotherhood by doing so. So the invisible man was not only adopting Wrestrum's rhetoric but emulating Wrestrum's acts, the acts of someone he knew to be a betrayer. If we identify Wrestrum with the Sambo dolls that Clifton handles, then the invisible man has accurately identified betrayal and done the right thing in spitting on the doll. But since the invisible man can be identified with Wrestrum, his accusations can also be seen as masking his own acts of betrayal.

To complicate matters further, the invisible man, as we have seen, also resembles the doll itself, the doll he renounces as the "obscene flouncing of everything human." Yet "humanity" has been one of his highest values, the trait he associated with his grandfather and his college instructor, Woodridge. It was even the term he first used as a Brotherhood spokesman to describe the effect of the Brotherhood on him. The inhuman, the electrified, and the mechanical, on the other hand—from the electric carpet in the first chapter to the nightmare of the mechanical man in the last—permeate the novel with menace. When the invisible man thus sees the dolls as an "obscene flouncing of everything human," he seems to be renouncing his own values.

This ironic self-incrimination lends even more irony to the term "My God!" Although it seems an appeal to heaven in a kind of shock or horror, we should remember that the invisible man's "God" in this passage is the Brotherhood, which, just before this scene, had again betrayed hirer. The invisible man, then, is calling to his betrayers (in the language of Wrestrum) about the outrage of flouncing everything human. Grammatically, "My God!" is in apposition to the noun phrase "everything human," and we could say that, at some level, "everything human" is the invisible man's God. "Everything human," however, is part of a larger gerund phrase, itself in apposition to "empty Sambo dolls," and the exclamation at another level can make us see "My God" as a synonym for the dolls, or at least make us ask in what way the two can be equated. The Sambo dolls thus suggest Tod and Wrestrum and the invisible man; they represent betrayer and betrayed, resiliency and emptiness, deity and fallen angel, humanity and mechanization. In other words, the Sambo dolls suggest infinite possibilities and show that the meaning of a black image depends upon its interpreters, just as the meaning of betrayal depends on one's loyalties.

Tod's spiel says so much:

> Shake it up! Shake it up!
> He's Sambo, the dancing doll, ladies and gentlemen.
> Shake him, stretch him by the neck and set him down,
> —He'll do the rest. Yes!
> He'll make you laugh, he'll make you sigh, si-igh.
> He'll make you want to dance, and dance
> Here you are, ladies and gentlemen, Sambo,
> The dancing doll.
> Buy one for your baby. Take him to your girl friend and she'll love you,
>   loove you!
> He'll keep you entertained. He'll make you weep sweet—
> Tears from laughing.
> Shake him, shake him, you cannot break him
> For he's Sambo, the dancing, Sambo, the prancing,
> Sambo, the entrancing, Sambo Boogie Woogie paper doll.
> And all for twenty-five cents, the quarter part of a dollar . . .
> Ladies and gentlemen, he'll bring you joy, step up and meet him,
>   Sambo the—. . . .
> What makes him happy, what makes him dance,
> This Sambo, this jambo, this high-stepping joy boy?
> He's more than a toy, ladies and gentlemen, he's Sambo, the dancing doll,
>   the twentieth-century miracle.
> Look at that rumba, that suzy-q, he's Sambo-Boogie,
> Sambo-Woogie, you don't have to feed him, he sleeps collapsed, he'll kill
>   your depression
> And your dispossession, he lives upon the sunshine of your lordly smile
> And only twenty-five cents, the brotherly two bits of a dollar because
>   he wants me to eat.
> It gives him pleasure to see me eat.
> You simply take him and shake him . . . and he does the rest.
> Thank you, lady . . . (326–27)

The invisible man, blinded by Tod's act of selling the dolls, apparently doesn't listen to the spiel, for there is nothing in it with which he would disagree. Tod accurately describes the images of the black for sale in America. When Tod suggests, furthermore, that the Sambo doll will "take it on the

lambo" (327), a phrase the invisible man will reiterate, he emphasizes the
sacrificial quality of the manipulated black image, a sacrifice Tod will manifest in human form a few moments later when he confronts the policeman
and invites his own death.

As we noted when we first saw Tod coming out of the shadow into
the light, in many ways he points the direction for the invisible man and
thus anticipates the journey of the novel. In much the same way, Tod's spiel
says what the invisible man will learn—about his image, his tradition, his
loyalties and betrayals—that necessitates his hibernation, his retreat to the
underground. His adamant aversion to Tod's spiel also anticipates what he
will learn about the reaction to his own spiels and acts: that "[he] was never
more hated than when [he] tried to be honest" (432).

Just as spiritually and psychologically Tod leads the invisible man to
enlightenment, his death physically directs the invisible man underground:
"I wandered down the subway stairs," he says after leaving the scene of Tod's
shooting, "seeing nothing, my mind plunging" (331). This plunge into the
subway also takes the invisible man outside "history," for while he is contemplating the meaning of history he sees some young men on the platform:

> What about those three boys ... tall and slender, walking stiffly
> with swinging shoulders in their well-pressed, too-hot-for-summer
> suits, their collars high and tight about their necks, their identical
> hats of black cheap felt set upon the crowns of their heads with a
> severe formality above their hard conked hair? It was as though
> I'd never seen their like before: Walking slowly, their shoulders
> swaying, their legs swinging from their hips in trousers that
> ballooned upward from cuffs fitting snug about their ankles; their
> coats long and hip-tight with shoulders far too broad to be those
> of natural western men. These fellows whose bodies seemed—what
> had one of my teachers said of me?—"You're like one of these
> African sculptures, distorted in the interest of design?" Well, what
> design and whose? (332–33)

This trinity, silent and ritualistic, suggests to the invisible man a new way
of reading history. In asking "what design and whose?" the invisible man
is starting to confront the basic issue—which I have called hermeneutics—that frames this novel. His question indicates that the terms "accu-
racy" and "distortion" become bogus once we realize that they presume
norms. With different presumption, we find the same object or narrative
reveals different distortions which in turn suggest different secrets, different spiritual readings.

The invisible man describes these young men, who for the first time have become significant to him, in language that associates them with some mystery play or pageant about the sacrificial death of Tod Clifton:

> I stared as they seemed to move like dancers in some kind of funeral ceremony, swaying, going forward, their black faces secret, moving slowly down the subway platform, the heavy heel-plated shoes making a rhythmical tapping as they moved. Everyone must have seen them, or heard their muted laughter, or smelled the heavy pomade on their hair—or perhaps failed to see them at all. For they were men outside of historical time, they were untouched, they didn't believe in Brotherhood, no doubt had never heard of it; or perhaps like Clifton would mysteriously have rejected its mysteries; men of transition whose faces were immobile. (333)

The consequences of his new spiritual reading overwhelm the invisible man but also enable him to connect disparate and seemingly irreconcilable details.

> But who knew (and now I began to tremble so violently I had to lean against a refuse can)—who knew but that they were the saviors, the true leaders, the bearers of something precious? The stewards of something uncomfortable, burdensome, which they hated because, living outside the realm of history, there was no one to applaud their value and they themselves failed to understand it. What if Brother Jack were wrong? What if history was a gambler, instead of a force in a laboratory experiment, and the boys his ace in the hole? What if history was not a reasonable citizen, but a madman full of paranoid guile and these boys his agents, his big surprise! His own revenge? For they were outside, in the dark with Sambo, the dancing paper doll; taking it on the lambo with my fallen brother, Tod Clifton (Tod, Tod) running and dodging the forces of history instead of making a dominating stand. (333)

The Sambo dolls, the running man, the underground man, the brothers (Brer) bear and rabbit all come together, in the last sentence, with the three dancerlike boys with taps on their shoes, the sacrificial lamb, and Tod Clifton. With this, the invisible man's language takes on ceremonial formality ("There were many seats and the three sat together" [334]), and the details he notices evoke, in both their symmetry and content, religious connotations:

I stood, holding onto the center pole, looking down the length of
the car. On one side I saw a white nun in black telling her beads,
and standing before the door across the aisle there was another
dressed completely in white, the exact duplicate of the zither except
that she was black and her black feet bare. Neither of the nuns was
looking at the other but at their crucifixes.... (334)

This scene causes the invisible man to paraphrase a verse he had heard "long
ago at the Golden Day" which strongly suggests the eucharist:

Bread and Wine,
Bread and Wine,
　　Your cross ain't nearly so
　　Heavy as mine ... (334)

He continues to notice the formal aspects of the young men's behavior,
which recall again the scene of Tod's death, and we see that Tod, in one
more way, anticipated the invisible man's behavior: " . . . Clifton would have
known them better than I. He knew them all the time" (334). As they leave,
the invisible man again acknowledges their spiritual significance: "I studied
them closely until they left the train, their shoulders rocking, their heavy
heel plates clicking remote, cryptic messages in the brief silence of the train's
stop" (335).

　　Studying these young men, the invisible man again assumes the role
of student, this time not at anyone's direct command, but as the self-willed
revolt against the imposed and institutionalized studies which have enslaved
and betrayed him. Emerging from the subway, outside the dictates of others'
presumptions—because of Clifton's death, outside of their versions of history—he views the people of Harlem differently:

Now, moving through the crowds along 125th Street, I was
painfully aware of other men dressed like the boys, and of girls
in dark exotic-colored stockings, their costumes surreal variations
of downtown styles. They'd been there all along, but somehow
I'd missed them. I'd missed them even when my work had been
most successful. They were outside the groove of history, and it
was my job to get them in, all of them. I looked into the design of
their faces, hardly a one that was unlike someone I'd known down
South. Forgotten names sang through my head like forgotten
scenes in dreams. I moved with the crowd, the sweat pouring off
me, listening to the grinding roar of traffic, the growing sound of

a record shop loudspeaker blaring a languid blues. I stopped. Was this all that would be recorded? Was this the only true history of the times, a mood blared by trumpets, trombones, saxophones and drums, a song with turgid, inadequate words? (335)

The word "design" takes us back to the question about the invisible man's past (what design and whose?), just as the faces themselves return him to it. This forgotten heritage takes the invisible man to the blues which, for Ellison, represent infinite possibilities, the possibilities seen by stepping outside History to repossess the forgotten folk culture, the signs of which can be discovered everywhere, once one understands that the secret is there. So Wilner is correct in seeing the thread as a sign of black cultural ties, but it is a sign intelligible only to those who know to look for the secret.

To reveal that secret, Tod died, and the doll thus becomes the key to interpreting his death. In that regard, one of its significant details is that it had "grinned back at Clifton as it grinned forward at the crowd, and their entertainment had been his death" (337), which is an emblematic restatement of the basic lesson in hermeneutics that I have been claiming is central to this novel.

Another important detail is that Tod had been controlling the doll all along with an invisible black thread. This is the black thread that has perplexed critics. It has raised questions about the informing context, the context which would tell us what the string represents, tell us, in other words, who is manipulating whom. That, however, may be the wrong question, the appropriate one focusing not on the manipulators but on the manipulation itself. Being both black and invisible the string becomes an emblematic lesson about the possibilities of black power. Clifton could make the image do anything he wanted it to, but, having gotten control of the invisible black string, he could not discover what to do with it because every choice was subject to interpretation by a world with different assumptions. So long as he lived in the realm of others' assumptions, his life could not have its own meaning, and the only alternative to selling his image was violently to assault the buyers. The only hope for freedom from that double bind—the double bind first acknowledged by the invisible man's grandfather—is to make others aware of that bind in which their sense of meaning is centered. To the cause of that decentering, Tod sacrifices himself and thus begins the invisible man on his road to salvation. "I could think of no justification for Clifton's having sold the dolls," he states, "but there was justification enough for giving him a public funeral, and I seized upon the idea, now, as though it would save my life" (338).

The invisible man's action precedes his understanding, because once he understands Tod's actions, he will already have found his salvation. For the time being, he understands that the dolls signify power: "[The other side] had the power to use a paper doll, first to destroy [Tod's] integrity and then as an excuse for killing him. All right, so we'll use his funeral to put his integrity back together again. . . . For that's all he had had or wanted. And now I could see the doll only vaguely and drops of moisture were thudding down upon its absorbent paper" (338). The doll's transformation, in the invisible man's eyes, from a sign of betrayal to a reminder of Tod's quest for integrity prefigures the invisible man's own transformation, as does the substitution of rainlike tears for the earlier shower of phlegm.

The funeral service itself is also rich with allusions to Christian mythology. Tod's coffin rests "upon the backs of its wobbly carpenter's horses" (343), and the word "mass" is used repeatedly in such a way as to suggest a Catholic service: "The sun shone down upon a mass of unbeared heads" (340); "I could see them winding up in a mass to the muffled sound of the drums" (341); "And now some of the older ones in the mass were joining in" (341); "I felt a wonder at the singing mass" (342). Although the word could also suggest the Brotherhood's call to the masses, it is never used in that way, almost calling our attention to the omission of the plural usage, especially when we remember not only Ellison's Joycean relish for puns but also that, in his own prenovelist days, Ellison published frequently for *New Masses*. Rather the invisible man fixes on individual faces—"a slender black man with his face turned toward the sun, singing through the upturned bells of the horn" (341), "a peanut vendor standing beneath a street lamp upon which pigeons were gathered, and now I saw him stretch out his arms with his palms turned upward, and suddenly he was covered, head, shoulders and outflung arms, with fluttering, feasting birds" (342).

The ritualistic quality, especially of this last crucifix image, would tend to suggest a spiritual reading of the text which reveals the ascension of Clifton's soul. In this context, the invisible man's references to the mountain from which he is speaking evoke associations with the sermon on the mount. The funeral is held in Mount Morris Park, where many of those reaching "the top of the mountain were spreading massed together" (342), and as the mass gathers, "the top of the little mountain bristled with banners, horns and uplifted faces" (342). The invisible man further calls attention to the fact that his nonsermon is given from a mount by saying, "Listen to me standing upon this so-called mountain!" (345).

These mount references, however, suggest that the invisible man, not Tod, is the Christ figure, or they suggest that Christ and/or Tod are somehow like Caesar, or they suggest that Jesus' sermon on the mount should be read as a subtle funeral oration. The content of the speech, moreover, is very different from that of the sermon on the mount. For although the speech suggests the

danger in failing to turn the other cheek, it emphasizes more the degrada-
tion involved in doing so. Exercising Christian tolerance, the speech implies
repeatedly, yields neither earthly nor heavenly reward and after the funeral we
are not allowed to see Tod as risen. Succinctly, the invisible man tells us: "They
filled the grave quickly and we left. Tod Clifton was underground" (347). Tod
(whose name, critics are quick to point out, means death) is, as the invisible
man repeatedly reminded his audience, completely mortal: "do you expect to
see some magic and the dead rise up and walk again? Go home, he's as dead
as he'll ever die. That's the end in the beginning and there's no encore" (343).

If the end of Tod's funeral oration is in the beginning, then that is one
more way in which Tod is like the narrator, who tells us in the prologue about
his own narration that "the end is in the beginning and lies far ahead" (5).
Thus Tod Clifton, buried in a density of allusion, from which he might or
might not rise, as Christ or anti-Christ, to save or reveal his friend or betrayer,
the invisible man, speaking a funeral sermon on the so-called mountain after
the death of his Tod. I asked early in this chapter: "Who is Tod Clifton?" The
answer I now want to suggest is: the enemy of dogma. For dogma is the real
devil of *Invisible Man*, no matter whose. When the invisible man subverts his
individuality to the cause of dogma, he indeed becomes the devil's henchman,
but when he sees himself or others as individuals he moves toward salvation. Because dogma makes people blind, it causes the narrator's invisibility;
it blocks the light and limits possibilities. Dogma is the dog that has undone
so many in this novel. When Peter Wheatstraw says "oh goddog daddy-o . . .
who got the damn dog?" (132) that dog-daddy is a dogma, too. Wheatstraw's
shift from "oh" to "o" echoes the implied shift in chapter 2, where Ellison
transfers his debt from Whitman to what the invisible man o, o, owes those
multimillionaires. As the goddog palindrome reminds us, furthermore, "god"
spelled backwards is "dog"; what we learn later is change the "g" to "t," and
God is dead.

Through Tod's death, the invisible man comes to see the victims of
dogma everywhere, and Tod's plunge outside that dogma—his route underground—means both violence and finality. For if Tod were guaranteed escape
or resurrection, he would simply be trading the body of one dogma for the
spirit of another. At the other extreme in this novel is Rinehart, who instead
of renouncing all dogma endorses it all. That is his "spiritual technology," his
mastery of religion and science, his dominion over every audience. For the
invisible man, this yea-saying means chaos, just as Tod's nay-saying means
death. The invisible man learns to substitute invisibility for death; that is, he
learns to follow his Tod symbolically and to oppose Rinehartism through an
awareness of the hidden assumptions that make Rinehartism possible in any
of its forms.

Invisibility thus casts a cold eye on the Brotherhood's dogma of the left as it does on the fascist dogma of the right.[4] Invisibility rejects equally the dogma of Bledsoe and that of Brockway, of Norton and of Ras, of Hambro, Kimbro, and Rambo. It also, as I hope to demonstrate in detail, rejects the dogma of historians and literary critics, and, as Joyce did, it challenges dogma about literary conventions themselves. Whereas, in 1952 (and very often today), allusions by convention refer to an accepted understanding, we have seen that potentially they can make us question that understanding and the reasons we might have accepted it.

NOTES

1. Although I have not done a statistical analysis of name frequency in *Invisible Man*, suffice it to say that simple empirical observation reveals this to be inordinately frequent in the text, much more frequent than any other name, especially given that Clifton does not appear until more than halfway through the novel.

2. See Bone ("Ralph Ellison and the Uses of the Imagination"); also Tischler ("Negro Literature and Classic Form," 352–65) and Cheshire (*"Invisible Man* and the Life of Dialogue," 19–34).

3. See Bennett and Nichols ("Violence in Afro-American Fiction," 173); Rupp (*Celebration in Post-War American Fiction*, 159).

4. Although New York City policemen dress in blue, Ellison makes Clifton's slayer a stiff armed, black-shirted, solidly (goose?-) stepping man to evoke connotations of fascism: "I could see the cop push Clifton again, stepping solidly forward in his black shirt, his arm shooting out stiffly, sending him in a head-snapping forward stumble . . ." (329).

ANDREW HOBEREK

Race Man, Organization Man, Invisible Man

> The organization had given the world a new shape, and me a vital role.
> —*Invisible Man*

Since the 1952 publication of Ralph Ellison's *Invisible Man*, one question has preoccupied its critics more than any other: Does Ellison's aesthetic individualism—his commitment to formally accomplished art that champions the ethical primacy of the individual—override his novel's racial and political concerns? The postwar humanists who first took up the novel's cause celebrated *Invisible Man* as a triumphant defense of the individual that masterfully transcended its "merely" racial subject matter. Robert Penn Warren, for instance, praised Ellison for being "more concerned with the way a man confronts his individual doom than with the derivation of that doom," while Saul Bellow commended Ellison's "brilliant individual victory" over the deindividualizing forces of modern society and his rejection of "a minority tone."[1] Subsequent critics concurred with this characterization of Ellison and his novel but saw it as cause for censure rather than praise. Irving Howe, who in an early review had decried *Invisible Man*'s "unqualified assertion of individuality," reiterated his claim in a famous exchange in which he criticized Ellison for deviating from the militant example of Richard Wright.[2] The Black Aestheticians of the late sixties and early seventies offered a similar argument; Ernest Kaiser, for instance, contended that

From *Modern Language Quarterly* 59, no. 1 (March 1998): 99–119. © 1998 by University of Washington.

Invisible Man was "a contrived novel [that supported] the existential notion that each person must solve his own problems."[3] Most recently, Jerry Gafio Watts, echoing Kaiser, has declared Ellison's "heroic" model of human achievement a self-interested valorization of individual artistic production at the expense of the struggle for racial equality.[4]

Other recent critics, however, have sought to provide a more complicated model of the relationship between Ellison's aesthetic and political commitments. For Houston A. Baker Jr., Ellison's ostensible devotion to modernist high culture is merely a mask behind which the author conceals his real devotion to an inevitably politicized African American vernacular culture. Phillip Brian Harper, on the other hand, accepts "*Invisible Man*'s relation to literary modernism" as genuine and grounded in "a metaphysical quest for individual identity" that mystifies political relations, but he argues that "politics" continually "reemerges in the problematic of race relations to disrupt" such mystification. Likewise, T. V. Reed finds that *Invisible Man* overcomes "the danger of aestheticizing racism" encapsulated in "the narrator's search for autonomy and authenticity" by "play[ing] between the universalizing element in literature (as Ellison's existential humanism conceived it) and the local, particular, historical conditions in which it is always rooted."[5]

But while Baker, Harper, and Reed all seem to reject the "easy aesthetic/political dichotomies" that have governed readings of *Invisible Man* (Reed, 59), I would argue that they do not, since for each critic literariness in general, and literary modernism in particular, plays the role of villain. The demonization of modernist aesthetic practice—which has a long, complex history of engagement with the political—makes it a self-evident target, whose specific historical manifestations need not be considered. By failing to address the very "local, particular, historical conditions" of literary form toward which Reed gestures, these critics reproduce the assumption underlying the humanist account of *Invisible Man*: Threatened individuality is a universal, human problem that "the special problems of the Negro writer" (Warren, 21) might influence but never quite equal in importance. Reed epitomizes this unintentional marginalization of the book's racial-political subject matter by asserting that *Invisible Man* ends with the narrator's realization of "how the particularities of American racism reinflect the more general philosophical and political problem of autonomy, of authorship of one's experience" (72).[6]

For reasons that are themselves historically specific, critics of *Invisible Man* have always failed to take into account that the "general philosophical and political problem of autonomy" assumes historically specific forms for everyone, black and white alike. I seek to correct their omission by showing that Ellison's aesthetic individualism can be understood as a version of the

"organization-man discourse," whose preoccupation with threatened individuality accompanies the postwar expansion of the white-collar workforce.
Within this discourse, the plight of the white-collar worker, whose agency and
autonomy is compromised by his role in large organizations, becomes representative of the plight of modern man per se: "Estranged from community
and society in a context of distrust and manipulation; alienated from work
and, on the personality market, from self; expropriated of individual rationality,
and politically apathetic—[white-collar workers] are the new little people, the
unwilling vanguard of modern society."[7] Thus C. Wright Mills writes in his
influential study *White Collar*. Although such ideas about modern identity find
their chief expression in works of cultural criticism like *White Collar*, David
Riesman's *Lonely Crowd*, and William H. Whyte Jr.'s *Organization Man*, they
also shape texts—including *Invisible Man*—that at first glance could not be
further removed from the framework of white-collar culture.[8]

Here I follow the lead of Richard Ohmann, who describes *Invisible Man*
as an example of the "illness story," which, he argues, appears throughout
postwar U.S. fiction as a formal reification of white-collar middle-class experience. That Ellison's novel "comprehends racism itself within the illness story
and the adolescent rite of passage," Ohmann suggests, accounts for its almost
immediate canonization.[9] I argue further that the white-collar concern with
threatened individuality is present in Ellison's novel not only in the symbolic
form of the illness story but explicitly. At the most basic level Ellison's novel
shares the plot of such popular treatments of white-collar angst as Ayn Rand's
Fountainhead and Sloan Wilson's *Man in the Gray Flannel Suit*: A young man,
anxious to find creative and fulfilling mental labor, instead encounters mysti-
fied, conformist organizations that threaten to rob him of his individuality,
agency, and autonomy. To offer an admittedly oversimplified formulation, the
organization-man narrative is what gives form to the novel's African American content.

Admittedly, this formulation runs the risk of subordinating *Invisible
Man*'s racial and political concerns to one extraneous framework even as it
gets rid of another. Surely, reading *Invisible Man* as an organization-man
narrative is no less dismissive of its African American subject matter than
reading it as an existential bildungsroman. However, understanding its universalist narrative of threatened individuality as the product of a historically
specific, class-based transformation of American culture provides us with
a more complex picture of how Ellison's racial concerns relate to the rest
of the book. Rather than something imposed on *Invisible Man* from the
outside, the organization-man discourse springs from Ellison's own complex
authorial identity. If few African Americans in the forties and fifties were
white-collar, Ellison in a way was. Postwar intellectuals underwent their own

process of *embourgeoisement* even as the larger society came to imagine all forms of mental labor as belonging under the white-collar umbrella.[10] As a writer and intellectual of his generation, Ellison had class and professional interests that, while they did not always tally with his "interests" as a black man, were no less authentic. Rather than see these two aspects of Ellison's authorial identity as mutually exclusive, we need to understand how the organization-man discourse shapes, and is shaped by, *Invisible Man*'s racial-political imaginary.

Certainly, Ellison's deployment of the organization-man narrative in *Invisible Man* attests to the postwar hegemony of white-collar culture. By severing the organization-man discourse from its white-collar origins, the novel helped generate this very hegemony by contributing to the confusion between white-collar interests and "those of society and indeed humanity at large."[11] Postwar critics did not so much ignore the novel's African American subject matter as perversely redeploy it to feed their own desire to see the organization-man narrative as universal: a crisis of individuality relevant to all people, not simply the white-collar middle class.

Read with a recognition of the historical contingency of white-collar universalism, however, *Invisible Man* can be seen to critique such universalism by highlighting "the intersection of 'white' collar vocabularies with the insidious languages of racism and ethnic exclusion."[12] If the novel's narrator voices a general postwar concern when he declares that he remains underground "because up above there's an increasing passion to make men conform to a pattern," his story repeatedly materializes the racial demarcations that, in the mid-century United States, forever forestall the achievement of absolute conformity.[13] From this perspective *Invisible Man* reads like an extended riff on a brief comment in Riesman's *Lonely Crowd* (written while Ellison was composing his novel and published two years earlier): "The peer-group can decide that there are certain outcasts, in class or ethnic terms, to whom the glad hand need not be extended, or who can (like the Negro in the South) be forced to personalize without the privilege of demanding a reciprocal response" (140). And not just in the South, as Ellison makes clear. *Invisible Man* is a novel written in the face of a historical paradox: a white-collar culture that simultaneously pretends to be universal while excluding a significant proportion of the postwar population. Thus Ellison's account of American racial identity has everything to do with the parts of the novel that postwar white-collar culture, and we its heirs, have read as transcending or avoiding race.

* * *

Early on in *Invisible Man* the unnamed protagonist accidentally escorts Mr. Norton, a rich, white trustee of the black southern college he attends, on a

series of misadventures involving the inhabitants of the surrounding countryside. After seeing the dazed Norton back to his room and obeying his
command to return with Dr. Bledsoe, the president of the college, Invisible
Man is startled to find himself reprimanded for having followed Norton's
orders to drive off the beaten path: "Damn what *he* wants. . . . Haven't you
got the sense God gave a dog? We take these white folks where we want
them to go, we show them what we want them to see." Then Invisible Man
receives "another shock" when Bledsoe prepares himself for the interview
with Norton by carefully adjusting his features in a hall mirror: "As we
approached a mirror Dr. Bledsoe stopped and composed his angry face like
a sculptor, making it a bland mask, leaving only the sparkle of his eyes to
betray the emotion that I had seen only a moment before. He looked steadily
at himself for a moment; then we moved quietly down the silent hall and
up the stairs" (102). As the narrative subsequently makes clear, careful self-
presentation masking calculated self-interest constitutes the key to Bledsoe's
administrative style: His constant performance of servile humility in the
presence of his school's wealthy white patrons (106) is what enables, even as
it belies, his power to tell them "how to think" (143).

Bledsoe's role-playing is hardly unique among *Invisible Man*'s characters. Rather, it is one of the novel's primary motifs. Bledsoe's advice to the
narrator to "get yourself power . . . then stay in the dark and use it!" (145)
both echoes his grandfather's deathbed injunction to "overcome [whites]
with yeses, undermine 'em with grins, agree 'em to death and destruction"
(16) and anticipates the counsel of the veteran who shares Bledsoe's wrath
following the Norton incident: "Play the game but play it your own way. . . .
You're hidden right out in the open—that is, you would be if you only realized
it" (153–4). The sharecropper Trueblood, as Baker and other commentators
have noted, crafts his horrific tale of incest to appeal to the sensibilities and
gain the favor of his white audiences. Trueblood's urban counterpart is the
con man Rinehart, whose protean manipulation of his "multiple personalities" (499)—"Rine the runner and Rine the gambler and Rine the briber and
Rine the lover and Rinehart the Reverend" (498)—is the source of his power.
Finally, all of these characters serve as counterparts to *Invisible Man*'s ultimate role-player: the nameless narrator himself, whose invisibility functions
as both source and symptom of his obsessive submersion into various roles.
Through this motif the novel blurs the line between role-playing as strategy
and role-playing as identity.

In his influential reading of *Invisible Man* Baker grounds the role-playing identity in the historical conditions of African American agency in the
white-supremacist United States: "Artful evasion and expressive illusion are
. . . traditional black expressive modes"; they constitute "the only resources that

blacks at any level can barter for a semblance of decency and control in their lives" (196). Yet Ellison's account of African American identity, considered in the postwar context, resembles nothing so much as the contemporaneous descriptions of white identity found in the organization-man discourse. If "Trueblood is ultimately merchandizing [*sic*] . . . an image of himself that is itself a product" (193), he is only mirroring the white-collar workers for whom traditional alienated labor is compounded by a new form of "self-alienation": "When white-collar people get jobs, they sell not only their time and energy but their personalities as well. They sell by the week or month their smiles and their kindly gestures, and they must practice the prompt repression of resentment and aggression" (Mills, xvii). Likewise, Whyte argues that the rise of "The Organization" and its accompanying "Social Ethic," which promotes consensus at all costs, is creating a society in which "adaptation has become . . . almost a constant" and organization men have become "interchangeables" (435, 437). Riesman, finally, argues that a new "other-directed" character type, emerging within and spreading out from "the 'new' middle class . . . engaged in white-collar work and the service trade" (20), is replacing the old "inner-directed" (13, passim) type of fixed goals with the tendency to continually adjust to the "signals" (21, passim) of peer group and mass media. Role-playing is central to the other-directed person, who "tends to become merely his succession of roles and encounters and hence to doubt who he is or where he is going," eschewing, that is, "the one-face policy of the inner-directed man for a multi-face policy that he sets in secrecy and varies with each class of encounters" (139). In the work of these cultural critics, as in *Invisible Man*, role-playing becomes the center of a new identity that is actually an anti-identity, because it is founded on absence.

Ellison concurs with his fellow postwar intellectuals, moreover, in setting his characters' role-playing in the context of organizations that assault identity by arrogating the power to confer it. This deindividualizing dynamic is first acted out when the protagonist is threatened with expulsion following the incident with Norton. "Here within this quiet greenness," the narrator recalls, "I possessed the only identity I had ever known, and I was losing it" (99). "Leaving the campus," he remembers thinking, "would be like the parting of flesh" (133). The classic organization in *Invisible Man* is, of course, the Brotherhood, which he approaches with the same mixture of professional self-interest—"It was the one organization in the whole coun-try in which I could reach the very top and I meant to get there" (380)—and evangelical fervor that critics like Whyte ascribe to organization men. Fur-thermore, the form of work that the Brotherhood undertakes is classically white-collar in that it involves the "manipulat[ion]" of *"people"* and *"symbols"* rather than *"things"* (Mills, 65). The scene in which the narrator is initiated into the Brotherhood makes the relationship between such work and role-playing explicit. The setting is, appropriately, an after-hours cocktail party, which suggests the blurring of work and play that characterizes modern labor: the encroachment of "glad-hand attitudes and values that stem in part from the sphere of leisure" onto "the day shift of work-mindedness" (Riesman, 141). Jack, the Brotherhood leader who has recruited Invisible Man, asks him if he "would . . . like to be the new Booker T. Washington" (305), then leads him into a side room and gives him an envelope containing his "new identity" (309). Afterward, the narrator recalls, the other brothers "smiled and seemed eager to meet [him], as though they all knew the role [he] was to play" (311).

If the parallels between *Invisible Man* and the organization-man discourse are too numerous to ignore, however, they are also somewhat odd, given the racial homogeneity of white-collar culture following World War II. A decade after *Invisible Man* was published, a U.S. Bureau of Labor Statistics survey noted that "nonwhite workers" (approximately 95 percent of whom were African American, according to the *Monthly Labor Review*'s account of the survey) made up a scant 3.7 percent of the white-collar workforce while accounting for 10.0 percent of the total nonagricultural workforce. Needless to say, African Americans were even less well represented in the high-paying, high-status managerial jobs that occupied the attention of figures like Mills and Whyte.[14] Indeed, white-collar culture did not simply reflect but helped generate the white-black racial schism in the postwar United States. The segregation of white-collar work, higher education, and suburban housing in the forties and fifties made possible a new multiethnic white identity that, feeding back into policy decisions, accelerated the growth of the African American urban underclass.[15]

Why then does the postwar period's preeminent literary account of African American identity hew so closely to what was becoming, when *Invisible Man* appeared, the standard sociological account of white American identity? Clearly, part of the answer lies in Ellison's desire to create a more three-dimensional, recognizably human African American protagonist than what he saw as Wright's dehumanized—because merely the product of his environment—Bigger Thomas. Ironically, however, Ellison's desire to transcend the "sociological vision of society" that he accused Irving Howe of admiring in Wright's work led him to yet another sociological vision (*Shadow*, 116). Because it was a vision of white and not black life, it was not so obviously tainted by the "anti-Negro assumptions" (307) that, in Ellison's estimation, accompanied the rise of social science as a technique of social control in the post-Reconstruction era (303–17). It was, however, implicated in the construction of a version of American identity whose material basis excluded

African Americans. White-collar culture, like the white-collar workforce at its core, was mostly white above the collar as well.

Ellison's inability to see that the narrative of threatened individuality derived from sociological accounts of white-collar life, even as he professed an explicit animus against the sociological, is characteristic of his generation of American intellectuals, which was shaped, more than any previous generation, by "the *embourgeoisement* of the ... intelligentsia" (Rahv, 306). The postwar expansion of universities, the mass media, and other similar institutions offered intellectuals increased "class, status, and self-image" (Mills, 156) at the same time that it threatened their autonomy by turning them into employees whose agendas were set by others. The same factors responsible for the expansion of white-collar work more generally turned intellectuals—who were, after all, the prototypical knowledge workers—into organization men par excellence: the "hired m[e]n of an information industry" (Mills, 150). Of course, the extent to which specific intellectuals lost their autonomy to white-collar organizations varied, but as an abstraction the fear of lost autonomy played a central role in shaping their identity as intellectuals. Within this framework, another abstraction—the white-collar organization man—provided a convenient straw man onto which intellectuals could displace their anxieties about white-collar work, thereby imagining themselves as autonomous individuals in relation to the white-collar masses. Like most acts of displacement, however, this one was less successful than those who performed it might have wished. Anticipating Ohmann's account of the "illness story," Mills recognized that humanist intellectuals for whom "the political psychology of the scared employee ha[d] become relevant" participated in a "cult of alienation" that obscured the institutional and ideological reorganization of their labor within a metaphysics of threatened individuality (160, 159). We have seen, though, how in *Invisible Man* this "personally tragic plot" (Mills, 160), with its narrative of lost autonomy and fragmented identity, produces a protagonist in many ways indistinguishable from the prototypical white-collar organization man.

What distinguishes *Invisible Man* from most postwar novels of alienation, however, is the way in which the drive to the metaphysical is continually interrupted by the poor fit between its implicitly white-collar narrative and its African American subject matter. While not reducible to any simple, a priori opposition, these two aspects of the novel are subject to a broad historical incompatibility that opens fault lines within the book. Tracing these fault lines, we begin to see how *Invisible Man* reproduces the organization-man narrative with a critical (in both senses of the term) difference.

Unsurprisingly, *Invisible Man* most explicitly foregrounds its protagonist's ambiguous position vis-à-vis The Organization when it focuses on the activity at the heart of white-collar culture's anxieties about individuality: work. In chapter 8 of the novel, Invisible Man, newly arrived in Harlem, comes across a Gideon's Bible in his room at Men's House and experiences a visceral rush of homesickness. But he puts the Bible and the homesickness aside with the thought "This was New York. I had to get a job and earn money" (162). In the remainder of the chapter he distributes the letters of introduction that Bledsoe has given him, ostensibly asking the prominent businessmen to whom they are addressed to find a place for him. The responses he receives confuse him. "Vaguely encouraged by secretaries" (168) but hearing nothing from their employers, he begins to suspect the former: "Maybe they destroyed the letters" (169). Paranoia sets in; Invisible Man experiences "a queer feeling that I was playing a part in some scheme which I did not understand" (170). He tells himself that his suspicions are "fantastic" (170) but considers the possibility that he is being tested for some arcane purpose. Unfortunately, he reflects, "they hadn't told me the rules" (170). Neither he nor, at this stage, the reader suspects the contents of the letters themselves, which warn their addressees not to hire him and ask them to say nothing about it to him, in order that "his severance with the college [may] be executed as painlessly as possible" (191).

In one sense this passage could not be more like the standard postwar accounts of white-collar life. Consider the parallels between it and the classic organization-man narrative, Wilson's bestselling *Man in the Gray Flannel Suit*, which tells the story of Tom Rath's decision to leave a low-paying but relatively comfortable job at a small foundation to go to work as a special assistant to the president of the United Broadcasting Corporation. Although he is immediately promoted to assistant to UBC's chief executive, he finds his position near the heart of the corporate world just as mystifying as Invisible Man does his own sojourn at its margins. Crucially, the world of business is paranoia-inducing for both characters. Relieved of his first task—writing a speech for UBC's president, Ralph Hopkins—and not immediately reassigned, Rath sees before him a gulf that his anxiety immediately fills with speculation: "Maybe that was the way Hopkins got rid of people. In this strange, polite world high in the sky above Rockefeller Center, maybe nobody ever really got fired. Maybe all Hopkins did was to give a man nothing to do, absolutely nothing to do, until he started to go out of his mind sitting uselessly in his office all day, and resigned. Maybe that was the polite, smooth way to get rid of a man nobody wanted."[16] Although he eschews Ellison's self-consciously modernist first-person narration in favor of a straightforwardly omniscient narration, Wilson's story is driven by the same implications of conspiratorial knowledge outside the protagonist's purview: "rules" he hasn't been told. This concern not only links *Invisible Man* and *The Man in the*

Gray Flannel Suit to each other but also demonstrates their shared centrality to the arc of literary history that would shortly lead to novels like Heller's *Catch-22* and Pynchon's *Crying of Lot 49*.

However, the parallels between *Invisible Man* and *The Man in the Gray Flannel Suit* can be taken only so far. That the protagonist finds himself with "nothing to do" means something very different in the two books. Even if Invisible Man were not carrying Bledsoe's treacherous letters—and even if his story were set in the booming fifties, rather than in the Depression thirties—he could hardly expect to land a job like Rath's, "high in the sky above Rockefeller Center." The best job Invisible Man *could* find on Wall Street is that of the black men he sees "hurr[ying] along with leather pouches strapped to their wrists" (164). To be white-collar means that "you carry authority, but you are not its source" (Mills, 80), but these men carry authority in a far more literal—and dehumanizing—sense. Invisible Man's stint at the margins of the business world functions as a kind of negative realism, to the extent that the novel can be read not only as an individual bildungsroman but also as an allegory of African American history from Reconstruction through the Harlem riots of 1943. The center of the white-collar world is as invisible in Ellison's novel as African Americans were in the midcentury white-collar workforce.

If this seems like a willful attempt to misread historical data into *Invisible Man*, it should be noted that the novel itself insistently marks the difference between the Wall Street episode and the others it comprises. A number of critics have pointed out that the following episode provides the novel's key symbol of American racial identity in the paint "as white as George Washington's Sunday-go-to-meetin' wig and as sound as the allmighty [*sic*] dollar," made with ten drops of "dead black" liquid (201–2, 200). The officially white final product, bound for "a national monument" (202), absorbs but is nonetheless impossible without the black liquid. "Ain't a continental thing that happens down here that ain't as iffen I done put my black hands in it," avows Lucius Brockway, the engineer in Liberty Paints' boiler room who prepares the "guts," the "*vee*-hicle," of the paint (218, 214). In the Wall Street episode, by contrast, the main symbol for national identity is a film to which Invisible Man treats himself during his abortive job search: "In the evening I went out to a movie, a picture of frontier life with heroic Indian fighting and struggles against flood, storm and forest fire, with the out-numbered settlers winning each engagement; an epic of wagon trains rolling ever westward. I forgot myself (although there was no one like me taking part in the adventures) and left the dark room in a lighter mood" (170). Here national identity is a projection on a flat white screen, rather than a white liquid with an invisible but nonetheless crucial black element; hybridity gives way to homogeneity, and the protagonist's relationship to the narrative of national history is one of (parenthetically repressed) exclusion.

Yet he does leave the dark theater "in a lighter mood." A standard metonym for white-collar culture more generally in postwar cultural criticism,[17] mass culture inserts itself into *Invisible Man*'s omnipresent pattern of chiaroscuro symbolism as an agency for the whitewashing of African American subjectivity. By implication, the protagonist's relationship to white-collar culture shapes as it excludes him. This dynamic is reinforced by other symbolically charged moments in this part of the book. While delivering his letters shortly before going to the movies, for instance, the protagonist happens to look up at a building and finds himself "challenged by the sheer height of the white stone with its sculptured bronze façade" (165). "Façade" suggests not only exclusion from but also adherence to the contours of an inescapable culture. The Organization shapes the individual's psyche even though the individual (being African American) cannot penetrate The Organization. In a subsequent scene, men's fashion stands in for white-collar culture. Leaving Men's House for the last time, Invisible Man describes among his former fellow tenants

> the business students from southern colleges, for whom business was a vague, abstract game with rules as obsolete as Noah's Ark but who yet were drunk on finance . . . and that older group with similar aspirations . . . who sought to achieve the status of brokers through imagination alone, a group of janitors and messengers who spent most of their wages on clothing such as was fashionable among Wall Street brokers . . . who never read the financial pages though they purchased the *Wall Street Journal* religiously and carried it beneath the left elbow, pressed firm against the body and grasped in the left hand. (256–7)

Later, of course, Wilson would make menswear central to the discourse of white-collar alienation through his eponymous protagonist, whose conventional uniform symbolizes—as he himself belatedly realizes—the colonization of individual identity by The Organization: "I really don't know what I was looking for when I got back from the war, but it seemed as though all I could see was a lot of bright young men in gray flannel suits rushing around New York in a frantic parade to nowhere. They seemed to me to be pursuing neither ideals nor happiness—they were pursuing a routine . . . it was quite a shock to glance down and see that I too was wearing a gray flannel suit" (300). Invisible Man's description of the Men's House tenants comments on *The Man in the Gray Flannel Suit* before the fact, as it were: Ellison anticipates Wilson's anxiety that clothes really *do* make the man but stresses the double remove at which it occurs for those excluded from white-collar culture. For the business students, janitors, and messengers loitering in the lobby of Men's House, pursuing a routine around New York would be not alienating; at the least, it would mean receiving a share of the postwar boom economy's spoils.

To the extent that *Invisible Man* functions as an allegory of African American history, then, the protagonist's desire to find a "new role" within The Organization—any organization—begins to seem far more legitimate. Indeed, such ambiguity is the keynote to *Invisible Man*'s portrayal of the relationship between the individual and The Organization. Early in his experience with the Brotherhood the narrator imagines his membership as "a way that didn't lead through the back door, a way not limited by black and white, but a way which, if one lived long enough and worked hard enough, could lead to the highest possible rewards ... a way to have a part in the big decisions, of seeing through the mystery of how the country, the world, really operated" (355). The narrator conceives of Brotherhood membership as offering him "the possibility of being more than a member of a race" (355), that is, of offering him a role as an individual, not as a black man.

From this perspective the problem with the Brotherhood is that it *fails* to make Invisible Man like its other members, as he discovers following the funeral he holds for Tod Clifton. Recalled to the Brotherhood's main headquarters, Invisible Man faces an angry Jack, who tells him, "You were not hired to think" (469). Although Jack asserts that for all of the Brotherhood's members, including himself, "the committee does the thinking. For all of us" (470), Invisible Man recognizes that this is untrue. "So here it is," he thinks, "naked and old and rotten. So now it's out in the open ..." (469; Ellison's ellipsis). What is out in the open, of course, is that he is subordinated not only to the group but to the group's white members, who lie on the other side of the preexisting hierarchy of race. Some people, to quote Riesman once again, can "be forced to personalize without the privilege of demanding a reciprocal response."

The ambiguity of Ellison's individualism is precisely the point missed by critics who see this side of his work as short-circuiting its political elements. For instance, Thomas Schaub contends that "the novel signals Invisible Man's lowest point when he 'organize[s] a drill team of six-footers [the "People's Hot Foot Squad"] whose duty it was to march through the streets striking up sparks with their hob-nailed shoes'" (112). This reading of *Invisible Man* as a Cold War text requires Schaub to see Ellison's depiction of organized group activity as a critique of totalitarianism. But in a 1961 interview Ellison relates a biographical anecdote that calls Schaub's interpretation into question. In the Oklahoma City of his boyhood, Ellison tells Richard Stern, there were many Negro veterans from the Spanish-American War who delighted in teaching the younger boys complicated drill patterns, and on hot summer evenings we spent hours on the Bryant School grounds ... learning to execute the commands barked at us by our enthusiastic drillmasters. And as we mastered the patterns, the jazz feeling would come into it and no one was satisfied until we were swinging. These men who taught us had raised a military discipline to the level of a low art form, almost a dance, and its spirit was jazz. (*Shadow*, 10–1)

This passage thus imagines the drill not as an unproblematically negative example of "military discipline" but as a form of "low art" whose "high" analogue is Louis Armstrong "bend[ing] that military instrument into a beam of lyrical sound" in *Invisible Man*'s prologue (8). Here Ellison specifically depicts art (popular art, but art nonetheless) as the product of organized *group* activity.

Schaub's misinterpretation of *Invisible Man* is itself symptomatic of an equally important, and perhaps even more persistent, legacy of the Cold War period: the logic, inherited from the organization-man discourse, of condemning everything inside The Organization and celebrating everything outside it. *Invisible Man* itself critiques this logic, which, Ellison recognized, could lead to a simplistic romanticization of those outside the white-collar mainstream, not least of all African Americans. Alice Echols and Eric Lott have described this "racial cross-dressing" as motivated by a crisis in middle-class masculinity, but they have not sufficiently stressed its structural dependence on the pathologization of middle-class normalcy in the organization-man discourse.[18] For instance, in Norman Mailer's 1957 essay "The White Negro," the postwar locus classicus of this tradition, the celebration of the Negro hipster gains its force through the juxtaposition of the hipster to the "Square cell[s] ... of American society"—that is, organization men: "Hated from outside and therefore hating himself, the Negro was forced into the position of exploring all those moral wildernesses of civilized life which the square automatically condemns as delinquent or evil or immature or morbid or self-destructive or corrupt."[19] Mailer's impact on the current critical scene is too often underestimated: The legacy of "The White Negro" can still be discerned in the tendency of cultural studies to celebrate "transgressive" politics of style, thereby romanticizing those excluded from power rather than seeking to open power up. As this tendency increasingly comes under critique from within cultural studies, we can learn from *Invisible Man* while learning how to read it.

Ellison presciently invokes and rejects the Mailerian dichotomy when he has his protagonist see and reject the hipster Rinehart as an alternative to the organizational world of the Brotherhood: "But what do *I* really want, I've asked myself. Certainly not the freedom of a Rinehart nor the power of a Jack, nor simply the freedom not to run" (575). Although a Rinehart-like manipulation of one's roles might serve as a useful "political instrument" (499), it becomes dangerous when elevated to an end in itself. The amoral manipulation of one's roles is, after all, precisely how one prospers within The Organization. When one of the Brotherhood's theorists attempts to jus-tify the group's tendency "to take advantage of the people," Invisible Man responds, "That's Rinehartism—cynicism . . ." (504; Ellison's ellipsis). To become Rinehart, then, is to become not the hipster opposite of the organi-zation man but his reflection.

From this perspective *Invisible Man* can be seen not as a mere displaced imitation of the organization-man narrative but as a critical reworking of it. By making his protagonist an African American organization man, Ellison rejects the romanticization of those excluded from the white-collar middle class. While his move carries the potential (realized in much of the *Invis-ible Man*'s critical reception) of subordinating the novel's racial concerns to a whitewashed existentialism, it can also be taken to reveal the racial uncon-scious of white-collar culture's construction of white identity. That is, the novel's narrative of alienation is subject to a functional reversibility through which its janitors and messengers who want to become executives can be read as executives who are afraid of becoming janitors and messengers.

Invisible Man suggests that the pervasive postwar desire for a romanti-cized African American lifestyle superior to the bureaucratized existence of the organization man overlays a deep-seated fear of racial downward mobility as the telos of organization life. Behind the white (-collar) desire to become black is the fear that one already is. The fear of racial downward mobility itself displaces class anxieties that have proven well founded. As early as 1951 Mills argued that while certain kinds of white-collar work provided the key to middle-class status in the midst of the postwar boom, white-collar work was structurally proletarianized because, unlike earlier forms of middle-class iden-tity based on small property ownership, it involved the by definition proletarian position of selling one's labor. While Mills's argument depended on a nostalgic regard of the free market as the matrix of uninhibited individualism (e.g., 9), and on a historically inaccurate account of the genealogy of the American middle class,[20] events since the early-seventies collapse of the postwar boom have largely confirmed his fears about white-collar proletarianization.

In a postwar climate that discouraged class analysis, fears of downward mobility reemerged here and there in a peculiarly racialized form. For instance, Cameron Hawley's *Executive Suite*—a bestselling 1952 novel about the power plays that take place in the Treadway Corporation following the unexpected death of its president—identifies J. Walter Dudley, Treadway's vice president of sales, as the organization man par excellence. Dudley is all appearance and no substance, a "perpetual beggar of friendship" whose professional success belies the fact that he is "a runner who [runs] without a goal."[21] In one scene Dudley has breakfast on the train between Chicago and Treadway's Pennsylvania headquarters. The steward assigns him to "old Henry," "a waiter who looked as if he had spent most of his long life in the service of a fine old Southern family." The other waiters are glad because tips are pooled and Dudley looks like a customer "who would really shell out for the Uncle Tom act." Dudley demands "fast service" in a voice of "brusque command," whereupon Henry gives him the patter—punctuated by many "Yassuh!"s—at which he excels. He offers Dudley a piece of melon he has "been saving special" and makes the rest of Dudley's order "sound like an inspired triumph." By juxtaposing Dudley and old Henry, *Executive Suite* draws an implicit parallel between their "acts" and suggests that Dudley himself engages in a kind of minstrelsy in his own job (239–40).

In a similar scene from Jack Finney's 1955 novel *The Body Snatchers*, the protagonist, Dr. Miles Bennell, and his old flame, Becky Driscoll, realize that the residents of Santa Mira are being taken over by pod-sprung alien duplicates. The pair has gone to Driscoll's house to see if her family has fallen victim as well, and, crouching on the front porch, they hear Driscoll's father, cousin, aunt, and uncle having an apparently normal conversation. But something alerts Bennell that all is not as it seems. Something in the Driscolls' voices reminds Bennell of Billy, a middle-aged black shoeshine man he knew in his college days. Billy "professed a genuine love for shoes" and appeared to enjoy the service he provided his patronizing white customers. But one morning, following "a student escapade," Bennell awoke to find himself in his car "in the run-down section of town" and overheard Billy engaging in a "quietly hysterical parody" of his own servility for another black man. "[N]ever before in my life," Bennell tells us, "had I heard such ugly, bitter, and vicious contempt in a voice, contempt for the people taken in by his daily antics, but even more for himself, the man who supplied the servility they bought from him." The narrative then flashes back to Driscoll's family, now obviously pod people, engaging in a similar parody of conversations they have had with Bennell. The shoeshine man Billy, *The Body Snatchers* suggests, is the white-collar middle class's alienated future.[22]

Within this framework *Invisible Man* offers a countergenealogy of white-collar alienation that explains its racial unconscious even as it undermines the peculiarly privileged position from which the organization-man discourse issues its complaints of middle-class angst. If the newness of the white-collar regime inheres in its shift of focus from the manipulation of things to the manipulation of people, the resulting self-alienating collapse between person and thing is long established for African Americans, brought to North America as commodities to produce other commodities. Even after the end of slavery, the history of African American labor in the United States remained a history of segregation into precisely the sorts of servile occupations feared by postwar white-collar workers. Crucially, the service sector grew at a slightly higher rate (although to considerably less fanfare) than the white-collar sector throughout the 1950s.[23] Although the service workforce remained disproportionately nonwhite at midcentury,[24] it had in some ways become harder to distinguish such service labor from the labor of the equally though oppositely segregated white-collar workforce.

But only in some ways. While the crucial differences between the kinds of work that white Americans and African Americans performed in these years are elided in the racial unconscious of the organization-man discourse, they remain explicit in *Invisible Man*. Ellison's novel thus avoids the twin errors of understanding white-collar work as the site of racial downward mobility or as a site of alienation whose relief lies in the non-"organized" world of the African American hipster. While offering an account of the way historically African American forms of labor anticipate the white-collar labor of the postwar period, *Invisible Man* insists on the differences that have separated, and continue to separate, white and black workers. It is in these complicated reflections on the parallels and disjunctions between postwar white-collar culture and African American experience that we may—indeed, must—grasp the unity of *Invisible Man*'s simultaneous tendencies toward "universalism" and racial specificity. While it would be absurd to read Ellison's novel as a work of economic history, we can appreciate its political and aesthetic strategies only by understanding the economic history in which it is embedded.

NOTES

Chris Looby, Ken Warren, and Christopher Wilson offered thoughtful critiques of earlier drafts of this essay, while Marshall Brown had helpful things to say about style. I owe Catherine Jurca a more thorough account of *Invisible Man*'s modernist aesthetics.

1. Warren, "The Unity of Experience," in *Ralph Ellison: A Collection of Critical Essays*, ed. John Hersey (Englewood Cliffs, N.J.: Prentice-Hall, 1974), 22; Bellow, "Man Underground," in Hersey, *Ralph Ellison*, 28–9.

2. Howe, "A Negro in America," *Nation*, May 1952, 454. For the exchange between Howe and Ellison, and the James Baldwin essays that motivated Howe's opening salvo, see Baldwin, "Everybody's Protest Novel" (1949) and "Many Thousands Gone" (1951), in *Notes of a Native Son* (1955; rpt. New York: Bantam, 1968), 9–36; Howe, "Black Boys and Native Sons" (1963), in *A World More Attractive: A View of Modern Literature and Politics* (New York: Horizon, 1963), 98–122; Howe, "A Reply to Ralph Ellison," *New Leader*, 3 February 1964, 12–4; and Ellison, "The

World and the Jug" (1963), in *Shadow and Act* (1964; rpt. New York: Vintage, 1979), 107–43.

3. Kaiser, "A Critical Look at Ellison's Fiction and at Social and Literary Criticism by and about the Author," *Black World* 20 (1970): 81–2, cited in Thomas Hill Schaub, *American Fiction in the Cold War* (Madison: University of Wisconsin Press, 1991), 93.

4. Watts, *Heroism and the Black Intellectual: Ralph Ellison, Politics, and Afro-American Intellectual Life* (Chapel Hill: University of North Carolina Press, 1994), passim.

5. Baker, "To Move without Moving: Creativity and Commerce in Ralph Ellison's Trueblood Episode," in *Blues, Ideology, and Afro-American Literature: A Vernacular Theory* (Chicago: University of Chicago Press, 1984), 172–99; Harper, *Framing the Margins: The Social Logic of Postmodern Culture* (New York: Oxford University Press, 1994), 122; Reed, *Fifteen Jugglers, Five Believers: Literary Politics and the Poetics of American Social Movements*, New Historicism, 22 (Berkeley: University of California Press, 1992), 71, 73. Reed, to be sure, credits Ellison's modernism with a politically progressive role in critiquing the earlier, implicitly humanizing mode of naturalism à la Wright. But this role remains compromised, as the quotes above make clear, by the structural dangers of depoliticization underlying *Invisible Man*'s "ambitions towards literary upward mobility" through modernism (71).

6. Reed's own notion of these conditions remains bound by the parameters of literary history, specifically the histories of "the white male literary and critical canon" and of literary naturalism (61), which he argues *Invisible Man* critiques. Taken in tandem with Reed's contention that the novel also critiques "black political/rhetorical strategies" (61), this move ironically perpetuates (and all the more firmly racializes) the distinction between aesthetics and politics that Reed sets out to overturn.

7. Mills, *White Collar: The American Middle Classes* (1951; rpt. New York: Oxford University Press, 1956), xviii.

8. Riesman, with Reuel Denney and Nathan Glazer, *The Lonely Crowd: A Study of the Changing American Character* (1950; rpt. New Haven, Conn.: Yale University Press, 1969); Whyte, *The Organization Man* (Garden City, N.Y.: Anchor, 1956).

9. Ohmann, "The Shaping of a Canon: U.S. Fiction, 1960–1975," in *Canons*, ed. Robert von Hallberg (Chicago: University of Chicago Press, 1984), 401 n. 43.

10. See Philip Rahv, "Our Country and Our Culture," *Partisan Review* 19 (1952): 306.

11. Jackson Lears, "A Matter of Taste: Corporate Cultural Hegemony in a Mass-Consumption Society," in *Recasting America: Culture and Politics in the Age of Cold War*, ed. Lary May (Chicago: University of Chicago Press, 1989), 50.

12. Christopher P. Wilson, *White Collar Fictions: Class and Social Representation in American Literature, 1885–1925* (Athens: University of Georgia Press, 1992), 4.

13. Ellison, *Invisible Man* (1952; rpt. New York: Vintage, 1989), 576.

14. Carol A. Barry, "White-Collar Employment: II—Characteristics," *Monthly Labor Review*, February 1961, 140–1.

15. Karen Brodkin Sacks, "How Did Jews Become White Folks?" in *Race*, ed. Steven Gregory and Roger Sanjek (New Brunswick, N.J.: Rutgers University Press, 1994), 78–102; George Lipsitz, "The Possessive Investment in Whiteness: Racialized Social Democracy and the 'White' Problem in American Studies," *American Quarterly* 47 (1995): 369–87.

16. Wilson, *The Man in the Gray Flannel Suit* (New York: Simon and Schuster, 1955), 153.

17. See Richard H. Pells, *The Liberal Mind in a Conservative Age: American Intellectuals in the 1940s and 1950s* (New York: Harper and Row, 1985), 216–32.

18. Echols, "'We Gotta Get Out of This Place': Notes toward a Remapping of the Sixties," *Socialist Review* 22, no. 2 (1992): 9–33; Lott, "White Like Me: Racial Cross-Dressing and the Construction of American Whiteness," in *Cultures of United States Imperialism*, ed. Amy Kaplan and Donald E. Pease (Durham, N.C.: Duke University Press, 1993), 474–95.

19. Mailer, "The White Negro: Superficial Reflections on the Hipster," in *The Portable Beat Reader*, ed. Ann Charters (New York: Viking, 1992), 585, 594.

20. For a corrective see Olivier Zunz, *Making America Corporate, 1870–1920* (Chicago: University of Chicago Press, 1990).

21. Hawley, *Executive Suite* (New York: Ballantine, 1952), 249, 135.

22. Finney, *The Body Snatchers* (New York: Dell, 1967), 116–20.

23. Carol A. Barry, "White-Collar Employment: I—Trends and Structure," *Monthly Labor Review*, January 1961, 15.

24. From 1950 through 1960 the percentage of white men who labored in the service sector varied from 6.5 to 6.3 percent, the percentage of white women from 17.9 to 90.3 percent. By contrast, the percentage of nonwhite male workers in the service sector varied from 24.0 to 17.4 percent in these years and that of nonwhite female workers from 72.5 to 63.6 percent (Barry, "White-Collar Employment: II," 142, table 3).

MORRIS DICKSTEIN

Ralph Ellison, Race, and American Culture

In the standard view of American culture after the war, and especially of the 1950s, the arts and intellectual life turned deeply conservative, reflecting the imperatives of the cold war, the migration to the suburbs, the new domesticity, and the rise of McCarthyism. A small academic industry has sprung up, linking every cultural development of the postwar period to the clenched mind-set of the cold war. At the same time, it has been more and more evident that the facile contrast between the fifties and the sixties is based on a deep simplification. The fifties were a far more restless, dynamic, and contradictory period than we have generally allowed. It can be easily shown how the roots of the sixties lay in the new energies of the postwar years, when writers, along with jazz musicians, abstract painters, and maverick filmmakers, contributed to a creative ferment that matched the growth of the economy and the spread of American influence. Working just outside the mainstream, often seemingly apolitical, these writers and artists helped shape a counterculture focused on the youthful dropout, the rebel without a cause, the disgruntled outsider who embodied new cultural values: improvisation, spontaneity, an experimental attitude.

This last phrase comes not from the Beats but, surprisingly, from Ralph Ellison describing his 1952 novel *Invisible Man* as he accepted the National Book Award. It may be hard to imagine Ellison, always so correct and elegant

From *Raritan* 18, no. 4 (Spring 1999): 30–50. © 1999 by *Raritan*.

in his personal demeanor, as any kind of radical, or as a forerunner of the counterculture. Moreover, no black writer was more warmly welcomed by the literary establishment or more reviled by his young successors when the catchwords of black nationalism took hold in the 1960s and '70s. Even before then, left-wing critics like Irving Howe had indicted Ellison and James Baldwin for turning their backs on the militant traditions of black anger associated with their mentor, Richard Wright.

Baldwin's damaging depiction of *Native Son* in his 1949 manifesto, "Everybody's Protest Novel," and again two years later in "Many Thousands Gone," dealt a major blow to Wright's reputation. It cleared the ground for writing that was far more personal than Wright's, more metaphysical, more concerned with individual identity, including sexual identity. Neither Baldwin nor Ellison ever challenged one essential conviction of Wright's, that the experience of African Americans was deeply conditioned by the traumatic effects of racial separation and discrimination. But this alone, they insisted, was insufficient to account for the varied ways that blacks had accommodated to their treatment and the complex lives they had shaped for themselves.

In his controversial 1963 essay "Black Boys and Native Sons," Howe looked approvingly at Baldwin's recent shift toward protest writing in *The Fire Next Time*. "Like Richard Wright before him, Baldwin has discovered that to assert his humanity he must release his rage." He accuses Ellison, however, of ending his only novel with a "sudden, unprepared and implausible assertion of unconditioned freedom," as if the Invisible Man in his basement hole spoke, without irony, for Ellison himself. Baldwin's newfound militance did little to endear him to the young black firebrands of the sixties, who attacked or dismissed him, and it seriously damaged his work, which at its best was grounded in introspection, not angry rhetoric. But Ellison responded to Howe and Baldwin—and, by implication, to his own later black critics—in a celebrated essay, "The World and the Jug," in which he wittily disparaged Baldwin for "out-Wrighting Richard" and minimized his own oedipal relationship to the author of *Native Son*. "Wright was no spiritual father of mine," he wrote. "I rejected Bigger Thomas as any final image of Negro personality" (something Wright himself had never intimated). Ellison explored the relationship more affectionately in a lecture about Wright a few years later, revealing how close he was to his mentor at least until 1940.

In essays like these, Ellison picked up where Baldwin faltered, insisting on the variety and complexity of black life and the range of influences, from Hemingway and T. S. Eliot to jazz, that had been enriching for black artists. Ellison was immune to the destructive force of black nationalism, perhaps because he had already reimagined it so well in *Invisible Man*. Black anger and black pride were only part of the broad constellation of Ellison's novel, which ranges over the whole terrain of African-American life, from folklore and dialect to urban hustling and pan-Africanism. This was why he reacted so strongly to Howe's well-argued but prescriptive essay. It seemed to confine the black writer to a path of anger, protest, and victimization. To a man who cherished his creative freedom, who had aspired to write the Great American Novel, this was a much narrower role than the one he wished to play.

The issue of freedom identified by Howe would become the keystone not only of Ellison's creative work but of his radical rethinking of the role of race and culture in American life. Howe, with his affinity for the European social novel, with his political commitments and his sense of the tragic, spoke up for the conditioned life, insisting that harsh circumstances define and limit the options available to individuals, especially those at the bottom of the social ladder. Ellison, on the other hand, was determined that his fiction and essays would reflect the widest range of encounters, the most abundant opportunities for self-making—in other words, a larger, more various American reality as he had known it.

Ellison's novel had already sent up every kind of ideological current in black life, from the Marxism of the thirties to Black Power notions that would only flourish more than a decade later. Born in Oklahoma in 1914, not long after its transition from Indian territory to statehood, Ellison had studied music at Tuskegee Institute between 1933 and 1936 before migrating to Harlem, where he began to write under Richard Wright's insistent prodding. Thus he not only knew Negro life in the West, in the South, and in the largest Northern ghetto, but was exposed (at Tuskegee) to the accommodationist ideas of Booker T. Washington ("the Founder"), which he would wickedly satirize throughout *Invisible Man*. All these, including his close links with the Harlem branch of the Communist Party, are among the autobiographical strands from which his novel is loosely woven. But these experiences appear even more directly in the essays which, as we now can see, form a major part of Ellison's literary legacy.

When Ellison first brought together his essays, reviews, lectures, and interviews in 1964 in *Shadow and Act*, they were gratefully received as revealing adjuncts to his novel, and as a promissory note for the fiction yet to come. A second collection, *Going to the Territory*, appeared with almost no fanfare in 1986. But well before the *Collected Essays* of 1995, it became clear that this impressive prose was not simply an assortment of personal opinions but a major body of cultural criticism that had inspired other black intellectuals and had begun to influence the national outlook on race, as Wright had done for the 1940s and Baldwin had done for the 1950s and early 1960s.

What once looked tame or apolitical in Ellison's work—his emphasis on identity, freedom, and the vast potential for diversity in American life—

has come to seem more radical than the political criticism that rejected it; this too has become part of our revised view of the postwar years. The key to Ellison's approach is his way of exploring his double consciousness, his sense of identity as a Negro and as an American. His answer to Baldwin's question, "Do I really want to be integrated into a burning house?" would surely have been, "Yes, because it's my house." And because not all of it is burning, not all the time: the property is still rich with undeveloped possibilities.

Of all African-American writers and intellectuals, Ellison stakes the greatest claims—not for a separate black culture or literary tradition, but for an inestimably great role within American culture. He acknowledges a debt to Jewish-American writers, but insists that they did not escape provinciality until they saw their experience in wider terms as part of the crazy quilt of American culture, by treating their protagonists as representative Americans, not simply as archetypal Jews.

Where others pay lip service to "diversity," Ellison shows in fascinating detail how different currents have merged into the mainstream of our culture—not simply how Anglo-Saxon culture was altered by the folkways and speech of outsiders but how the children of immigrants and slaves adapted remote customs to their own usage. Cultural appropriation is the great theme of Ellison's essays, which explore the mixed origins and improvisational strategies of both black and American identity. Through half a century of lecturing and writing, Ellison never tired of describing how different cultural forms, high and low, classical and vernacular, eastern and western, northern and southern, were braided together into an authentic American creativity. In the varied traditions of early Du Bois, Dewey, Randolph Bourne, Horace Kallen, and Alain Locke, Ellison's is a classically pluralist defense of cultural diversity. In a revealing tribute to Locke, Ellison stressed the danger of becoming "unconsciously racist by simply stressing one part of our heritage," the genetic, racial part.

> You cannot have an American experience without having a black experience. Nor can you have the technology of jazz, as original as many of those techniques are, without having had long centuries of European musical technology, not to mention the technologies of various African musical traditions. . . .
>
> What I am suggesting is that when you go back you do not find a pure stream; after all, Louis Armstrong, growing up in New Orleans, was taught to play a rather strict type of military music before he found his jazz and blues voice. Talk about cultural pluralism! It's the air we breathe; it's the ground we stand on.

Part of Ellison's story was about how a culture could be created by people who were neither free nor equal—by despised immigrants or oppressed slaves. In one example, he describes how slaves adapted European dance fashions brought over by their masters:

> First the slaves mocked them, and then decided, coming from dancing cultures, that they could do them better—so they went on to define what is surely the beginnings of an American choreography.

He goes on to show that what began in rags in the slave yards eventually found its way into Negro dance halls and juke joints until it finally reached the stage. In Ellison's picture, popular and vernacular culture, located at the fringes of the social hierarchy, provides the pores through which the main body of culture breathes and renews itself. Blacks had "the freedom of experimentation, of trying out new things no matter how ridiculous they might seem," because "there was no one to take them too seriously." Oppression and dislocation had imposed "a great formlessness" on Negro life. They needed to experiment, to develop a new language, because they were forced into tight corners where they had to improvise, to recreate themselves, and because the cultural mainstream reflected no honest images of their own lives—or mirrored them only in distorted or one-dimensional forms, as in minstrel culture or in Hollywood movies.

To Ellison, white Americans have always "suffered from a deep uncertainty as to who they really are." On one hand this led them to seek a unified identity by scapegoating "outsiders." But the same national uncertainty gives these outsiders exceptional leverage—politically, to recall the majority to its professed ideals; culturally, to work within the many popular forms of expression that make America different from an old and traditional culture. "On this level," says Ellison, "the melting pot did indeed melt, creating such deceptive metamorphoses and blending of identities, values, and lifestyles that most American whites are culturally part Negro American without even realizing it." And he shows how, beginning as far back as Huckleberry Finn, the black presence led to "certain creative tensions" that had a decisive effect on the high culture as well.

In the opening piece of his second collection, "The Little Man at Chehaw Station," Ellison wrote a definitive (if idealized) meditation on the American audience, which he saw embodied in the little man behind the stove at a small railroad station near Tuskegee—the random individual whose judgment matters, who sees through the bogus performance, whose culture is at once eclectic and classical, popular yet demanding. If *Invisible Man* had a single ideal reader, it would be this man, completely ordinary yet protean and adventurous. "Possessing an American-vernacular receptivity to change, a healthy delight in creative attempts at formalizing irreverence, and a Yankee trader's respect for the experimental, he is repelled by works of art that would strip human experience—especially American experience—of its wonder and stubborn complexity." This figure is the artist's creative conscience—the surprisingly knowledgeable, innately skeptical Everyman. Whether such a man actually exists, for Ellison he is a paradigm of democratic life, in which culture and education have spread through mysterious channels and "certain assertions of personality, formerly the prerogative of high social rank, have become the privilege of the anonymous and the lowly."

Such a man can also become the agent rather than simply the consumer of culture; in a different guise he reappears later in the essay as a classic "American joker," a cool ghetto customer who performs some astonishing bits of personal theater before delighted onlookers outside Ellison's home on Riverside Drive. After describing this street-smart character's antics, including his flamboyant dress and body language, Ellison calls him "a home-boy bent on projecting and recording with native verve something of his complex sense of cultural identity." This man—or Ellison's projection of him—represents culture as pragmatic improvisation, for he is putting together his own personality out of bits and pieces of different traditions. Making himself up as he goes along, he demonstrates "an American compulsion to improvise upon the given." He "was a product of the melting pot and the conscious or unconscious comedy it brews." To Ellison, Americans have "improvised their culture as they did their politics and institutions: touch and go, by ear and by eye; fitting new form to new function, new function to old form." This emphasis on improvisation links Ellison not only to the counterculture of the 1950s, but to a wider American tradition that extends from Emerson and pragmatism to jazz and picaresque fiction—the Huck Finn-style road novels, steeped in the vernacular, that made a breakthrough for many fifties writers. It also connects him, as Ross Posnock shows in his new book *Color & Culture*, to postmodern, anti-essentialist notions of identity.

In this account of our eclectic forms of self-invention, Ellison is at once expounding the technique of *Invisible Man*, situating it within American culture, and perhaps explaining why it was so hard for him to complete his second novel. Two years later he developed these ideas in an autobiographical lecture, "Going to the Territory," the title piece of the same collection. Here Ellison gave one of the most forceful descriptions of how our culture and identity have been shaped by a constant process of cultural assimilation. The very title alludes to Huck Finn's metaphor for reclaiming his freedom. Recalling his own school days in Oklahoma, not long after the Territory had become a state, Ellison describes young Negroes learning European folk dances, a sight which some might find "absurd" but to him is part of a salutary process of appropriating the Other, making creative use of what seems alien. Rather than expressing "a desire to become white," we were narrowing "the psychological distance between them and ourselves," as well as "learning their dances as an artistic challenge." This skill, this discipline, would be the black children's secret weapon as well as their key to an unnoticed freedom—"our freedom to broaden our personal culture by absorbing the culture of others," something that could develop and grow even "within our state of social and political unfreedom."

For Ellison himself this was a special gift, for it introduced him "to the basic discipline required of the artist." Ellison's musical education would shape his vision of American literature as the cultural expression of democracy, an ongoing process of transformation mediated by the vernacular. He sees the vernacular not simply as "popular or indigenous language," but as a "dynamic process in which the most refined styles of the past are continually merged with the play-it-by-eye-and-by-ear improvisations which we invent in our efforts to control our environment and entertain ourselves." On one level this is a demotic version of Eliot's "Tradition and the Individual Talent," with its account of how the tradition is constantly being altered by new voices and creative departures. On another level it's a well-articulated example of a fluid and functional pragmatist aesthetic within a democratic culture.

Far from treating the vernacular as a dumbing-down of high culture, a view common among critics of popular culture in the 1950s, Ellison sees it as part of an ongoing process of self-renewal. "While the vernacular is shy of abstract standards," he says, "it still seeks perfection in the form of functional felicity. This is why considerations of function and performance figure so prominently in the scale of vernacular aesthetics." This, of course, is a description of jazz, for Ellison the very epitome of how vernacular artists refine and transform traditional materials. But it applies equally well to a writer like Twain, who showed how to turn regional speech into art "and thus taught us how to capture that which is essentially American in our folkways and manners."

Ellison's versions of Twain, of jazz and the blues, and of his own early musical education are also accounts of the creative process that shaped *Invisible Man* and made it an archetypal American novel. In his previously mentioned 1953 speech accepting the National Book Award, Ellison gives prime importance to the book's "experimental attitude," that phrase out of the pragmatist lexicon that would apply equally well to a modernist or a jazz aesthetic. Explaining why he turned away from the spare language of naturalism, he notes that "despite the notion that its rhythms were those of everyday speech,

I found that when compared with the rich babel of idiomatic expression around me, a language full of imagery and gesture and rhetorical canniness, it was embarrassingly austere." In its place he sought a language and form that were richer, more varied, and more mysterious, full of word-play and allusion, metaphoric in plot as well as verbal style, so as to convey the fluidity and complexity of the world as he had experienced it. With its protean form and exuberant style, *Invisible Man* would exemplify the vernacular process through which American culture had explored its contradictions, including its racial conflicts.

One of Ellison's most strongly held views was that race itself is hardly more than a mystification, that skin color and blood kinship are of little help in explaining the complexity of human culture. Ellison's aim is to put aside "the insidious confusion between race and culture." Whether seen as a source of pride (by nationalists), of shame (by racists), or of solidarity (by communal boosters), race alone determines little about what human beings can achieve. It is not a fate to which individuals have been ineluctably condemned, or an essence that defines or delimits them. In his response to Irving Howe, he complains that "Howe makes of 'Negroness' a metaphysical condition, one that is a state of irremediable agony which all but engulfs the mind." Ellison's pragmatic response—to Howe, to Baldwin, to white supremacists and black nationalists alike—is that identity is fashioned rather than given, created rather than determined by biology or social statistics. "It is not skin color which makes a Negro American but cultural heritage as shaped by the American experience."

For Ellison the construction of identity is analogous to the hard work of making art, involving a mixture of personal discipline and subtle cultural influences. In *Invisible Man* he gives us an anonymous protagonist with no identity except what others are continually trying to impose on him, no strategy except his eagerness to please. In the whole spectrum of postwar fiction he is the ultimate outsider, telling his story from his underground lair. But through most of the novel he is also the man who most wanted to be an insider, to fit in and to be accepted. The novel's episodic structure, prismatic language, and fluid technique reflect the process through which he tests and gradually sheds these imposed definitions, with all the illusions that came with them.

Like Voltaire's Candide, whose experience continually belies his teacher's insistence that this is "the best of all possible worlds," Ellison's protagonist is an unshakable innocent, immature, eager to get ahead, trained in the habits of deference and humility through which blacks in America had traditionally gotten by. But life itself tells him otherwise, beginning with the death of his grandfather, who, after a long, quiet, humble existence, calls himself a spy and a traitor in the enemy's country, and urges him to "overcome 'em with yeses, undermine 'em with grins, agree 'em to death and destruction." Near the end of the book, the hero bitterly determines to do just that: "I'd let them swoller me until they vomited or burst wide open. . . . I'd yes them until they puked and rolled in it. All they wanted of me was one belch of affirmation and I'd bellow it out loud. Yes! Yes! YES! That was all anyone wanted of us, that we should be heard and not seen, and then heard in one big optimistic chorus of yassuh, yassuh, yassuh!"

The whole novel is a test of his grandfather's double message of humility and enmity, seeming accommodation and inner resistance—the first of many bits of advice he takes in without fully understanding them. Like the heroes of other picaresque novels, the young man is less a full-blooded character than a convenience of a symbolic, often surreal plot. Ellison uses narrative as a freewheeling vehicle for ideas, word-play, wild satire, ideological burlesque, and striking realistic detail. His grandfather's words serve as a chorus or leitmotif recurring from episode to episode. The novel is tied together by many other such texts that reappear musically, a theme and variations marking the stages of the narrator's progress. Another text like this is "To Whom It May Concern—Keep This Nigger-Boy Running," which he understands to be the message he carries as he tries to make his way in the world. At every step he's given the illusion of progress only to keep running in place, to get nowhere. He needs to break with received messages, socially ascribed roles, conventional restraints, and respectable ambitions in order to come into his own.

The typical bildungsroman is about the passage from innocence to experience, a process that turns the naive or callow protagonist into the substantial person who narrates the book. The hero of *Invisible Man*, however, ends up nowhere, in a state of articulate hibernation, in some well-lit Dostoevskyan hole in the ground, not in Harlem but in some "border area" where he can see without being seen. The novel is not about the shaping of a life but the unshaping of illusions, about breaking through to a new awareness of what you can do and be. When the hero eventually puts his innocence behind him—the naivete he had resumed in nearly every episode—it is not to make a life but to shed all the false lives for which he had been pointlessly striving. Along with the "running" metaphor, this suggests *Invisible Man*'s kinship to other picaresque fiction of the 1950s, such as *The Catcher in the Rye, On the Road, Lolita*, and *Rabbit, Run*. In these novels, the protagonist's deepest need is not to become a success, to settle into an ordered life, but to escape the one he already has—not to take on responsibility but to slough it off. Like Holden Caulfield, Ellison's hero eventually sees through the phoniness of nearly everyone around him, the fakery inherent in social role-playing. He rejects the 1950s mantra of maturity, the demand for affirmation, and reaches for something that makes him an outsider, even a pariah. He wants to live his discontent, even if it is only half understood.

One thread of *Invisible Man* is Ellison's lively mockery of every kind of respectability, black or white, corporate or communist, middle class or working class. The good white citizens who organize the "battle royal" are lechers and sadists, treating the black boys like gladiators in a Roman arena. At college the young man tries but fails to live by the visionary ideals of the Founder and Dr. Bledsoe. Expelled, he learns what those so-called ideals really add up to—a way of manipulating whites into thinking that you serve and respect them. Up north, he seeks help from a trustee of the college named Emerson—the names in the book are broadly symbolic—but is disabused by the man's fretful son. He is a spoof of a well-meaning white liberal—patronizing, neurotic, and self-absorbed; he urges the young man to study another Emerson's ideas about self-reliance, and seeks plaintively to be his friend, but ends up asking him to become his valet.

Each episode is dominated by a false God exacting tribute, a would-be mentor trying to determine his path. "Everyone seemed to have some plan for me, and beneath that some more secret plan." At the paint factory he is under the authority of an old Uncle Tom, Lucius Brockway, underpaid, overqualified, submissive to whites, vicious to other blacks especially those connected with the union. After an explosion reminiscent of Fritz Lang's sci-fi masterpiece *Metropolis*, he enters a surgical "white" world and is subjected to surreal experiments by men probing his sense of reality. In trying to deprive him of his identity, to lobotomize him, they unwittingly open him up to a new, more fluid sense of identity that will flourish in the big city.

At the other extreme are the few characters who nurture him without an agenda of their own, or simply help open his eyes. Trueblood's tragicomic tale of incest introduces him to the earthy world of the shacks and sharecropper cabins that lie outside the purview of the respectable college. When he shows this world to one of the white trustees, he is cast out—for introducing a touch of reality onto a painted set. Another helpful figure is the vet who echoed his grandfather's advice as the young man headed north: "Play the game, but don't believe in it—that much you owe yourself." In Harlem he boards with Mary, whose maternal concern is as anchored and authentic as Trueblood's ribald comedy of love and lust. She is a warm-hearted specimen of the common people, the substratum of personal reality that social theories ignore or suppress. The hero's mentors claim to be putting him in touch with history, but it is only a conveyor belt towards an unwanted future, an abstract process that takes no account of his wishes or needs. "Look at me! Look at *me!*" he finally shouts, in what could be the motto for the whole novel. "Everywhere

I've turned somebody has wanted to sacrifice me for my good—only *they* were the ones who benefited."

In one of the novel's richest scenes, he buys baked yams from a Harlem street-vendor and is flooded with nostalgia for the home he left behind, a distant pastoral world he has been taught to rise above. Yet going back to this early world is no answer. He must see its value—must accept the common life, the sensory plenitude from which he sprang—but also must put it behind him. Just as the college is the false Eden from which he had to fall in order to become himself, Mary's home is only a temporary shelter from the swirl of the city streets. Eating the yams makes him not only homesick but reflective. "What a group of people we were, I thought. Why, you could cause us the greatest humiliation simply by confronting us with something we liked." This leads him to a delicious fantasy in which he accuses Bledsoe of being "a shameless chitterling eater! . . . of relishing hog bowels!"

> Bledsoe would disintegrate, disinflate! With a profound sigh he'd drop his head in shame. He'd lose caste. The weekly newspapers would attack him. The captions over his picture: *Prominent Educator Reverts to Field-Niggerism!* . . . In the South his white folks would desert him. . . . He'd end up an exile washing dishes at the Automat.

This goes on much longer—it's the kind of wild riff that marks the hero's moments of recognition—and it leads to a moral: "to hell with being ashamed of what you liked." But the mind keeps turning, and within a page or two he begins to see the limits of the yam view of life. "Continue on the yam level and life would be sweet—though somewhat yellowish. Yet the freedom to eat yams on the street was far less than I had expected upon coming to the city. An unpleasant taste bloomed in my mouth now as I bit the end of the yam and threw it into the street; it had been frostbitten." In the end he typically resolves his conflict with an outrageous pun, "I yam what I yam."

This yam scene is one of several turning points at the center of the book. It's preachy—Ellison is always making his points—yet full of the sensory exuberance that gives this novel its gusto. Much of the commentary on the novel has focused on the brilliant set-pieces of the first half, especially the Trueblood episode, making up a darkly comic American equivalent of *The Pilgrim's Progress*. But readers have sometimes stumbled over the seemingly overlong Brotherhood sections that follow, which are clearly based on Ellison's (and Wright's) experiences with the Communist Party. It is only here, however—and in the Harlem riots that follow—that Ellison begins to pull the many threads together, bringing the novel to its exhilarating conclusion. Just as the hero must leave Mary behind, he must give up the sanctuary of the Men's House, a temple of hollow propriety and foolish dreams and ambitions. (The Men's House is Ellison's version of the Harlem Y, where he stayed when he first came to the city in 1936.) By dumping the foul contents of a cuspidor over the head of a Baptist reverend whom he takes for Bledsoe, the hero throws away the crutch that protected him from a world "without boundaries"—from the fluid reality of Harlem and the city. If in earlier episodes he is slowly shedding illusions, only to deal with new ones right afterward, now he gradually yields to the flux as he comes to recognize and relish his own invisibility. In his own way he enacts the process of self-making described in Ellison's (and Emerson's) essays.

The narrator's growth of awareness, his willingness to go with the urban flow, is played out through metaphors, such as the images of blindness and vision that run through the whole novel: the blindfolded boys at the battle royal, the college sermon about the Founder by the blind preacher Barbee, the torn photograph of a boxer who had been blinded in the ring, and finally the glass eye of Jack, the Brotherhood leader, which pops out at an unfortunate moment and reminds us of the limits of his vision. In the Brotherhood the young man learns to see beyond race, as Richard Wright did, but he is mocked and chastised when what he sees doesn't fit the current line. The Brotherhood liberates him at first, introducing him to a wider world, giving him both work to do and a fully developed set of ideas, along with a sense of hope, a solidarity with others. But finally, like every other institution, it tries to impose its outlook on him. The Brotherhood pretends to a scientific grasp of history; it claims to know what Harlem needs better than Harlem itself. But this is ultimately exposed as another example of whites patronizing blacks—and of inflexible organizations stifling spontaneity and individuality.

As the novel's epilogue makes clear, Ellison is giving us a black-accented version of the anticonformist discourse of the 1950s, the social critique of the lonely crowd and the organization man. But because he is black, the narrator is faceless in a special and vivid way. He is invisible because no one really sees him; the Brotherhood recruits him but does not want him to think. "You made an effective speech," they tell him. "But you mustn't waste your emotion on individuals, they don't count. . . . History has passed them by." They object when he makes any appeal to color, yet he wonders whether he is being used simply because he's black. "What was I, a man or a natural resource?"

The second half of *Invisible Man* is also closely linked to midcentury novels and memoirs of disillusionment with communism, including Koestler's *Darkness at Noon*, the suppressed second half of Wright's *Black Boy*, and the collective volume *The God That Failed*, which included both Koestler and

Wright along with Ignazio Silone and others. Since Ellison was young and marginal to the Harlem branch of the Party and Wright was famous and central to it, it's fair to assume that this part of *Invisible Man* is heavily indebted to Wright's experiences, as described in both *American Hunger* and Ellison's "Remembering Richard Wright." There Ellison expresses gratitude to Wright for his willingness to confide in him about his problems with the Party, "especially his difficulty in pursuing independent thought." When Ellison's narrator is brought up on trial, the charges echo those directed against Wright—that he trusts his own judgment over the Party's, that he speaks *for* blacks rather than *to* them, that he is too concerned with race. *Invisible Man* takes us far beyond the anticommunist confessional, however; the young man's disillusionment is part of a much larger process of casting off misconceptions and exploring his own identity.

When the narrator decides that his political patrons are simply white men with yet another plan for him, he realizes that even in the Brotherhood he needs to live a double life. He learns to live within a shifting sense of who he actually is. Standing before an audience on his Party assignment, decked out in a new suit and a new name, he experiences a sense of vertigo, as if caught with his identity down. He fears that he might forget his name, or be recognized by someone in the audience. "I bent forward, suddenly conscious of my legs in new blue trousers. But how do you know they're your legs? . . . For it was as though I were looking at my own legs for the first time—independent objects that could of their own volition lead me to safety or danger." He feels that he is standing simultaneously at opposite ends of a tunnel, both in the old life he has left behind and in a new world that's still disturbingly vague and unformed.

> This was a new phase, I realized, a new beginning, and I would have to take that part of myself that looked on with remote eyes and keep it always at the distance of the campus, the hospital machine, the battle royal—all now far behind. Perhaps the part of me that observed listlessly but saw all, missing nothing, was still the malicious, arguing part; the dissenting voice, my grandfather part; the cynical, disbelieving part—the traitor self that always threatened internal discord. Whatever it was, I knew that I'd have to keep it pressed down.

Like so much else in the novel, this at once exemplifies and parodies Emersonian notions of self-transformation. As a spokesman for the Brotherhood, the narrator is shedding his old skin, exercising his power over language and people. Yet he is also simply playing another assigned role, keeping the dissenting parts of himself "pressed down." With a flash of panic he sees that "the moment I walked out upon the platform and opened my mouth I'd be someone else." But he also senses that he could become simply a Party hack with an assumed name, someone arbitrarily forced to deny his past.

Only when he puts on dark green glasses and is everywhere taken for Rinehart, the hustler and trickster, the man of many faces and roles, is he willing to step outside history, acknowledge his invisibility, and yield to the fluidity of the world around him. Both the Brotherhood and the nationalists—personified by Ras the Exhorter, with his impassioned Garveyite rhetoric of racial pride—are locked into the hard lines of history as they each see it. Only Rinehart, who is everywhere and nowhere at once, can negotiate the chaos of the ghetto, the boundary-free world of modern urban identity.

> Could he be all of them: Rine the runner and Rine the gambler and Rine the briber and Rine the lover and Rinehart the Reverend? Could he himself be both rind and heart? What is real anyway? ... His world was possibility and he knew it. He was years ahead of me and I was a fool. The world in which we lived was without boundaries. A vast seething, hot world of fluidity, and Rine the rascal was at home. Perhaps *only* Rine the rascal was at home in it.

This is the novel's version of the malleable, self-fashioned identity that Ellison invokes in his essays, a way of stepping out of imposed roles or shaping them to your needs. His friend Tod Clifton, the poster boy for the Harlem Brotherhood, has turned his back on the organization and plunged out of history. In midtown he hawks Sambo dolls, whose fine strings symbolize how he himself felt manipulated. After Tod is shot down by a policeman, the narrator pursues a less suicidal way of reclaiming his individuality. Rinehart, the man of the city, provides him with a clue. "My entire body started to itch, as though I had been removed from a plaster cast and was unused to the new freedom of movement." He sees that compared to the South, where everyone knew him, the urban world can offer him freedom. "How many days could you walk the street without encountering anyone you knew, and how many nights? You could actually make yourself anew. The notion was frightening, for now the world seemed to flow before my eyes. All boundaries down, freedom was not only the recognition of necessity, it was the recognition of possibility."

* * *

Many of the midcentury works of deradicalization convey a wounded quality, a sense of apocalyptic combat, as in Whittaker Chambers's *Witness*

(1952), or a deep sense of loss, as in much of *The God That Failed*. Many former radicals portrayed communism as a lost or spoiled idealism, something precious they would never be able to recover. But a heady exhilaration spills over in the last hundred pages of *Invisible Man*, the thrill of a man reclaiming his own life—the food that embarrassed him, the experiences that formed him, the music "that touched upon something deeper than protest, or religion." What does the Brotherhood know of "the gin mills and the barber shops and the juke joints and the churches . . . and the beauty parlors on Saturdays when they're frying hair. A whole unrecorded history is spoken there." For these people it was not the Brotherhood but Rinehart, with his dodges and disguises, his endlessly resourceful maneuvers, that represented "a principle of hope, for which they gladly paid. Otherwise there was nothing but betrayal."

The narrator reasserts his solidarity with those who lie outside history, the "transitory ones": "birds of passage who were too obscure for learned classification, too silent for the most sensitive recorders of sound." As in his recognition of a world "without boundaries," Ellison, through his character, is expressing his commitment to becoming an artist, at once shaping his own identity and keeping in touch with common experience. The Brotherhood's line, like other white views of Negro life, is enjoined from above, not experienced from below. "It was all a swindle, an obscene swindle. They had set themselves up to describe the world. What did they know of us, except that we numbered so many, worked on certain jobs, offered so many votes, and provided so many marchers for some protest parade of theirs." As he recognizes how he's been used, his Dostoevskyan sense of humiliation helps him repossess his own experience:

> I began to accept my past and, as I accepted it, I felt memories welling up within me. It was as though I'd learned suddenly to look around corners; images of past humiliations flickered through my head and I saw they were more than separate experiences. They were me; they defined me. I was my experiences and my experiences were me, and no blind men, no matter how powerful they became, even if they conquered the world, could take that, or change one single itch, taunt, laugh, cry, scar, ache, rage or pain of it.

Through images of sight and insight, he gives us what seems like the novel's actual point of origin, the writer's own moment of recognition that catapulted him from the blindness of politics, ideology, and sociological abstraction to a grasp of the complexity of his own experience. Suddenly, all his old mentors merge into a single figure trying to bend him to their will—an external force that he must overthrow. "I looked around a corner of my mind and saw Jack and Norton and Emerson merge into one single white figure. They were very much the same, each attempting to force his picture of reality upon me and neither giving a hoot in hell for how things looked to me. I was simply a material, a natural resource to be used." This is Ellison's declaration of independence, his personal emancipation proclamation. The thrill he feels in writing it we also feel in reading it, not least because it provides the novel with such a strong formal resolution.

Did Ellison imagine that ordinary people, especially black people, could find freedom in the same way, as some artists can, by recognizing that reality and identity were malleable, that they are free to create themselves? He believes that blacks have a culture, a way of life, in which they already have done so. He dislikes deterministic visions of entrapment like the portrait of Bigger Thomas in *Native Son*, and insists that Richard Wright, in creating Bigger, had not done justice to his own wide experience. But Ellison's emphasis is always on imaginative freedom within political and social unfreedom, within limits that can be only partly transcended. Writing about *The Great Gatsby* he describes "the frustrating and illusory social mobility which forms the core of Gatsby's anguish," yet he argues that the novel's black readers could not make Gatsby's mistakes. Accepting the National Book Award for *Invisible Man*, Ellison, despite his feeling that social mobility can be "illusory," appealed to the shape-changing figure of Proteus as his paradigm for coping with America's "rich diversity and its almost magical fluidity and freedom." In his essays he tells us repeatedly that the effort that creates art—that requires craft, discipline, and a mastery over reality—is the same as the process that shapes individual identity and ultimately culture itself.

In one of many discursive texts set into *Invisible Man*, the narrator remembers a literature teacher's comments on Stephen Dedalus in Joyce's *Portrait of the Artist*: "Stephen's problem, like ours, was not actually one of creating the uncreated conscience of his race, but of creating the uncreated features of his face. Our task is that of making ourselves individuals. The conscience of a race is the gift of its individuals who see, evaluate, record.... We create the race by creating ourselves and then to our great astonishment we will have created something far more important: We will have created a culture." Since *Invisible Man* is in many ways modeled on Joyce, and since Joyce himself highlights the word race, this is an especially momentous statement of purpose. *Invisible Man* is linked not only to the postwar discourse of anticommunism but to the closely related defense of liberal individualism and cultural pluralism in the work of social critics like Lionel Trilling, Reinhold Niebuhr, and Arthur Schlesinger, Jr. The case Trilling makes for the inwardness and complexity of art as against ideology is echoed by both Baldwin and

Ellison. Yet Ellison gives it a radical, not a conservative edge. His arguments for the diversity of both black and American life, for a cultural rather than a strictly political approach, for discipline and self-mastery, and for an acceptance of complexity and contradiction have in recent years provided black artists and intellectuals like his close friend Albert Murray, Toni Morrison, Michael Harper, Wynton Marsalis, James Alan McPherson, Stanley Crouch, Gerald Early, and Henry Louis Gates, Jr. with a vigorous alternative to both black nationalism and Marxism.

Powerful as Ellison's essays are, his novel is even more impressive, a veritable *Ulysses* of the black experience, rich with folklore, verbal improvisation, mythic resonance, and personal history, in his words, "a raft of hope, perception and entertainment" that does justice to the variety of African-American life. Though a novel of the civil rights years, its perspective is neither integrationist nor rights-oriented but cultural. As angry as any text of black nationalists, it charts an odyssey through a whole way of life, a study of attitudes rather than abuses, deliberately written, as he recalled much later, in a voice of "taunting laughter," in a tone "less angry than ironic."

The novel is rich with moments that are neither realistic nor allegorical but emblematic, such as the yam-eating scene or the hero's one-man uprising at the Men's House or the splendid vision of Ras on a great black horse, dressed in the garb of an Abyssinian chieftain, with fur cap, shield, and cape ("a figure more out of dream than out of Harlem"). Ras makes great speeches, but when the narrator, defending himself, throws a spear that locks his jaws together, Ellison is doing something that few other postwar novelists could get away with—creating a charged image that is at once an event, a metaphor, and a statement. Baldwin in "Notes of a Native Son" had looked at the Harlem riots of 1943 through the lens of his own family history; Ellison, no less effectively, makes it emblematic of all the crosscurrents of African-American life.

In the typology of *Invisible Man*, Marcus Garvey foreshadows the Black Panthers, thirties Marxism anticipates post-sixties Marxism, and a midcentury conception of America's cultural diversity, marked by a fluid, malleable sense of identity, proves remarkably germane to an end-of-century debate over pluralism and multiculturalism. After steering us through every kind of emotional and ideological excess, Ellison's work represents the triumph of the center, the victory of moderation. Summing up every ideology roiling the turbulent waters of black life, Ellison wrote a great ideological novel, perhaps the single best novel of the whole postwar era, at once his own inner history and the complex paradigm of a whole culture.

JAMES M. ALBRECHT

Saying Yes and Saying No: Individualist Ethics in Ellison, Burke, and Emerson

The writings of Ralph Ellison constitute one of American literature's most sophisticated explorations of the doubleness that W. E. B. Du Bois described as central to African American identity. While testifying to the "longing" of the African American to overcome the social and psychic divisions imposed by American society, to "merge his double self into a better and truer self," Du Bois envisioned that truer self as one in which the doubleness of African and American elements would continue to coexist: "In this merging he wishes neither of the older selves to be lost. He would not Africanize America, for America has too much to teach the world and Africa. He would not bleach his Negro soul in a flood of white Americanism, for he knows that Negro blood has a message for the world" (215). Similarly, Ellison always asserted that, as an artist and an individual, he was heir both to a distinctive African American culture and to the American heritage within the Western European tradition. "I was taken very early," he recalled of his youth, "with a passion to link together all I loved within the Negro community and all those things I felt in the world which lay beyond" ("That Same Pain" 71). As an aspiring musician, for example, Ellison "felt no need to draw a line between the two traditions" of jazz and classical music: "our ideal was to master both" (69). Even in segregated America, Ellison found that, "[c]ulturally, everything was mixed": "we wanted to share both: the

From *Publications of the Modern Language Association of America* 114, no. 1 (January 1999): 46–63. © 1999 by the Modern Language Association of America.

65

classics and jazz, the Charleston and the Irish reel, spirituals and the blues, the sacred and the profane" (70). Without minimizing the "all too real" obstacles designed to deny blacks opportunities (72),[1] he insisted on the complexity of the experience that African Americans achieved in spite of and in resistance to those obstacles. Consequently, he criticized writers such as Richard Wright for portraying African Americans as too determined, too defeated by their social environment.[2]

The individualism behind this critique of Wright is itself a prime example of Ellison's desire to "master both" traditions, a product of that border space of doubleness where things are culturally mixed, where traditional American institutions become inflected by the unique perspective of African American experience.[3] Ellison's individualism draws on a central Emersonian tradition of American individualism yet revises that tradition by placing it firmly in the context of American race relations. I hope to illustrate this genealogy by exploring a complex scene of intertextual allusion: Ellison's satire of Emerson in *Invisible Man*. Critics have tended to read this satire as evidence of Ellison's scathing rejection of Emersonian individualism.[4] Such a reading accepts— and constructs Ellison as accepting—the traditional and resilient idea that Emerson's philosophy ignores the material and historical reality of evil. In contrast, I want to argue that Ellison's parody is aimed at a highly mediated version of Emerson—the Emerson canonized in Lewis Mumford's 1926 study *The Golden Day*, an influential precursor to F. O. Matthiessen's *American Renaissance*. Moreover, even as Ellison lampoons this canonical Emerson, the ethic of self-expressive action dramatized by the career of Ellison's narrator extends a pragmatic tradition of individualism running from Emerson through writers such as William James and Kenneth Burke. The canonical portrait of an idealist Emerson who affirms the transcendent autonomy of the individual mind has too often obscured the more pragmatic self described in Emerson's writings, a self that exists only within the limitations of the material world, including the pervasive limitations of culture, society, and language, and that therefore is always socially implicated and indebted. It is this Emersonian tradition, concerned with the individual's complex relations to social resources and responsibilities, that Ellison extends. Thus, *Invisible Man*'s parody of Emerson is best read, I believe, as a dual gesture of critique and affiliation: Ellison rejects canonical Emersonianism, as well as the political blindnesses commonly associated with it, in order to appropriate the ethical possibilities of a more pragmatic Emersonian individualism.[5]

While Mumford is the mediating figure in *Invisible Man*'s parody of Emerson, Ellison's affiliation with a more pragmatic Emerson can be traced through the mediating figure of Ellison's friend Kenneth Burke, who Ellison claimed greatly influenced *Invisible Man* ("Art of Fiction" 218–19).[6] Both Ellison and Burke revise Emerson's individualism as they extend it, adding a more political notion of social responsibility to Emerson's ethic of self-expressive activity, or self-culture. Such critiques offered from within the pragmatic tradition are far more cogent, I would argue, than more traditional interpretations that depict Emerson as an absolute idealist or an apologist for capitalism.[7] Moreover, following Du Bois's and Ellison's insistence that the African American experience is quintessentially American, I would argue that a truly American sense of an Emersonian tradition must include African American writers like Ellison who have both claimed and reshaped that tradition.[8]

I

Ellison, named Ralph Waldo Ellison by his father, could hardly help perceiving Emerson as an imposing American precursor (Ellison, "Hidden Name" 194–97). Indeed, Emerson occupies a prominent position in *Invisible Man*: Mr. Norton, a white New England industrialist and a philanthropic trustee of the black state college the narrator attends, repeatedly recommends Emerson's philosophy to the narrator. Norton dwells particularly on the idea of fate, which he says links him to the narrator: "[Y]ou are my fate," he insists, "upon you depends the outcome of the years I have spent in helping your school" (41). Ellison heavily ironizes Norton's vision of his connection to black youth, making clear that Norton's philanthropy is blatantly self-aggrandizing:

> I have wealth and a reputation and prestige—all that is true, but your great Founder had more than that, he had tens of thousands of lives dependent upon his ideas and upon his actions. What he did affected your whole race. In a way, he had the power of a king, or in a sense, of a god. (44–45)

It is a desire for such godlike power that underlies Norton's notion of a destiny that connects him to the narrator: "Through you and your fellow students I become, let us say, three hundred teachers, seven hundred trained mechanics, eight hundred skilled farmers, and so on" (45). In contrast, Norton's actual effect on the narrator is disastrous.

Norton asks the narrator to drive him on a tour of the countryside, where he hears a story of incest from a black farmer, Jim Trueblood, that mirrors Norton's incestuous feelings for his own daughter and pushes him to a physical collapse. When Norton calls for whiskey to restore himself, the narrator takes him to a local saloon and bordello named, significantly, the Golden Day. There Norton meets a group of black war veterans on furlough from a local asylum who treat him with anger and disdain, and that anger boils over into a riot. Norton's self-serving vision of himself and of black–white relations thus is shaken, and the narrator is expelled from college, upbraided by the college president, Dr. Bledsoe, for being stupid enough to show a white person the reality of black experience. Moreover, the narrator, sent north with what he thinks are letters of recommendation from Bledsoe, seeks employment from a character named Mr. Emerson. The narrator does not meet Emerson, but at Emerson's office he sees one of Bledsoe's letters, which reveals that the college and its white trustees have conspired to expel him permanently, to "hope him to death, and keep him running" (191).

Not surprisingly, readers often see these allusions as a bitter indictment of Emersonian individualism. Alan Nadel, in his insightful study of *Invisible Man*'s allusions to American literature, argues that the inaccessible Mr. Emerson represents the abstract idealism of Emerson's philosophy, while Mr. Norton represents the absurdity of attempting to apply those ideals to real life (115). This parody rejects Emerson, Nadel concludes, as an "author of false hopes" who is unable "to recognize evil [. . . in] the complicated form it takes in the actual world" (118, 116). The limitation of this interpretation is that it largely accepts *Invisible Man*'s parodic characters as a sincere and accurate criticism of Emerson's philosophy. Yet the version of Emerson being lampooned is, after all, a highly mediated one: Mr. Norton's vague platitudes confidently cite Emerson to validate Norton's role as an industrialist and philanthropist, but Ellison's satire surely invites readers to discount this self-serving appropriation. Indeed, Nadel quotes in a footnote a letter Ellison wrote Nadel in which Ellison cautions that he was satirizing not Emerson's "oracular stance" but, rather, "some of the bombast that has been made of his pronouncements" (15n7). The narrator's relationship to Mr. Norton is indeed crucial for understanding how *Invisible Man* both extends and revises Emerson's ethics, yet it is important to resist concluding that the parody in Norton's bombastic reduction of Emerson indicates Ellison's true relationship to Emerson.

Another argument for interpretive caution is that Lewis Mumford, as well as Norton, mediates the version of Emerson satirized by Ellison. The name of the whorehouse where the narrator takes Norton, the Golden Day, clearly alludes to Mumford's study of the same title. Mumford uses the term *golden day* for the years 1830–60, which he celebrates as an era in which writers like Emerson, Thoreau, Whitman, Melville, and Hawthorne transformed the material facts of American life into higher expressions of artistic or spiritual truth. What is remarkable about Mumford's book is the pessimism and nostalgia of its historical narrative—an interpretation stressed both by Nadel (86–89) and by James Livingston in his excellent study of pragmatism (225–55).[9] Mumford portrays the golden day as a fleeting cultural moment when the American mind had escaped the materialism of the pioneer era but had not yet become mired in the materialism of the Gilded Age: "That world was the climax of American experience. What preceded led up to it: what followed, dwindled away from it" (91). In this scheme, America's development into an industrial society, accelerated by the Civil War, can appear only as a tragic fall in which the American imagination succumbed to the materialism of the machine age. Mumford locates this imaginative failure in the literature of realism and naturalism and especially in the philosophy of William James, whose focus on utility, Mumford charges, amounts to a "pragmatic acquiescence" to material reality (183–93).

It seems that the object of Ellison's parody, then, is Mumford's idealized construction of Emerson and Mumford's narrative of the relation between American literature and history. Most obviously, by presenting the Golden Day as a whorehouse for disenfranchised black soldiers, Ellison is ridiculing Mumford's history: 1830–60 was no golden day for African Americans. Mumford makes only passing reference to the sectional struggle over slavery that increasingly dominated the American scene in the 1840s and 1850s, and his only real interest in the Civil War is that it hastened the industrialization that ended the golden day: "the war was a struggle between two forms of servitude, the slave and the machine. The machine won, and the human spirit was almost as much paralyzed by the victory as it would have been by the defeat" (136). By contrast, Ellison, in his 1946 essay "Twentieth-Century Fiction and the Black Mask of Humanity," praises writers such as Emerson, Thoreau, Whitman, Melville, and Twain not for imaginatively transcending history—the achievement Mumford valorizes—but for confronting the central dilemma of American history embodied in the oppressed humanity of the African American (88).[10]

Nadel provides a cogent interpretation of Mumford's role in *Invisible Man*'s literary allusions, arguing that Ellison's whorehouse symbolizes the historical reality repressed by Mumford's study (94–103). Unfortunately, when Nadel moves on to assess Ellison's allusions to Emerson, Mumford vanishes from the account. Having persuasively argued that Ellison advocates rejecting Mumford's reductive literary history, Nadel is content to rehearse conventional interpretations of Emerson. Nadel's readings of Ellison's characters Mr. Norton and Mr. Emerson paint Emerson as an absolute optimist who effaces evil—either by celebrating a transcendent ideal beyond material reality or by celebrating the material as ideal, blithely ignoring the less-than-ideal aspects of that reality. The problem is not Nadel's interpretations of Ellison's characters; they seem right on the mark—if one reads the characters as lampooning stereotypical misreadings of Emerson, if one recalls Ellison's claim to be satirizing the "bombast that has been made of" Emerson. Nadel acknowledges but then erases this basic yet crucial distinction: he admits that Mr. Norton's platitudes are distortions of Emerson but then argues that Mr. Norton's absurd applications reveal absurdities in Emerson. For example, Nadel sees Mr. Norton's reductive notion of fate as an extension of Emerson's reductiveness:

> [Emerson] asserts that Fate is Nature, which is good, and failure to see that good in any given event is the failure of human understanding to penetrate the underlying natural cause [...]. The implication here is that all human remedy and redress is attitudinal. Some may regard this as rationalizing, but that may not be a bad choice for problems which admit no other solution. The problem with this philosophy is that it does not differentiate—in fact encourages not differentiating—between natural evils and correctable human error. Such a lack of distinction enables wealthy Mr. Norton to oversimplify Emerson [...]. (113)

Nadel is correct in noting that Emerson's philosophy is attitudinal; indeed, as I argue below, one of the central pragmatic views connecting Emerson to Burke and Ellison is the attitudinal aspect of Emerson's ethics. However, when Nadel claims that Emerson's philosophy is merely attitudinal, that it fatalistically renounces acts that might redress correctable evils, it is Nadel and not Emerson who is failing to differentiate.

In particular, how can the concept of fate Mr. Norton espouses (and Nadel accepts) be squared with Emerson's exhorting individuals throughout his writings to action that will both realize their human potential and reshape the world around them? Emerson's essay "Fate," belying its title, explicitly rejects fatalism in favor of activism. Even as Emerson acknowledges that limitation is a central "element running through entire nature" (952), he affirms that creative change occurs within and against the limits of the material world:

> But Fate has its lord; limitation its limits; is different seen from above and from below; from within and from without. For though Fate is immense, so is power, which is the other fact in the dual world, immense. If Fate follows and limits power, power attends and antagonizes Fate. (953)

Emerson insists that power and limitation are inextricably linked, that particular limits are often transcended, that today's obstacle may be the occasion for or source of tomorrow's power. He stresses that dangerous and limiting natural forces—water, cold, steam, electricity, disease—at least serve as stimulants to human ingenuity, while at best they are "convertible by intellect into wholesome force": "The water drowns ship and sailor, like a grain of dust. But learn to swim, trim your bark, and the wave which drowned it, will be cloven by it, and carry it, like its own foam, a plume and a power" (958). As this statement makes clear, Emerson neither ignores evil nor fatalistically accepts it: instead, he accepts a world of limits in order to affirm our limited yet sufficient ability to act on and transform that world: "We can afford to allow the limitation, if we know it is the meter of the growing man" (957).

Given the history of Emerson's critical reception (see Lopez 19–52, 165–89; Buell), it is not surprising that readers—even ones as astute as Nadel—should accept Ellison's parodic figures Mr. Norton and Mr. Emerson as an accurate and sincere critique of Emerson. Emerson has traditionally been accused of a transcendentalist fascination with the absolute that ignores or subsumes the tragic limits of existence. Curiously, this supposed absolutism has been described as taking two nearly contradictory forms. As the title of Stephen Whicher's influential study *Freedom and Fate* suggests, critics have charted a shift in the course of Emerson's career, from a naive idealism celebrating the individual's access to absolute unity and power, to a more sober skepticism or fatalism celebrating the absolute forces of nature that determine and limit individual acts. This conventional construction of two Emersons clearly parallels the two figures in Ellison's parody: Mr. Emerson, with his inaccessible idealism, and Mr. Norton, with his naively benign vision of our actual fates.

The key question is, how much sense does it make to conclude that Ellison is endorsing these conventional readings of Emerson? The biting energy that *Invisible Man* expends on parodying Emerson suggests an anxiety of influence that should encourage critics to look past the apparent rejection of Emerson to other, more significant connections between the two writers. In discussing his literary namesake, Ellison acknowledged just such a complex sense of indebtedness. As a youth, he changed his middle name from Waldo to an anonymous W. and "avoided [Emerson's] works like the plague" ("Hidden Name" 197). As an adult artist, however, he stressed that he "did not destroy" but "only suppressed" that "troublesome middle name of [his]": "I could suppress the name of my namesake out of respect for the achievements of its original bearer, but I cannot escape the obligation of attempting to achieve some of the things which he asked of the American writer" (208–09).

When Ellison's allusions are seen as directed at Mumford's literary history, *Invisible Man*'s satire can be read as rejecting Mumford's idealized portrait of Emerson, even as the novel extends a pragmatic tradition of individualism rooted in Emerson. In opposing Emersonian transcendence to Jamesian acquiescence, Mumford essentially replicates the split critics have posited in Emerson's career—from the naive prophet of freedom to the stern prophet of fate. Those who read Emerson in such absolutist terms—whether, like Mumford, praising him for transcending historical limits or, like Nadel, blaming him for ignoring them—erase the pragmatic Emerson who profoundly influenced James, Burke, and Ellison. There is, of course, a counter tradition in American criticism—starting with John Dewey and James and extending through more contemporary critics like Burke, Richard Poirier, and Stanley Cavell—that views Emerson as a founding figure in American pragmatism.[11] *Invisible Man's* parody of and its indebtedness to Emerson place Ellison in this pragmatic tradition as well. If Ellison sends Mr. Norton to the Golden Day saloon in order to reject Mumford's idealized Emerson and thus to affiliate himself with another, more politically useful Emerson, one place to look for such an affiliation is in the pragmatic aspects of Emerson's individualism that are effaced by Mumford's narrative.

II

Two aspects of the individualist ethics that connect Emerson to Ellison and Burke can be termed tragic and comic, following Burke's definition of those attitudes. Though often accused of ignoring tragic limits, Emerson in fact insists that our acts are always limited by the cultural media with which they must be articulated and by the material environment they strive to reshape. As cultural beings, we depend on inherited ideas and tools so profoundly that even our efforts to reform or transcend traditional constructs must make use of tradition: "so deep is the foundation of the existing social system" that we "are under the necessity of using the Actual order of things, in order to disuse it" ("Conservative" 178). Moreover, though our acts can change our environment, any changes in turn become part of a new environment that reacts on us: "Every spirit makes its house; but afterwards the house confines the spirit" ("Fate" 946). To see one's acts in this perspective, as expressing both one's will and the limits on it, is, Burke argues, a tragic vision:

> The act, in being an assertion, has called forth a counter-assertion in the elements that compose its context. And when the agent is enabled to see in terms of this counter-assertion, he has transcended the state that characterized him at the start. In this final state of tragic vision, intrinsic and extrinsic motivations are merged. That is, although purely circumstantial factors participate in his tragic destiny, these are not felt as exclusively external, or scenic; for they bring about a *representative* kind of accident, the

kind of accident that belongs with the agent's particular kind of character. (*Grammar* 38–39)

Emerson expresses a similar insight when he claims that the individual "comes at last to be faithfully represented by every view you take of his circumstances" ("Spiritual Laws" 314). Emerson's individualist ethic of self-expressive action, or self-culture, is a response to these tragic limits on the self. It is against the resistances of our environment that we know and develop our individuality: "We must have an antagonism in the tough world for all the variety of our spiritual faculties, or they will not be born" ("Man the Reformer" 140). Viewing individuals as alienated from both the sources and the products of their acts, Emerson argues that the primary value they can find in life, their only inalienable property, resides in the development of self achieved through the act of doing: "that which a man is does always by necessity acquire, and what the man acquires is living property" ("Self-Reliance" 281); "[t]he goods of fortune may come and go like summer leaves," but "[w]hat a man does, that he has" ("Spiritual Laws" 311).

But if Emerson locates value in self-expressive acts, there is also a social component to his individualist ethics. For Emerson—as for the pragmatists who follow him—the self is inescapably social. For example, when Emerson in "Self-Reliance" exhorts the reader, "Trust thyself," the gloss he provides may surprise some: "Accept the place the divine providence has found for you, the society of your contemporaries, the connection of events" (260). The self here exists through its social and historical engagements, by participating in the events that define a historical moment. Emerson is acutely aware that human intelligence is cultural; perhaps his central insight, as well as his preoccupation, is that our acts and even our perceptions depend on what he often calls "history" or "society"—in short, on language. There is a social division of labor inherent in the cultural sources of all human acts: no individual can perform all the actions culture makes available; each must focus on some specialized area of activity. Accordingly, though Emerson exhorts the reader, "[D]o your work, and I shall know you" (264), he celebrates individuals who let culture work for them, who best manipulate the resources supplied by others. In his essay on Shakespeare, he describes "the greatest genius" as "the most indebted man": "he finds himself in the river of the thoughts and events, forced onward by the ideas and necessities of his contemporaries"; "all have worked for him, and he enters into their labors" ("Shakspeare" 710–11).

Emerson's model of the self thus acknowledges that individual acts are socially indebted and that they imply a social responsibility. Emerson attempts to deal with this social implication by asserting that a rigorous and sincere

pursuit of the work or vocation that best utilizes and develops one's talents is
a moral end that sufficiently fulfills one's duties to others:

> You may fulfill your round of duties by clearing yourself in the
> *direct*, or in the *reflex* way. Consider whether you have satisfied
> your relations to father, mother, cousin, neighbour, town, cat, and
> dog; whether any of these can upbraid you. But I may also neglect
> this reflex standard, and absolve me to myself. I have my own stern
> claims and perfect circle. ("Self-Reliance" 274)

Indeed, extending the audacious claim that one can absolve oneself through
the "stern claims" of individualized work, Emerson insists that we have our
most beneficial effect on others through the example of our individualized
actions. Arguing that our most precious and stable value lies in developing
our individual faculties, Emerson asserts that others can truly aid us only by
pushing us to our own work: "Activity is contagious," he writes in "The Uses
of Great Men"; "men are helpful through the intellect and the affections.
Other help, I find a false appearance" (620). Though Emerson has complex
and conflicting attitudes toward community,[12] he views the influence of
others as essential to the self. This belief is evident in his intense preoccupation with friendship and with the inspiration geniuses offer. In Emerson's
vision, a healthy community is one in which active individuals inspire and
antagonize one another through their diverse activities.

It is on this issue of social responsibility that both Burke and Ellison depart from Emerson. In opposition to Emerson's claim that individual acts—despite their social indebtedness—can attain an autonomous or
independent moral integrity, Burke argues that an individualist ethics must
include gestures of communication and self-analysis that are more directly
political. Responsibility cannot be measured only by the isolated requirements of a specialized vocation. "The human agent, *qua* human agent, is
not motivated solely by the principles of a specialized activity [...]. Any
specialized activity participates in a larger unit of action. 'Identification' is a
word for the autonomous activity's place in this wider context, a place with
which the agent may be unconcerned"—but should be concerned (*Rhetoric* 27). That is, the ethics of an activity cannot be measured solely by an
individual's intentions or competence: "one's morality as a specialist cannot
be allowed to do duty for one's morality as a citizen" (31). We must consider
how our individual acts participate in larger social contexts, contexts that
may imbue those efforts with unintended consequences. Burke illustrates
this point with a brutal pastoral metaphor that strikes at the heart of a narrow professionalism: "The shepherd, *qua* shepherd, acts for the good of the

sheep, to protect them from discomfiture and harm. But he may be 'identi-fied' with a project that is raising the sheep for market" (27). Similarly, Burke often criticizes the complicity between science and the military-industrial complex: one can be a technically excellent physicist yet be helping to cre-ate weapons of mass murder. The need to rethink individual responsibility, Burke emphasizes, has become imperative: since the "extreme division of labor under late capitalist liberalism [has] made dispersion the norm and [has] transformed the state of Babel into an ideal" (30–31), it has become increasingly easy to absolve oneself of any broad responsibility, even as the destructive power of technology has made it increasingly urgent that people confront injustice and conflict peacefully.

Burke here shares Mumford's concern over the dangers posed by mod-ern technology, though he moves beyond Mumford's reactionary response to those dangers.[13] Burke acknowledges that the "generic divisiveness" inherent in humankind's nature as a "symbol-using animal" is exacerbated by the "high state of occupational diversity" in modern industrial societies—communist as well as capitalist (*Rhetoric* 146, 110). Yet instead of imagining (as Mumford does) a self that imaginatively transcends the material conditions of modern society, Burke pragmatically envisions an ethical self that is capable of dealing with such divisions. Viewing individuals as inevitably existing in a state of social division, Burke argues, need not require that one see them as essentially alienated, combative, or deceptive: one can also choose to see individuals as essentially rhetorical—as "humane word-slingers" committed to "persuasion by words, rather than by force" (72).

The complex and divisive social context of individual acts, Burke insists, requires a comic ethics. Both comedy and tragedy provide ways of under-standing human limitation, but, Burke stresses, they reflect crucially differ-ent attitudes toward individualism. Tragedy, which he links to historical eras of nascent individualism, portrays human limitation in relation to natural and supernatural forces such as fate or the gods, treating individualism—and its attendant ethical blindnesses—in terms of criminal transgression or hubris (*Attitudes* 37–39). In contrast, comedy deals with the limitations of "man in society" (107); it analyzes human motives with "the maximum of forensic complexity" required by "sophisticated social structures" (42, 107), treating individualization as an inescapable result of the diversity of social roles and positions:

> The progress of humane enlightenment can go no further in picturing people not as *vicious*, but as *mistaken*. When you add that people are *necessarily* mistaken, that *all* people are exposed to situations in which they must act as fools, that *every* insight

contains its own special kind of blindness, you complete the comic
circle, returning again to the lesson of humility that underlies great
tragedy. (41)

A comic awareness of human limitation endorses a pluralistic tolerance of
diversity and conflict. Every social position has "its own special kind of
blindness," and thus human beings are "necessarily mistaken" but not necessarily vicious. Our conflicts with others do not result only from overt ill will,
since the diversity of occupation and lifestyle inherent in culture ensures that
individuals will have different and conflicting needs. Accordingly, a comic
ethics provides a mandate for rhetoric, for confronting our differences and
communicating across them. This ethics encourages "charitability" toward
the motives of others—indeed, the alternative is an assumption of universal cunning and hypocrisy that would make social cooperation impossible.
However, Burke also insists that charitability must not be "gullibility": we
must denounce overt deception and oppression, and crucially, we must strive
to recognize how our own social position may subtly implicate us in conflicts
with others (107). Burke's concept of identification combines these rhetorical responsibilities (*Rhetoric* 27–29): we must identify with others across
social divisions while also confronting how our own position may identify
us—like the shepherd who is identified with the slaughterhouse—with
divisive social forces.

Yet if Burke rejects Emerson's vision of the moral independence of individual action, Burke's comic ethics at the same time extend a pragmatic tradition leading back through William James to Emerson. In *Attitudes toward
History*, Burke argues that Emerson, Whitman, and James offer "[p]erhaps the
three most well-rounded [...] frames of acceptance in American literature"
(5). Frames of acceptance are ways of describing and approaching reality: they
"name both friendly and unfriendly forces" and "fix attitudes that prepare for
combat." A frame of acceptance is "not the same as *passiveness*" (20), Burke
insists, for it articulates attitudes of both acceptance and rejection, saying yes
and saying no, naming what we can or must accept and what we can or must
struggle to change. For Burke, pragmatism exemplifies a well-rounded frame
because it refuses to accept limitation without also affirming our ability to
act in response to limits—an attitude Burke locates in the Jamesian motto
"Where resignation *must* be, it will be 'provisional' [...] afford[ing] 'ground
and leisure to advance to new philanthropic action'" (3). This activist attitude
closely parallels the logic of Emerson's essay "Fate," and indeed Burke cites
Emerson as a precursor to James. Emerson's doctrine of compensation—the
idea that "[i]n all evil, there is inevitably some compensatory good"—does
not ignore evil, Burke argues, but articulates a pragmatic response to evil, a

"project for living" that views the limits of our world as occasions for action: "Calamities arise, and by compensation, they force us to turn them into benefits, lest we perish" (18, 19).

It is a desire to strike a pragmatic stance of acceptance and rejection toward the ethical blindnesses of individualism that motivates Burke's comic balance between charitability and gullibility. To accept charitably that all individuals are "necessarily mistaken"—implicated in social conflicts of which they are unaware—is not simply to excuse or exonerate them. Precisely the opposite is true: the comic frame, by insisting that individuals are always in danger of being mistaken, obligates us to scrutinize the various ways our lives are identified in larger social contexts. Burke pragmatically accepts the inevitability of social conflicts in order to adopt an activist mandate of confronting and resolving those conflicts: his comic frame "promotes the realistic sense of one's limitations [. . .] yet the acceptance is not passive" (107). Indeed, the Emersonian roots of Burke's comic ethics become evident when one compares Burke's view of individuals as necessarily mistaken with Emerson's description of the individual in "Experience":

> The individual is always mistaken. He designed many things, and drew in other persons as coadjutors, quarrelled with some or all, blundered much, and something is done; all are a little advanced, but the individual is always mistaken. It turns out somewhat new, and very unlike what he promised himself. (484)

While Emerson is capable of brazenly asserting, "I may [. . .] absolve me to myself," he is also—as this passage shows—acutely conscious of how the individual's actions participate in larger social processes of change over which no individual has complete control. If Burke rejects the former Emersonian mood, his comic ethics still extend the Emersonian project of critically analyzing the inescapably social context of individual action.

III

Ellison perhaps most clearly illustrates his affiliation with the individualist ethics of both Emerson and Burke in a speech he delivered to Harvard alumni in 1974. Ellison opens by expressing his uncanny sense of the ironies involved in speaking at the university where his literary namesake delivered the famous "Divinity School Address," then reports how this unease was compounded: "I received a letter from Harvard addressed to Ralph Waldo Emerson! Lord, but what tenacious memories you Harvards have!" ("Address" 418). This anecdote provides a winning humorous gambit to warm up the audience, but lurking in the joke is a serious point about the relationships among individuals and across social divisions in a pluralistic society:

> [N]ow that I stand before you, how fortunate for me that my unmistakable pigmentation shines forth no less as sign than as symbol. I assure you that even though I've insisted for years that our American obsession with practical joking was originally not intentional, but arose out of the incongruities abounding in a man-and-mammy-made society set up within an unexplored and alien land, it was still somewhat shocking to find, under the most decorous of circumstances, the image of a Negro American novelist made to show forth through the ghostly (and I hope benign) lineaments of a white philosopher and poet. (418–19)

This striking image of double consciousness, Ellison's "Negro" face "show[ing] forth" through Emerson's "ghostly lineaments," abounds in possible meanings. One hears a writer expressing his sense of appropriating a precursor's voice or, more uncomfortably, of having that precursor speak through him—an anxiety of influence complicated by race. Following Houston Baker's lead, one can hear Ellison self-consciously donning a "Western critical mask" in his pronouncements about literature (844). Above all, one hears Ellison's sense of the unexpected intersections of identity in America's pluralistic culture: what "show[s] forth" in this image is not only the stubborn perception of race that divides Ellison from Emerson but also the shared aspects of cultural identity that reach across racial categories. Ellison's shock is a shock of recognition, for his connection to Emerson aptly reflects the democratic and individualist ideals shared by the two writers, ideals that led African American parents to name their sons Ralph Waldo. "There were, and are, a number who are named Waldo," Ellison notes in "The Novel as a Function of American Democracy." "Amusing as this is," he continues, "it reveals something of how the insight and values of literature get past the usual barriers in society and seep below the expected levels" (760).

Ellison uses his uncanny affiliation with Emerson as an opening example of the complex social relationships that any truly democratic individualist ethics must take into account. A recurrent theme in Ellison's work is that if America is ever to fulfill its democratic promise, individuals must recognize more fully how they are connected to one another—both by the social relations of inequality that create conflict and by the shared democratic ideals that may inspire attempts to remedy those inequities. Ellison's Harvard speech invokes such connections, exemplified in the memorial to Harvard's

Civil War dead that links Ellison and his audience in the unfinished struggle for civil rights ("Address" 419–20). This vision of America embodies the social complexity—and the potential for conflict and miscommunication—assumed by Burke's comic frame: "Such mysteries arise out of the difficulty of communicating across the hierarchical divisions of American society, and a great deal of our misunderstanding springs from our failures of communication" (418).

Similarly, as Ellison describes the individualist ethics required by this pluralistic complexity, he explains his connection to Emerson in terms that closely parallel those of Burke's comic and tragic frames. Much as Burke warns that insidious motives can be identified with seemingly benign acts, so Ellison focuses on the potential ethical blindnesses of individualism. Discussing the familiar notion of "American innocence" often applied to Emerson—the "tendency to ignore the evil which can spring from our good intentions" (420)—Ellison argues that *innocence* is a misnomer for the ethical dilemmas of individualism, which are better understood through a tragic terminology of "hubris" and "nemesis" (420–21). Crucially, however, Ellison does not rehearse the commonplace that Emerson naively ignores evil. On the contrary, he insists that "neither tragic arrogance nor insolence is limited to Americans": echoing Burke's comic assumption of inevitable mistakenness, Ellison asserts that "these flaws arise from the nature of the human animal and from the limitations encountered by human consciousness when asserting itself against the vast multiplicity of the universe" (421). Moreover, while he admits that Emersonian individualism is liable to this human "forgetfulness that leaves us vulnerable to *nemesis*," he twice cites Emerson as exemplifying the "conscience," "consciousness," and "conscientiousness" that offer the only remedy to such ethical lapses (423):

> [R]emember that the antidote to *hubris*, to overweening pride, is irony, that capacity to discover and systematize clear ideas. Or, as Emerson insisted, the development of consciousness, consciousness, consciousness. And with consciousness, a more refined conscientiousness, and most of all, that tolerance which takes the form of humor, for when Americans can no longer laugh at each other, they have to fight one another. (425)

Revealing his close affinity to Burke, Ellison here asserts that the best ethical response to the potentially tragic results of human limitations is a comic consciousness of the complexity of human motives and an accompanying humorous tolerance (Burke's charitability) toward conflict. Even as Ellison warns against the threat of ethical blindness implicit in Emersonian individualism, he lays claim to an Emersonian sense of the complexity of the

individual's social implication—affiliating himself with the Emerson who
knew that "the individual is always mistaken," or, in Ellison's words, the
Emerson who was well "aware of the labyrinth in which Americans walk"
("Novel" 760).

Ellison's use of a Burkean terminology of tragedy and comedy to discuss
Emerson suggests that readings of *Invisible Man*'s parody of Emerson should
be informed by Ellison's claim that his fiction expresses a "tragicomic" attitude toward life ("That Same Pain" 80):

> [T]here is a value for the writer in trying to give as thorough
> a report of social reality as possible. [... T]he small share of
> reality which each of our diverse groups is able to snatch from the
> whirling chaos of history belongs not to the group alone, but to all
> of us. It is a property and a witness which can be ignored only to
> the danger of the entire nation. ("Hidden Name" 208)

Ellison's mandate to give "as thorough a report of social reality as possible" is a tragic ethic of self-expression in the Emersonian vein, locating
value in the character we achieve in struggling against the resistances of
our environment. In essays and interviews, Ellison repeatedly voices the
deeply Emersonian idea that expressing the complexity of one's experience
is a moral duty that requires nonconformism. "I learned that nothing could
go unchallenged," he relates, especially the "formulas" of "historians, politi-
cians, sociologists," and even the "older generation of Negro leaders and
writers," formulas that threatened to "deprive both humanity and culture of
their complexity" (Introduction 57). By expressing the particularity of one's
individual and communal experience, one can disrupt the totalizing ideological narratives that render that experience invisible. Ellison here revises
Emerson by broadening self-expression into an act of social communication
and political assertion. Self-expression is a way to take personal responsibility for making one's own invisibility visible; it is also a social act that reveals
the reciprocity of human responsibility: to make one's own invisibility visible
is to challenge others both to "see" that invisibility and to acknowledge how
their identity and social position depend on the invisibility of others. Here
Ellison, like Burke, adds a social, or comic, component to his individualist
ethics, insisting that self-expression must serve as an act of political communication: it is a "property and witness" that "belongs not to the group alone,"
a reality that all in a democratic society must acknowledge.

Invisible Man charts its narrator's progression toward this tragicomic
model of self-expression, a progression that can be traced in the narrator's
relationship with Mr. Norton. As Ellison observes in his "Working Notes

for *Invisible Man*," Jim Trueblood—the farmer whose tale of incest forces Norton and the narrator to retreat to the Golden Day bordello—serves as one model of a possible tragicomic attitude and as an indicator of how far Norton and the narrator must travel to achieve more-accurate knowledge of themselves and of their relationship to each other: "Life is either tragic or absurd," Ellison claims, "but Norton and the boy have no capacity to deal with such ambivalence" (344). Baker has argued that Trueblood's tragicomic ambivalence lies in his status as a trickster or blues figure who rejects the logic of guilt and of punishment/castration implicit in the dominant Western tragic myths.[14] Trueblood's attitude toward his transgression is comic in Burke's terms: seeing himself not as vicious but as mistaken, Trueblood gains comic insight into the complex social context of his act. As Baker insists, the entire Trueblood episode is inextricably grounded in the socioeconomic relations of the Jim Crow South: the incest occurs, for example, after a lack of firewood forces daughter and parents to sleep together for warmth. Moreover, by telling the tale for eager white audiences, Trueblood gains insight into—and even some control over—the workings of race and class that define his social situation. In rejecting the symbolic castration of mainstream Western culture, Baker argues, Trueblood resists the social castration visited on black men in Ellison's America (832). Exploding Norton's placid vision of the fate connecting him to African Americans, Trueblood's tragicomic tale exposes the reality of race relations that exists behind the college's ideology of racial uplift.

Yet Trueblood is a problematic model of tragicomic ethics, for as Baker acknowledges, he gains insight and control by donning a minstrel mask for his white auditors, playing a stereotype whose function, Ellison insists, is "to veil the humanity of Negroes" and thereby to "repress the white audience's awareness of its moral identification with its own acts and with the human ambiguities pushed behind the mask" ("Change the Joke" 103). The resonances between Ellison's and Burke's terminologies of "identification" here are salient: an attitude that allows individuals to obscure how their acts identify them with others is an ethical failure. Baker reads Trueblood's shortcomings as Ellison's acknowledgment that it is perhaps impossible for the African American artist to escape such compromises—that there is no space for African American expression that is free of the distortions of the market and racism. Baker's argument is convincing. Indeed, Ellison's narrator comes to learn that even in his heady career as a political orator he has not escaped Trueblood's dilemma: like Trueblood's tale, the narrator's speeches are manipulated for the purposes of a white audience (the Brotherhood's leadership). Baker's conclusion does not take into account, however, Ellison's narrator's attempt, in his final confrontation with Norton, at an act of tragicomic expression that avoids the compromises of the minstrel mask.

The narrator's development in the novel can be read as preparation for his adoption of a tragicomic mode of action in his final encounter with Norton. The narrator learns that he must assert the particularity of his experience against the competing ideologies of racial uplift and economic determinism he encounters at the black college and in his experience with the socialist Brotherhood, respectively. This step requires narrating how those ideologies rendered him invisible—he becomes visible only by naming his invisibility. The narrator's presence in the prologue and epilogue as one who has gained insight through narrating his experience is the true culmination of the novel—a fact that critics have often discussed[15] and that Ellison himself indicates by describing the narrator as progressing from "invisibility to visibility" and "from ranter to writer" ("Art of Fiction" 215; "Change the Joke" 111). Many readers have been troubled that this act of self-narration is also an act of "hibernation" (*Invisible Man* 13): achieving insight through naming one's own invisibility seems to require an ironic detachment and paralysis. The narrator is driven underground by the bitter realization that even when he felt he was most effectively expressing the particular plight of the black community—when he spoke at Tod Clifton's funeral or when he helped Harlem residents burn down their tenement—his acts were manipulated and lost in larger political struggles: "I [...] had been a tool," he writes, "[a] tool just at the very moment I had thought myself free" (541). Thus, despite his insistence that his hibernation is a "covert preparation for a more overt action" (13) and despite his decision to emerge from his hole (567–68), his ironic awareness of his past invisibility seems to preclude future actions that would not involve him in a similar invisibility—a similar futility and vulnerability to manipulation.

Indeed, the narrator acknowledges this possible connection between insight and paralysis when he describes himself, on entering his hibernation, as "caught like Trueblood's jaybird that yellow jackets had paralyzed in every part but his eyes" (556).[16]

The narrator's claim that his act of self-narration does not lead to ironic paralysis can be read as a pragmatic assertion that a tragicomic awareness of human limits does not discourage action but, rather, encourages action that responds to those limits. As I argue above in relation to Emerson, a tragic attitude affirms that we express our humanity only by engaging the resistant world, even though such engagement implies a loss of autonomy. Ellison's narrator exemplifies this tragic view. The deepest despair of his hibernation is symbolized in a nightmare in which Jack and the Brotherhood, Mr. Emerson, Norton, and Bledsoe—"*all of whom,*" the narrator says, "*had run me*" and "attempt[ed] to force [their] picture of reality upon me" (556, 497)—make the narrator "*free of illusions*" by castrating him (557). This dream suggests that one cannot escape illusion simply by avoiding action: one could avoid illusion only if one could be stripped (castrated) of all human desire. Thus, the narrator finds it impossible to remain ironically detached: "I couldn't be still even in hibernation. Because, damn it, there's the mind, the *mind*. It wouldn't let me rest" (560). Being human requires acting, even though acting involves blindnesses and embarrassments. The narrator accepts "all past humiliations" as "precious parts of my experience" (496): to accept one's own particular history, even its humiliations, is to affirm the character one has developed in coping with that history. Ellison adopts the agonistic view of identity that is central to Emerson's ethic of self-reliance—the idea that "[w]e must have an antagonism in the tough world for all the variety of our spiritual faculties, or they will not be born."

Yet Ellison, characteristically, adds a social component to Emerson. He insists that to accept a tragic history is also to align oneself with the resources of a particular cultural heritage—with a set of attitudes, styles, myths, symbols, rhetorical strategies, and political concerns:

> [W]hat I have tried to commemorate in fiction is that which I believe to be enduring and abiding in our situation, especially those human qualities which the American Negro has developed despite, and in rejection of, the obstacles and meannesses imposed upon us. [... S]o much which we've gleaned through the harsh discipline of Negro American life is simply too precious to be lost. I speak of the faith, the patience, the humor, the sense of timing, the rugged sense of life and the manner of expressing it which all go to define the American Negro. These are some of the things through which we've confronted the obstacles and meannesses of which you speak, and which we dare not fail to adapt to changed conditions lest we destroy ourselves. [...] I am unwilling to see those values which I would celebrate in fiction as existing sheerly through terror; they are a result of a tragicomic confrontation of life. ("That Same Pain" 79–80)

The tragic side of Ellison's tragicomic ethics is expressed in the view he takes here toward communal identity. He of course wants to eradicate the injustices imposed on African Americans, but at the same time he wants to celebrate and preserve the character, the cultural sensibility, forged in the experience of resisting those injustices. As a number of critics have noted[17] and as Ellison always insisted, *Invisible Man* is not simply the story of the narrator's disastrous infatuation with the ideologies of racial uplift and socialism; it is also an exploration of the rich African American traditions available to the narrator—embodied by his grandfather, True-blood, the Vet, Mary, Brother Tarp, Tod Clifton, Frederick Douglass, and Louis Armstrong, as well as by the more troubling examples of Bledsoe, Rinehart, and Ras.

One characteristic of African American sensibility that Ellison valued highly was the ability to "suffer the injustice which race and color are used to excuse without losing sight of either the humanity of those who inflict that injustice or the motives, rational or irrational, out of which they act" ("World" 178). This claim points to the comic side of Ellison's tragicomic ethics. In describing the African American ability to confront racial conflict yet still acknowledge a human connection across that conflict, Ellison parallels Burke's definition of the comic balance between charitability and gullibility. In fact, Ellison credits Burke with greatly influencing the structure of *Invisible Man*: he claims that the narrator's development follows the Burkean progression from "purpose to passion to perception" ("Art of Fiction" 218–19)—purpose being an act, passion the resistance or limitation the act meets, and perception the self-knowledge the actor gains in seeing the extent and limit of his or her act.

Ellison's self-proclaimed debt to Burke is significant for what it suggests about the narrator's hibernation in *Invisible Man*. Burke—in a passage Ellison quotes in "An Extravagance of Laughter" (647)—insists that the progression to a comic perception of the limits of every action does not lead to ironic paralysis but enables individuals to act more consciously: by becoming "student[s] of [themselves]," even on "occasions when [they have] been tricked or cheated," individuals can be "*observers of themselves, while acting*"; the "ultimate" comic attitude "would not be *passiveness*, but *maximum consciousness*" (Burke, *Attitudes* 171). Ellison's narrator echoes this logic when he says, "I'm shaking off the old skin [...]. I'm coming out, no less invisible without it, but coming out nevertheless [...] since there's a possibility that even an invisible man has a socially responsible role to play" (568). In shaking off the skin of his old delusions, the narrator accepts that new actions risk new delusions; he emerges "no less invisible" but more conscious of the invisibility against which he must struggle. The ironic consciousness the narrator attains is not a sign of paralysis: instead, it signals his pragmatic acceptance that the self is never finished (much less absolute) but fluid and provisional—that continued growth can occur only through subsequent acts and the embarrassments they entail.

Instead of being a retreat from social action, the self-expression Ellison's narrator achieves in his hibernation is, like Burke's identification, a social act of communication, confrontation, and self-analysis. Ellison stresses this point by including in his epilogue one "overt action" that the narrator undertakes in his hibernation—the final confrontation of Mr. Norton.[18] Since the action occurs in the subway, it clearly depends on the ironic awareness the narrator has achieved "underground." In this prominent encounter, the narrator revises the notion of fate that Norton had espoused at the black college. Norton's assertion that his destiny as a philanthropist depends on the success of those he helps is not only transparently egocentric; more important, it reflects an ideology of social uplift that falsifies his true connection to the narrator. This ideology renders the narrator invisible because it ignores the reality of seg-regated America. It also effaces Norton's true identity, allowing him to deny that his status as a white industrialist implicates him in the systemic oppres-sion of persons like the narrator. In Norton and the narrator's final meeting, Norton is lost on the subway platform but is ashamed to ask a white person for directions. He approaches the narrator, whom he does not remember:

> "Don't you know me?" I said.
> "Should I?" he said.
> "You see me?" I said, watching him tensely.
> "Why, of course—Sir, do you know the way to Centre Street?"
> "So. Last time it was the Golden Day, now it's Centre Street. You've retrenched, sir. But don't you really know who I am?"
> "Young man, I'm in a hurry," he said, cupping a hand to his ear. "Why should I know you?"
> "Because I'm your destiny."
> "My destiny, did you say?" He gave me a puzzled stare, back-ing away. "Young man, are you well? Which train did you say I should take?"
> "I didn't say," I said, shaking my head. "Now, aren't you ashamed?"
> "Ashamed? ASHAMED!" he said indignantly.
> I laughed, suddenly taken by the idea. "Because, Mr. Norton, if you don't know *where* you are, you probably don't know who you are. So you came to me out of shame. You are ashamed, now aren't you?" (564–65)

In this exchange—which ends as the narrator erupts in laughter and Norton escapes into a subway train—the narrator's response to Norton exemplifies a model of social connectedness that imposes responsibilities of communica-tion and self-analysis on both parties. In the subway, a setting that symbol-izes the narrator's underground self-awareness and Norton's blindness, the narrator attempts to make Norton see the dynamic of invisibility that truly

connects their destinies. The narrator, by naming his invisibility, accepts
the responsibility of self-expression: "[A]fter years of trying to adopt the
opinions of others I finally rebelled. I am an *invisible* man" (560). Crucially,
this act of self-expression imposes similar responsibilities of self-awareness
and social awareness on Norton: Norton cannot know "who he is" until he
acknowledges "where he is"—until he acknowledges how his social position
is identified, in Burke's sense, with the forces that render others invisible.

The narrator here displays Burke's comic balance of connection and
confrontation or, in Ellison's terms, the dual ability to see the injustice and
humanity of one's oppressor. Even in rejecting Norton's notion of fate, the
narrator acknowledges that his and Norton's identities are indeed connected.
In one sense, the narrator is approaching Norton in a spirit of kindness, really
trying to help the lost Norton find his way, to help him know his true social
and individual identity. This effort is no easy claim of democratic fraternity
but a complex assertion of the connection between oppressor and oppressed.
As the narrator explains elsewhere in the epilogue:

> I condemn and affirm, say no and say yes, say yes and say no.
> [...] I sell you no phony forgiveness, I'm a desperate man—but
> too much of your life will be lost, its meaning lost, unless you
> approach it as much through love as through hate. So I approach
> it through division. So I denounce and I defend and I hate and I
> love. (566–67)

The vocabulary of yes and no resounds throughout *Invisible Man*. The narrator learns the futility of saying yes to dominant ideologies—like Norton's
and the Brotherhood's—that render him invisible (497–98), but when he
attempts to sabotage the Brotherhood by following his grandfather's advice
to "overcome 'em with yeses, undermine 'em with grins, agree 'em to death
and destruction" (16), the results are equally disastrous. Trueblood, Bledsoe,
and the Vet constitute other unsatisfactory models of yessing duplicity. The
narrator's final confrontation with Norton offers an alternative to these
strategies of duplicity, a way to say yes *and* no in a direct political act of communication—to assert the democratic connection of all American citizens
and confront the systemic discrimination that separates them. Finally, this
attempt to say yes and no echoes Burke's balance of acceptance and rejection,
linking the ethics of Ellison's novel with a comic attitude that is charitable
but not gullible in confronting social divisions and conflicts.

It is in this individualist ethics of self-expression, not in the parodic
figures of Mr. Norton and Mr. Emerson, that Ellison's most cogent critique
of Emerson lies. In "Twentieth-Century Fiction and the Black Mask of

Humanity," Ellison argues that American literature has failed to offer meaningful models of democratic individualism precisely because it too often has
rendered invisible the humanity of those excluded from America's promise
of freedom. Ellison asserts that the "individualist" impulse to rebel against
society's constrictions and corruptions must be "dialectically" tempered by a
"humanist" acceptance of the social order (89–90): specifically, the individual
must accept his or her own responsibility for the social order and its injustices.
As an example of such a balance, he cites the famous moment in *The Adventures of Huckleberry Finn* when Huck decides to "emancipate" Jim. By having
Huck accept "the judgment of his superego—that internalized representation
of the community—that his action is evil," Twain suggests that the individualist desire to reject the injustices of society is inescapably compromised by
the individual's profound implication in society: "Huck Finn's acceptance of
the evil implicit in his 'emancipation' of Jim represents Twain's acceptance of
his personal responsibility for the condition of society" (Ellison, "Twentieth-
Century Fiction," 88, 89). All too frequently, Ellison claims, the social protest voiced by American literature remains "shallow" because it "seldom turns
inward upon the writer's own values; almost always it focuses outward, upon
some scapegoat with which he is seldom able to identify himself as Huck Finn
identified himself with the scoundrels who stole Jim, and with Jim himself"
(91). Ellison here insists that an individualist ethics must include Burkean
acts of identification. We can understand our own democratic identity—our
freedoms, our tyrannies, and our responsibilities—only if we understand how
our social position identifies us with social structures that oppress others: this
truth has found its most powerful symbol, Ellison argues, in the figure of the
enslaved or disenfranchised African American.

   Ellison's discussion of American literature illuminates his dual attitude
toward the possibilities of Emersonian individualism. On the one hand,
Ellison asserts that individualism must guard against a false sense of independence: he criticizes the American tendency toward "[narrow] artistic individualism" that devolved, in writers such as Hemingway, into personalized
myths of merely individual tragedy (92–96). *Invisible Man*'s parody denounces
the Emerson appropriated by this tradition of individualism, which evades
the historical and social connections that define the American self. Yet Ellison simultaneously reclaims a different Emerson: he lists Emerson among
the nineteenth-century American writers who were led by their commitment
to individualism—by the "passion for personal freedom" and "revolt against
the old moral authority"—to reconceive the "Negro as a symbol of Man"
(88). Like Burke, Ellison is drawn to the Emerson whose obsession with
self-reliance is based on the pragmatic insight that the individual's actions
are always socially implicated and indebted. Ellison's writings suggest that

the positive promise of American individualism can be realized only if the Emersonian ethic of nonconformist self-expression includes the political task of exploring the individual's connections to and conflicts with others—only if the danger of individualist hubris is tempered by an Emersonian ethic of consciousness, conscience, and conscientiousness. This tension is summed up in the distance between Emerson's brazen claim "I may [...] absolve me to myself" and the hard-won sense of democratic identity Ellison's narrator expresses when he wonders in the novel's famous closing line, "Who knows but that, on the lower frequencies, I speak for you" (568).

NOTES

1. "I came to understand, in other words, that all that stood between me and writing symphonies was not simply a matter of civil rights, even though the civil rights struggle was all too real" ("That Same Pain" 72).

2. For Ellison's criticisms of Wright, see Ellison, "That Same Pain" (73–75), "Richard Wright's Blues," and "World."

3. Gilroy's *The Black Atlantic* also theorizes a culturally mixed identity that cuts across racial and national lines. Gilroy depicts the "transcultural, international formation" (4) of the African diaspora—characterized by "hybridity" and "homeless-ness" (2, 111–12), by "routes" instead of "roots" (19)—as a "counterculture" to the dominant Western paradigm of enlightenment and modernity and its underlying dualism of purity and exclusion (2, 45–46). He does not offer a sustained discussion of Ellison, focusing instead on writers like Du Bois and Wright whose trans-Atlantic expatriation catalyzed their sense of transcultural identity (17–19). There are, none-theless, clear affinities between Ellison's and Gilroy's views of black cultures as existing at once inside and outside mainstream Western culture (following Du Bois's model of double consciousness)—in spaces characterized both by exclusion and by freedom to appropriate and mix cultural styles. Ellison uses the autobiographical trope of the Oklahoma Territory to describe his border space ("Going to the Terri-tory" 600–05), while Gilroy uses the international space of the Atlantic Ocean and the ships that traversed it (16–17).

4. This interpretation has gained ascendancy in the work of recent critics such as Nadel and Lee. Lee, following Cornel West's lead, argues that Ellison's satire is aimed at the inability of Emerson's individualism to deal with the reality of racism. Earlier assessments of Ellison's allusions to Emerson, such as studies by Deutsch, Rovit, and Nichols, focus mainly on literary or philosophical affinities between the two writers, instead of on Ellison's political revision of Emerson. I offer an alterna-tive to both these approaches, one that acknowledges the philosophical tradition connecting Ellison and Emerson, as well as the way Ellison turns this inheritance to his own political concerns.

5. For a different analysis of Ellison's individualism, see Watts. Focusing not on Ellison's fiction but on his career as an African American intellectual and on his public statements about the purposes and responsibilities of art, Watts discusses Ellison in the light of the conflict between "hyperpoliticized" and "depoliticized" approaches to African American cultural studies (11). Watts admires Ellison for championing the complexity of African American cultural and individual experience

against a reductive Marxism or black nationalism yet also faults his individualism for veering too far in the opposite direction (57, 71). According to Watts. Ellison's cultural pluralism (62, 105) and his commitment to a vision of the exceptional, heroic individual as a measure of freedom and possibility (116) remain trapped in a bourgeois, meritocratic elitism that ignores or underestimates the determining force that structures of inequality have on the individual (81, 85, 108). While Watts offers a valuable discussion of Ellison's debate with Irving Howe (and Richard Wright) over the politics of literary practice, his conclusion that Ellison retreats into an apolitical individualism is influenced too much by the polemics of the debate. My reading of the individualist ethics dramatized in *Invisible Man* and of the responsibilities of democratic art that Ellison outlines in "Twentieth-Century Fiction and the Black Mask of Humanity" is intended to show that Ellison had a more coherent and politically engaged vision of individualism—and literary practice—than Watts seems to allow.

6. For discussion of Ellison's connection to Burke, see Ellison, "Essential Ellison"; Burke, "Ralph Ellison's Trueblooded *Bildungsroman*"; Adell; Parrish; and O'Meally, "Burke."

7. See, e.g., Bercovitch; Gilmore; Jehlen; and Newfield. For an analysis of how these political critiques of Emerson accept and perpetuate the traditional dichotomies of Emerson criticism, see Albrecht.

8. West's *The American Evasion of Philosophy* constitutes the most ambitious attempt to map a genealogy of American pragmatism that includes African American writers. West does not, however, include either Burke or Ellison in his study. Moreover, West is ultimately dismissive of the political potential of the Emerson–James trajectory of pragmatism, arguing that both thinkers are hindered by a "bourgeois" commitment to individualism that prevents them from "taking seriously fundamental social change" (60). West further argues that Emerson's commitment to egalitarianism is seriously "circumscribed" by racist determinism (34). I offer this reading of the Emerson–Burke–Ellison line of influence in part to suggest alternatives to West's assessment of the political trajectory of pragmatic individualism.

9. Nadel's and Livingston's criticisms of Mumford's historical nostalgia are by no means representative of Mumford's reception—especially by critics on the left. For a more reverent reading of Mumford, see Blake.

10. As recent scholarship has stressed, though Emerson felt that his talents and temperament made him ill-suited for politics, he took an increasingly active role in voicing public support for the abolition movement throughout the 1840s and 1850s (see Gougeon; Emerson, *Emerson's Antislavery Writings*).

11. A representative but not exhaustive list of major works that stress Emerson's position in the pragmatic tradition includes James; Burke, *Attitudes toward History* 3–33 and "I, Eye, Ay"; Dewey; Carpenter; Poirier, *Poetry, Renewal,* and *World*; Cavell, "Mood" and "Thinking"; West; and Bloom. My approach to Emerson extends, and is deeply indebted to, many of these works.

12. For discussions of Emerson's relation to community, see Kateb 222–29 and Albrecht 198–201.

13. Burke's attitude toward technology here is firmly in the Jamesian pragmatic tradition. As Livingston cogently argues, it is ironic that Mumford should target pragmatism in his polemic against modern threats to human agency, for one of James's central concerns is to reaffirm human will, belief, and action. As

Livingston asserts, pragmatists did not "surrender the genuine self or the moral personality to the empiricists and positivists" but, rather, accepted the modern industrial order as an accomplished historical fact—as "the premise of their thinking about the meaning and the moral stability of the human personality"—in order to appropriate the possibilities for future transformation inherent in that new order (278–79). Where "Mumford saw only symptoms of disease," pragmatists saw "attempted cures as well" (246).

14. In contrast to Baker, who describes Trueblood as a trickster figure of phallic power, Spillers stresses that the socioeconomic forces splintering the black family make the Western oedipal myth inapplicable to African American fathers and daughters.

15. For example, Stepto; Smith; and Callahan all provide readings that stress the importance of the act of narration in *Invisible Man*.

16. This paralysis, Burke might suggest, reflects tragedy's tendency to associate insight with punishment and even death; comedy, in contrast, tends to symbolize insight as rebirth in which the "mistaken" blindnesses of the old self are left behind (*Grammar* 39). Accordingly, in a short essay on *Invisible Man*, Burke describes Ellison's novel as a kind of bildungsroman in which the narrator develops a more mature comic consciousness in response to the complexities of race relations ("Ellison's Trueblooded *Bildungsroman*").

17. For example, Smith discusses how Bledsoe, Brother Tarp, Rinehart, Trueblood, and Tod Clifton represent model identities for the narrator to emulate, models that place Ellison's protagonist "in a tradition of Afro-American letters" whose writers "name themselves before a culture that ha[s] denied their full humanity" (27); Stepto places Ellison's novel in the rhetorical tradition of slave narratives; and Callahan argues that the political themes of Ellison's narrator reflect the particular experiences of southern blacks and that the rhetoric of the narrator's speeches echoes the communal call-and-response form of African American worship.

18. Strictly speaking, the narrator performs another confrontational act in his hibernation: as described in the novel's prologue, he assaults and almost kills a white man who insults him with a racial epithet. Though both acts occur during the narrator's hibernation, this confrontation from the prologue provides a symmetrical contrast to the narrator's confrontation of Norton in the epilogue. Ellison thus seems to offer rhetorical confrontation as an alternative to violent confrontation and thereby again aligns himself with Burke, who argues in *Attitudes toward History* and *A Rhetoric of Motives* that the comic and rhetorical attitudes advocate persuasion and compromise instead of violence.

Works Cited

Adell, Sandra. "The Big E(llison)'s Texts and Intertexts: Eliot, Burke, and the Underground Man." *CLA Journal* 37 (1994): 377–401.

Albrecht, James M. "'Living Property': Emerson's Ethics." *ESQ* 41 (1995): 177–217.

Baker, Houston A., Jr. "To Move without Moving: An Analysis of Creativity and Commerce in Ralph Ellison's Trueblood Episode." *PMLA* 98 (1983): 828–45.

Benston, Kimberly W. *Speaking for You: The Vision of Ralph Ellison*. Washington: Howard UP, 1987.

Bercovitch, Sacvan. "Emerson, Individualism, and the Ambiguity of Dissent." *South Atlantic Quarterly* 89 (1990): 623–62.

Blake, Casey Nelson. *Beloved Community: The Cultural Criticism of Randolph Bourne, Van Wyck Brooks, Waldo Frank, and Lewis Mumford.* Chapel Hill: U of North Carolina P, 1990.

Bloom, Harold. *Agon: Towards a Theory of Revisionism.* New York: Oxford UP, 1982.

Buell, Lawrence. "The Emerson Industry in the 1980's: A Survey of Trends and Achievements." *ESQ* 30 (1984): 117–36.

Burke, Kenneth. *Attitudes toward History.* 1937. Los Altos: Hermes, 1959.

———. *A Grammar of Motives.* 1945. Berkeley: U of California P, 1969.

———. "I, Eye, Ay—Emerson's Early Essay 'Nature': Some Thoughts on the Machinery of Transcendence." *Emerson's Nature: Origin, Growth, Meaning.* 1969. 2nd ed., enlarged. Ed. Merton M. Sealts, Jr., and Alfred R. Ferguson. Carbondale: Southern Illinois UP, 1979. 150–63.

———. "Ralph Ellison's Trueblooded *Bildungsroman.*" Benston 349–59.

———. *A Rhetoric of Motives.* 1950. Berkeley: U of California P, 1969.

Callahan, John F. "Frequencies of Eloquence: The Performance and Composition of *Invisible Man.*" O'Meally, *New Essays* 55–94.

Carpenter, Frederic. "William James and Emerson." *American Literature* 11 (1939): 39–57.

Cavell, Stanley. "In an Emerson Mood." Cavell, *Senses* 141–60.

———. *The Senses of Walden: An Expanded Edition.* San Francisco: North Point, 1981.

———. "Thinking of Emerson." Cavell, *Senses* 128–38.

Deutsch, Leonard J. "Ralph Waldo Ellison and Ralph Waldo Emerson: A Shared Moral Vision." *CLA Journal* 16 (1972): 159–78.

Dewey, John. "Emerson." *Characters and Events.* Ed. Joseph Ratner. New York: Octagon, 1970. 69–77.

Du Bois, W. E. B. *The Souls of Black Folk.* 1903. *Three Negro Classics.* New York: Avon, 1965. 207–389.

Ellison, Ralph. "Address to the Harvard College Alumni, Class of 1949." Ellison, *Collected Essays* 415–26.

———. "The Art of Fiction: An Interview." With Alfred Chester and Vilma Howard. Ellison, *Collected Essays* 210–24.

———. "Change the Joke and Slip the Yoke." Ellison, *Collected Essays* 100–12.

———. *The Collected Essays of Ralph Ellison.* Ed. John F. Callahan. New York: Mod. Lib., 1995.

———. "The Essential Ellison." Interview with Steve Cannon, Ishmael Reed, and Quincy Troupe. *Y'Bird Reader* 1.1 (1977): 130–59.

———. "An Extravagance of Laughter." Ellison, *Collected Essays* 613–58.

———. "Going to the Territory." Ellison, *Collected Essays* 591–612.

———. "Hidden Name and Complex Fate." Ellison, *Collected Essays* 189–209.

———. Introduction to *Shadow and Act.* Ellison, *Collected Essays* 49–60.

———. *Invisible Man.* 1952. New York: Random, 1972.

———. "The Novel as a Function of American Democracy." Ellison, *Collected Essays* 755–65.

———. "Richard Wright's Blues." Ellison, *Collected Essays* 128–44.

———. "That Same Pain, That Same Pleasure." Interview with Richard G. Stern. Ellison, *Collected Essays* 63–80.

———. "Twentieth-Century Fiction and the Black Mask of Humanity." Ellison, *Collected Essays* 81–99.

———. "Working Notes for *Invisible Man.*" Ellison, *Collected Essays* 341–45.

———. "The World and the Jug." Ellison, *Collected Essays* 155–88.

Emerson, Ralph Waldo. "The Conservative." Emerson, *Essays* 173–89.
———. *Emerson's Antislavery Writings*. Ed. Len Gougeon and Joel Myerson. New Haven: Yale UP, 1995.
———. *Essays and Lectures*. New York: Lib. of Amer., 1983.
———. "Experience." Emerson, *Essays* 471–92.
———. "Fate." Emerson, *Essays* 941–68.
———. "Man the Reformer." Emerson, *Essays* 135–50.
———. "Self-Reliance." Emerson, *Essays* 259–82.
———. "Shakspeare; or, the Poet." Emerson, *Essays* 710–26.
———. "Spiritual Laws." Emerson, *Essays* 303–23.
———. "The Uses of Great Men." Emerson, *Essays* 615–32.
Gilmore, Michael. *American Romanticism and the Marketplace*. Chicago: U of Chicago P, 1985.
Gilroy, Paul. *The Black Atlantic: Modernity and Double Consciousness*. Cambridge: Harvard UP, 1993.
Gougeon, Len. *Virtue's Hero: Emerson, Antislavery, and Reform*. Athens: U of Georgia P, 1990.
James, William. "Address at the Emerson Centenary in Concord." *The Writings of William James: A Comprehensive Edition*. Ed. John J. McDermott. 1967. Chicago: U of Chicago P, 1977. 581–86.
Jehlen, Myra. *American Incarnation: The Individual, the Nation, and the Continent*. Cambridge: Harvard UP, 1986.
Kateb, George. *The Inner Ocean: Individualism and Democratic Culture*. Ithaca: Cornell UP, 1992.
Lee, Kun Jong. "Ellison's *Invisible Man*: Emersonianism Revised." *PMLA* 107 (1992): 331–44.
Livingston, James. *Pragmatism and the Political Economy of Cultural Revolution, 1850–1940*. Chapel Hill: U of North Carolina P 1994.
Lopez, Michael. *Emerson and Power: Creative Antagonism in the Nineteenth Century*. Dekalb: Northern Illinois UP 1996.
Matthiessen, F. O. *American Renaissance: Art and Expression in the Age of Emerson and Whitman*. New York: Oxford UP, 1941.
Mumford, Lewis. *The Golden Day: A Study in American Experience and Culture*. New York: Liveright, 1926.
Nadel, Alan. *Invisible Criticism: Ralph Ellison and the American Canon*. Iowa City: U of Iowa P, 1988.
Newfield, Christopher. *The Emerson Effect: Individualism and Submission in America*. Chicago: U of Chicago P, 1996.
Nichols, William W. "Ralph Ellison's Black American Scholar." *Phylon* 31.1 (1970): 70–75.
O'Meally, Robert. *New Essays on Invisible Man*. New York: Cambridge UP, 1988.
———. "On Burke and the Vernacular: Ralph Ellison's Boomerang of History." *History and Memory in African-American Culture*. Ed. Genevieve Fabre and O'Meally. New York: Oxford UP, 1994. 244–60.
Parrish, Timothy L. "Ralph Ellison, Kenneth Burke, and the Form of Democracy." *Arizona Quarterly* 52 (1995): 117–48.
Poirier, Richard. *Poetry and Pragmatism*. Cambridge: Harvard UP, 1992.
———. *The Renewal of Literature: Emersonian Reflections*. New York: Random. 1987.
———. *A World Elsewhere: The Place of Style in American Literature*. 1966. Madison: U of Wisconsin P, 1985.

Rovit, Earl H. "Ralph Ellison and the American Comic Tradition." *Wisconsin Studies in Contemporary Literature* 1.3 (1960): 34–42.

Smith, Valerie. "The Meaning of Narration in *Invisible Man*." O'Meally, *New Essays* 25–53.

Spillers, Hortense. "'The Permanent Obliquity of the In(pha)llibly Straight': In the Time of the Daughters and the Fathers." *Changing Our Own Words: Essays on Criticism, Theory, and Writing by Black Women*. Ed. Cheryl A. Wall. New Brunswick: Rutgers UP, 1989. 127–49.

Stepto, Robert B. "Literacy and Hibernation: Ralph Ellison's *Invisible Man*." Benston 360–85.

Watts, Jerry Gafio. *Heroism and the Black Intellectual: Ralph Ellison, Politics, and Afro-American Intellectual Life*. Chapel Hill: U of North Carolina P, 1994.

West, Cornel. *The American Evasion of Philosophy: A Genealogy of Pragmatism*. Madison: U of Wisconsin P, 1989.

Whicher, Stephen E. *Freedom and Fate: An Inner Life of Ralph Waldo Emerson*. Philadelphia: U of Pennsylvania P, 1953.

BERTRAM D. ASHE

Listening to the Blues: Ralph Ellison's Trueblood Episode in Invisible Man

O n the front porch of his house, on an unseasonably warm Southern spring day in the middle of the century, Jim Trueblood told a long tale to a young Negro college student and one Mr. Norton, a wealthy donor to the college. Trueblood's tale occupies the majority of chapter two of Ralph Ellison's *Invisible Man*. In Charles Chesnutt's *The Conjure Woman* the short stories are rendered with a textual frame, as is Zora Neale Hurston's *Their Eyes Were Watching God*. Their length differences notwithstanding, in both Chesnutt's and Hurston's texts the relationship between teller and listener inside the text seems to mirror the hoped-for relationship between text and reader. In *Invisible Man*, once again there is an inside-the-text teller and inside-the-text listeners; however, this is an *embedded* narrative rather than a formal "frame" narrative.[1]

Embedded narratives must be considered in the context of the events of a novel that happen before and after the storytelling event. For example, in *Invisible Man*, the Trueblood episode is a distinct text unto itself, but it is also an early "adventure" in Invisible Man's quest to understand himself. Adventure" is the term Susan Rubin Suleiman uses in *Authoritarian Fictions: The Ideological Novel As a Literary Genre*. She defines a "story of apprenticeship"[2]

as two parallel transformations undergone by the protagonist: first, a transformation from *ignorance* (of self) to *knowledge* (of

From *From Within Frame: Storytelling in African-American Fiction*. © 2002 by Routledge.

self); second, a transformation from *passivity* to *action*. The hero
goes forth into the world to find (knowledge of) himself, and
attains such knowledge through a series of "adventures" (actions)
that function both as "proofs" and as tests. The adventures in
which the hero triumphs are the means whereby he "discovers
his own essence"—they thus fulfill the traditional function of a
text; but they constitute, at the same time, a "proof" of his new-
found knowledge of self, which is the necessary precondition for
authentic action in the future. In effect, the hero's "adventures" are
but the prelude to genuine action: a story of apprenticeship ends
on the threshold of a "new life" for the hero—which explains why,
in the traditional *Bildungsroman*, the hero is always a young man,
often an adolescent. (65)

Suleiman's "story of apprenticeship" theory describes the actions of the hero
of *Invisible Man* from the Battle Royale, his earliest "adventure," through
the epilogue, where the demonstration of his "new-found knowledge of self"
suggests a "prelude to genuine action." His readiness to emerge from his
"hole" at novel's end does signal a "'new life' for the hero."

The Trueblood episode is, indeed, an "adventure" that is vital to the reading of the novel as Invisible Man's growth from a naive college student to
a mature, knowledgeable individual. But it is the episode's execution of the
blues mode[3] that allows Invisible Man to demonstrate his transformation in
the epilogue after his "adventures" pile on top of each other. For both Invisible Man-the-listener and the reader of his autobiography, the episode shows
Trueblood as a model of what Invisible Man would become: a bluesman. Mr.
Norton, on the other hand, listens differently and emerges as a problematic
model for readers who identify with him. Norton, too, makes an appearance
in the epilogue. But Invisible Man goes beyond merely providing "the rest
of the story" to the Trueblood episode; much as Hurston does in the closing
pages of *Their Eyes Were Watching God*, Ellison's narrator discusses the very
nature of audience itself. As we shall see, Invisible Man ponders his readers'
possible reception of his narrative, and in the process he reveals his "fictional-
ization" of his readers. His discussion of his intended audience in the epilogue
speaks to his models inside the text, and the connection between Trueblood
and Invisible Man becomes even more evident when viewed through these
novel-ending comments.

Like Ong, Suleiman sees inside-the-text listeners as models for readers.
In a discussion of the novel *L'Etape*, Suleiman writes that when one character
"reads" the stories of his brother and sister, he "occupies a position analogous
to that of the reader of their stories and of the novel as a whole. His act

of interpretation is a mimesis of the general activity of the reader—and the consequence of this interpretation, which is a change in his whole way of being and acting, is also presumably supposed to function as a model, or as a mirror image, for the reader" (79). As we have seen in Hurston's novel, where Pheoby acts as model for both the porch-sitters and the readership, Ellison, in his "Working Notes for *Invisible Man*," envisions Trueblood as a model for the narrator:

> Against the tragic-comic attitude adopted by folk Negroes (best expressed by the blues and in our scheme by Trueblood) [Invisible Man] is strictly, during the first phase of his life, of the nineteenth century. Thus neither he nor Mr. Norton, whose abolitionist father's creation he is, can respond to Trueblood's stoicism, or to the Vet's need to get close to the naked essence of the world as he has come to see it. Life is either tragic or absurd, but Norton and the boy have no capacity to deal with such ambivalence. The boy would appease the gods; it costs him much to discover that he can satisfy the gods only by rebelling against them. (344)

Ellison holds Trueblood up as an example of a stoic bluesman who adopts a tragic-comic attitude to grapple with the absurdities of African-American life.[4] And when Ellison provides Trueblood as an additional "invisible man"—one who, "when they approach [him] they see only [his] surroundings, themselves, or figments of their imagination—indeed, everything and anything except"[5] the individual that Trueblood truly is—Ellison also imbues Trueblood with a stoicism that outlasts and transcends the obstacles placed before him.[6] The early "point" to the novel's latter "counterpoint," then, is made through storytelling. Trueblood is, according to Robert Stepto, a "master storyteller."[7] Invisible Man writes that Trueblood "told the old stories with a sense of humor and a magic that made them come alive" (46). And through his storytelling, Trueblood embodies what Henry Louis Gates, Jr. calls "the improvisatory prehistory of the blues."[8]

Trueblood tells his tale to a double audience—literally, he repeatedly tells the tale to both black and white audiences. These storytelling events constitute Trueblood's "adventures," in the Suleiman sense, and they prefigure Invisible Man's "adventures" as well. The first telling happens the morning after the incident, when Kate, after leaving the house to go down the road, "comes back with some women to see 'bout Matty Lou. Won't nobody speak to me," says Trueblood, "though they looks at me like I'm some new kinda cottonpickin' machine. I feels bad. I tells them how it happened in a dream, but they scorns me" (65–6). After that first futile telling, Trueblood "goes to see the preacher and even he don't believe me. He tells me to git out of his house, that I'm the most wicked man he's ever seen and that I better go confess my sin and make my peace with God" (66). As a result of telling his stories, Trueblood undergoes a transformation, as will Invisible Man much later. At the preacher's behest, Trueblood goes off to be alone with God. This religious retreat includes fasting and denial of fluids, until the transcendence of the blues intervene:

> I leaves tryin' to pray, but I caint. I thinks and thinks, until I thinks my brain is go'n bust, 'bout how I'm guilty and how I ain't guilty. I don't eat nothin' and I don't drink nothin' and I caint sleep at night. Finally one night, way early in the mornin', I looks up and sees the stars and I starts singin'. I don't mean to, I didn't think 'bout it, just start singin'. I don't know what it was, some kinda church song, I guess. All I know is I *ends up* singin' the blues. I sings me some blues that night ain't never been sang before, and while I'm singin' them blues I makes up my mind that I ain't nobody but myself and ain't nothin' I can do but let whatever is gonna happen, happen. (66)

Before Trueblood's retreat, his storytelling attempts were futile, and he was frustrated by his audiences' refusal to believe his tale.[9] After the retreat, however, where Trueblood "makes up [his] mind," the reaction to his tale differs somewhat. He still gets an understandably negative reaction when he next "tells Kate and Matty Lou 'bout the dream" (66), but when Kate's first words are "How come you don't go on 'way and leave us?," Trueblood reacts by saying, "I'm a man and a man don't leave his family" (66).

The retreat thus provides the tale with a turning point, a point that occurs with Trueblood's singing of the blues. The movement from religious to secular, from singing a church song that "ends up [with] singin' the blues," signals Trueblood's transformation from what Ellison calls a "pre-individu-alistic state" to that of being an individual who does what he feels he must. As Houston Baker, Jr. writes, "The first unpremeditated expression that True-blood summons is a religious song. But the religious system that gives birth to the song is, presumably, one in which the term "incest" carries pejorative force. Hence, the sharecropper moves on, spontaneously, to the blues" (187–88).

The three specific black audiences he talks to (the women taking care of Kate, the preacher, and Kate and Mattie) all react negatively to his tale. He finds more rejection when he tells the tale to other blacks, including those at the school, who are, perhaps, most hostile to Trueblood and his act. They offer to send Trueblood and his family out of the county, but Trueblood refuses, and an interesting power play develops as a result of his refusal: both Trueblood and the "biggety school folks" use the threat of white influence as instruments of power in order to get their way. In a scene somewhat reminiscent of Chloe's going to her slavemaster to get satisfaction from Hannibal's autonomous revenge plot in Chesnutt's "Hot-Foot Hannibal," the school officials threaten to "turn the white folks loose on" Trueblood. Trueblood admits that "Them folks up there to the school is in strong with the white folks and that scared me" (52), but after they call him a "disgrace" he "got real mad [and] went down to see Mr. Buchanan, the boss man . . ." (52).

He then begins to tell his tale to whites, with much more "positive" results than he has with his earlier black audiences. He moves from Buchanan to Sheriff Barbour, who, in turn, "called in some more men" to hear it again. "They wanted to hear about the gal lots of times and they gimme somethin' to eat and drink and some tobacco" says Trueblood. "Surprised me, 'cause I was scared and spectin' somethin' different. Why I guess there ain't a colored man in the county who ever got to take so much of the white folkses time as I did" (53). The revelation that he was "scared" telling his tale to whites echoes the way he was "scared" when the blacks from the school threatened to exercise their influence with powerful whites. Obviously, however, he was willing to tell the whites himself because he was either less afraid of white reaction than he was of the school administrators' connection with whites, or because, regardless of what happened, he insisted on retaining agency and carrying the message himself. More than likely it was a combination of both.

At bottom, his white audience's reaction to his tale is astonishingly different from the black reaction:

[T]he white folks took to coming out here to see us and talk with us. Some of 'em was big white folks, too, from the big school way cross the State. Asked me lots 'bout what I thought 'bout things, and 'bout my folks and the kids, and wrote it all down in a book. (53)

It would be a mistake, however, to assume that Trueblood's repeated tale is told virtually verbatim at each telling. Baker writes that the

multiple narrative frames and voices in Ellison's Trueblood episode include the novel Invisible Man, the protagonist's fictive autobiographical account, Norton's story recalled as part of the fictive autobiography, Trueblood's story as framed by the fictive autobiography, the sharecropper's own autobiographical recall, the dream narrative within that autobiographical recall. All these stories reflect, or 'objectify,' one another in ways that complicate their individual and composite meanings. (176)

But when Trueblood tells his tale to the different facets of the black community, "the tale" is actually Trueblood talking about "the dream" in an
effort to explain how it is that he managed to impregnate both his daughter and his wife at approximately the same time. By the time he tells the
tale to Norton and Invisible Man, he is talking about the dream *and the
aftermath* to explain not just how they became pregnant but how his life
has changed in the interim. As such, it is important to note that the tale
Trueblood tells to the women, to the preacher, and to Kate and Matty
Lou is not the same tale Invisible Man records in his memoir. The tale he
tells to the whites, on the other hand, has expanded to a discussion of the
night it happened, the economic context of that night's winter, his state of
mind *regarding* the economic context of that winter, the dream, and the
incest act itself.[10]

Trueblood, master storyteller that he is, shapes and adapts his story to
his audience. Still, the difference between white reaction and black reaction is
something that does not get past Trueblood, even as he claims not to understand it:

> Things got to happenin' right off. The nigguhs up at the school
> come down to chase me off and that made me mad. That's what I
> don't understand. I done the worse thing a man could ever do in his
> family and instead of chasin' me out of the country, [whites] gimme
> more help than they ever give any other colored man, no matter
> how good a nigguh he was. Except that my wife an' daughter won't
> speak to me, I'm better off than I ever been before. (67)

Trueblood reveals the various audience reactions to his tale over the eight-
plus months since the incident itself and they mirror the white/black reaction to the audience before him as he sits and talks to Invisible Man and
Mr. Norton.

Indeed, Mr. Norton brings all of the contradictions, confusions, and,
perhaps above all, *guilt* of the paternalistic white aristocracy to his hearing of
the tale. As Ellison makes clear in his "Notes," Trueblood is not speaking to
an audience that can "respond" when he tells his tale to Mr. Norton and Invisible Man. Recall that Ellison asserts that "Norton and the boy have no capacity to deal with such ambivalence" (344). Invisible Man describes Norton as a
"multimillionaire," with "A face pink like St. Nicholas' topped with a shock of
silk white hair. An easy, informal manner. . . . A Bostonian, smoker of cigars,
teller of polite Negro stories, shrewd banker, skilled scientist, director, philanthropist, forty years a bearer of the white man's burden, and for sixty a symbol
of the Great Traditions" (37).

Co-listener Invisible Man, however, is by turns ashamed, disgusted, and embarrassed because he is (still) trapped in his double-consciousness: he sees Trueblood through Mr. Norton's eyes. Wolfgang Iser writes, "The traditional hero of the novel is endowed with a quite specific function: he is the focal point of reference for virtually all events in the world he represents, and he gives the reader the opportunity to participate in these events."[11] So it is important that Invisible Man, early in chapter two, writes of Mr. Norton, "I felt that I was sharing in a great work and, with the car leaping leisurely beneath the pressure of my foot, I *identified myself* with the rich man reminiscing on the rear seat . . ." (39, italics added). Mr. Norton, in fact, becomes the "focal point" for "virtually all [of the] events" that follow in the chapter.

It is in connection with his "fate" that Invisible Man identifies with Mr. Norton; importantly, his lack of identification with Trueblood extends further narrative identification to Mr. Norton. This identification is important since, as I will discuss below, Invisible Man revisits his relationship with Mr. Norton in the epilogue, after the bulk of his narrative has been related and after he has come to understand and reconcile his double consciousness. At this early stage, however, the reader can only "read" Invisible Man by paying attention to his comments about the way the school administrators view Trueblood. The school officials called Trueblood's music "primitive spirituals" (47). Invisible Man adds, "We were embarrassed by the earthy harmonies they sang, but since the visitors were awed we dared not laugh at the crude, high, plaintively animal sounds Jim Trueblood made as he led the quartet" (47). These statements are further examples of the difference between the black audience and the white audience's possible reception of Trueblood's performance—both musical *and* storytelling. Whenever the black middle class (signified in this instance by Invisible Man, the rest of the students, and the school's officials) is confronted with an example of black folk expression, it blanches.

For Trueblood's tale is spliced with comments by Invisible Man that speak to his discomfort in the white gaze, to his "sense of shame" (68) at hearing Trueblood's sometimes ribald narrative in the presence of a white person: "How can he tell this to white men, I thought, when he knows they'll say that all Negroes do such things?" (58). (This question is a precursor to a question Invisible Man would ask himself much later in the novel. Just as Invisible Man asks himself why Trueblood would tell his tale to Mr. Norton, he later asks himself why, indeed, he would tell his own tale [579].) In his "Notes," Ellison sees Trueblood's "stoicism" and the Vet's pursuit of "the naked essence of the world" as values to be emulated; he makes it clear that Invisible Man, at least early on, and Norton have "no capacity" to "deal with such ambivalence." Ellison's "Notes" position Trueblood and the Vet as legitimate polar opposites of Norton and "the boy," emphasizing that Norton is a product of a socioeconomic climate that doesn't demand that he grapple with the "absurd predicament" in which Negroes find themselves. Invisible Man, however, as Ellison states, "represents the Negro individualist, the personality that breaks away from the pre-individual community of southern Negro life to win its way in the jim crow world by guile, uncletomming, or ruthlessness. In order to do this he must act within the absurd predicament in which Negroes find themselves upon the assumption that all is completely logical" (344).

Invisible Man has, by narrative's end, achieved some semblance of individuality. There are two instances in the second chapter, shortly before Trueblood tells his tale, that remind the reader that Invisible Man is recalling these events and interpreting them from the individualist stance he has achieved by the end of the narrative.[12] These two moments help ground the events in the correct time. The first reference point occurs when Mr. Norton hands his daughter's miniature to Invisible Man. "She was very beautiful, I thought *at the time* . . . ," he writes. "I know *now* that it was the flowing costume of soft, flimsy material that made for the effect; today . . . she would appear as ordinary as an expensive piece of machine-tooled jewelry and just as lifeless. *Then*, however," he concludes, "I shared something of his enthusiasm" (43 italics added). The juxtaposition of "at the time" and "now," and of "today" and "then," emphasizes the fact that Invisible Man-the-character shares duties with Invisible Man-the-narrator. The character serves the narrator's ideological ends, and this short reference to time reminds the reader that this is not simply the telling of a linear story but the recounting of a series of events that is being interpreted from the perspective of a man who has come to understand his invisibility.

This brief reminder of the narrator's perspective remains a momentary pause in the narrator's concentration on Invisible Man's school experiences until the narrator pauses again in the midst of relating how the college's inhabitants were embarrassed by Jim Trueblood as he led the quartet. When Invisible Man writes, "That had all passed now with his disgrace," the word "now," no longer means as-I-sit-in-my-basement; it refers to the episode-specific time when Trueblood was no longer welcome at the school after impregnating his wife and daughter. But the next sentence again situates the narrator underground, as he clearly marks the difference between the present and the past he writes about: "I didn't understand in those pre-invisible days that their hate, and mine too, was charged with fear" (47). Further, Invisible Man uses this additional time-shift-reference to comment on how much he's learned in between the past and the present-day writing of his autobiography. He also refers to a nonspecific "we" that could be taken more than one way:

"How all of us at the college hated the black-belt people, the 'peasants,' during those days! We were trying to lift them up and they, like Trueblood, did everything it seemed to pull them down" (47).

This reference to "those days" is relayed in first person plural. He could simply be referring to "us" because of the obvious fact there were a plurality of students at the school. However, that sentence could also possibly hint that what Invisible Man has undergone in between the time he spent at school and the writing of the narrative in his room is a transformation in how he views the black folk, the "peasants." The first person plural point of view could, additionally, speak to a hoped-for massive, class-crossing alteration of how African-Americans deal with "the absurd predicament" in which they find themselves upon assuming that "all is completely logical" (344), given that Trueblood and the Vet are mature bluesmen.

I read the Trueblood episode as a way for Ellison to suggest to black middle class readers an alternative reaction to the Truebloods—and the Mr. Nortons—of America. And white readers who have, for reasons I discuss above, identified with Mr. Norton, can see how far they have *not* come.[13] My sense is that Ellison inserted these two time-shift reminders so that when Invisible Man returns to real time in the epilogue the readers (black and white) can see how far he's come, and how far they, as readers, may have come as well. Through the same process of identification, at the end of the novel, the black middle class could glimpse the idea of a progression of their own.

This second time-reference also suggests that the Trueblood episode is, in fact, incomplete as an episode in and of itself, that it is actually a crucial setup that will show the reader the contrast between a naive Invisible Man and the Invisible Man who has grown into the realization that all is not "completely logical." The reader, as a result of watching and hearing Trueblood-the-model's "stoicism" in action, can begin to glimpse the transformation Invisible Man has gone through by the time the epilogue appears. The critical moment in that epilogue, for the purposes of this discussion, comes when Invisible Man recalls seeing Mr. Norton in the subway:

> He's lost, I thought, and he'll keep coming until he sees me, then he'll ask for direction. Maybe there's an embarrassment in it if he admits he's lost to a strange white man. Perhaps to lose a sense of where you are implies the danger of losing a sense of *who* you are. That must be it, I thought—to lose your direction is to lose your face. So here he comes to ask his direction from the lost, the invisible. Very well, I've learned to live without direction. Let him ask. (577)

Over the course of the novel, Invisible Man has come to recognize his invisibility, and as a result he has learned to "live without direction." But here he implies that Mr. Norton has also lost a sense of who he is during his absence from the real time of the novel.

In fact, Invisible Man, as his "adventures" pass one after the other, has himself come to realize the critical "loss" of those who deny the richness of black contributions to American culture. Gates, in a profile of Albert Murray, called Ellison's insistence on a black core to the American way of life as "perhaps the most breathtaking act of cultural chutzpa this land had witnessed since Columbus blithely claimed it all for Isabella":

> In its bluntest form, [Murray and Ellison's] assertion was that the truest Americans were black Americans. For much of what was truly distinctive about America's "national character" was rooted in the improvisatory prehistory of the blues. The very sound of American English "is derived from the timbre of the African voice and the listening habits of the African ear," Ellison maintained. "If there is such a thing as a Yale accent, there is a Negro wail in it." (76)

In James Alan McPherson's "Indivisible Man," Ellison says emphatically, "I recognize no American culture which is not the partial creation of black people. I recognize no American style in literature, in dance, in music, even in assembly-line processes, which does not bear the mark of the American Negro" (*Collected Essays* 356).

Ellison, in *Invisible Man*, prefigures his non-fiction writings that confirm African-Americans' place at the center of American culture. "But I'm your destiny," says Invisible Man to Mr. Norton in the epilogue, "I made you. Why shouldn't I know you?" He goes on to suggest that Norton "Take any train; they all go to the Golden D[ay]" (578), metaphorically implying that the totality of American culture is inextricably entwined with African-American life and folkways. If some white readers were identifying with Mr. Norton during the Trueblood episode, the assumption here is that those whites have, as well, lost a sense of who they are since they don't realize their "black" cultural roots. Ellison says as much in the closing pages of the novel:

> America is woven of many strands; I would recognize them and let it so remain. It's "winner take nothing" that is the great truth of our country or of any country. Life is to be lived, not controlled; and humanity is won by continuing to play in the face of certain defeat. Our fate is to become one, and yet many—This is not prophecy

but description. Thus one of the greatest jokes in the world is the spectacle of the whites busy escaping blackness and becoming blacker every day, and the blacks striving towards whiteness, and becoming quite dull and gray. (577)

It is this intercultural comment that prompts Invisible Man to a recollection of Norton. Invisible Man, then, effectively turns Norton's chapter two statement ("you are involved in my life quite intimately, even though you've never seen me before. You are bound to a great dream and to a beautiful monument" [43]), into an example of how far Invisible Man has come since then. When first uttered, the words confuse Invisible Man because he still identified with Norton. Now he is clear about its meaning. Norton, in the earlier chapter, makes a paternal reference to his "first-hand organizing of human life" (42). But by the end of the narrative, Invisible Man understands that it is the influence of the American Negro which has, in part, influenced Norton. By taking Norton's comments and turning them on their head, Invisible Man exhibits the combination of white–black culture that accurately reflects the history between blacks and whites in this country.

But the novel-ending meeting between Norton and Invisible Man does far more than that. It re-contextualizes the Trueblood episode, modulating and expanding it in a fashion that frame texts such as Chesnutt's and Hurston's can only accomplish by projecting beyond the text. *Invisible Man* provides a storytelling event in the second chapter and then allows its readers the rest of the book to view its results.

The embedded narrative allows readers to glimpse a tangible growth process as the novel plays out. As the readers—white and black, with their myriad patterns of identification—read on to witness Invisible Man grappling with the Brotherhood and Lucius Brockway, Mary Rambo and Ras the Destroyer, even Rinehart, the possibility exists that their worldview will be altered. The early-on Trueblood episode and the book-ending reprisal of the Norton–Invisible Man connection highlight this possible growth.

However, Invisible Man puzzles with the idea of exactly who his audience is in the closing pages of the book. The closing five paragraphs of the novel, beginning with "So why do I write, torturing myself to put it down?" (579) to the last, one-sentence paragraph that ends the book, "Who knows but that, on the lower frequencies, I speak for you?" (581), address the notion of audience—in effect, he discusses who he means by "you," even though he never explicitly says so. Michel Fabre, in "The Narrator/Narratee Relationship in *Invisible Man*," makes a compelling case for the narratee, or the "fictional construct [who] should not be confused with the actual reader,"[14] being "a member of the white West" (541). Fabre bases his conclusion on Ellison's

use of the narratee-addressed "you," reading closely for clues as to whether
Ellison belongs to the addressed group or not.

> That the novel does address itself to white America is made clear
> in other, equally important sections of the Epilogue. During the
> last attempt at interpreting the grandfather's riddle . . . the narrator
> asks: "Did he mean to affirm the principle which they themselves
> (i.e., the men who did the violence) . . . had violated . . . ? Or did he
> mean that we had to take the responsibility for all of it . . . because
> we, with the given circumstances of our origin, could only thus
> find transcendence?" (574). This sounds like an inner monologue
> in response to the grandfather's question, not like an address to
> the reader, but it clearly identifies "they" as the racists, the white
> American oppressors, and "we" as the Black community. (542)

Here Fabre selects an excerpt that does more than suggest whites as the
audience. This passage suggests that while the narrative might be *addressed*
to white readers, it *assumes* black readers as well. Otherwise, the above question containing the "we" has no one to ponder an answer. This stance—the
familiar difficulty of the dual-audience—is yet another quandary that Invisible Man must overcome.

The audience discussion hinges upon the position Invisible Man takes
when he wishes to "at least *tell* a few people about" his experiences (579),
even as he imagines he knows how the (white) reader will react: "'Ah,' I can
hear you say, 'so it was all a build-up to bore us with his buggy jiving. He only
wanted us to listen to him rave!'" (581). Through his narrator, at the end of his
novel, Ellison is wrestling with one of the chief conundrums of the African-
American artist: how to communicate with an audience that would "refuse to
see me. . . . [T]hey see only my surroundings, themselves, or figments of their
imagination—indeed, everything and anything except me" (3). Invisible Man
sees the problem, and its tenable solution, this way:

> The very act of trying to put it all down has confused me and
> negated some of the anger and some of the bitterness. So it is that
> now I denounce and defend, or feel prepared to defend. I condemn
> and affirm, say no and say yes, say yes and say no. I denounce
> because though implicated and partially responsible, I have been
> hurt to the point of abysmal pain, hurt to the point of invisibility.
> And I defend because in spite of all I find that I love. In order to
> get some of it down I *have* to love. I sell you no phony forgiveness,
> I'm a desperate man—but too much of your life will be lost, its

meaning lost, unless you approach it as much through love as through hate. So I approach it through division. So I denounce and I defend and I hate and I love. (579–80)

With this statement, Invisible Man demonstrates that he has adopted the blues mode; he has, through great trial and error, attained Trueblood's sense that, having found himself "in a tight spot like that there," trying to figure a way "to git myself out of the fix I'm in," he had to "move without movin'" (59). Baker writes, "If desire and absence are driving conditions of blues performance, the amelioration of such conditions is implied by the onomatopoeic *training* of blues voice and instrument. Only a *trained* voice can sing the blues" (8). Baker's pun is obvious, as Invisible Man has been properly "trained," over the length of the novel to sing the blues. John S. Wright puts it this way:

Rinehart and Trueblood are ultimately the *nonpolitical* poles of sensibility between which the narrator must mediate his own ambiguous sense of freedom as necessity and as possibility. Despite Rinehart's unmediated freedom and Trueblood's subjection to psychic and social necessity, what Rinehart and Trueblood share is their existential awareness that to be free one must be able to "move without moving," a problem that Rinehart masters but Trueblood *transcends*.[15]

Although Ellison's "Notes" are undated and are thought to have been written sometime "after beginning *Invisible Man* in 1945" (*Collected Essays* 341), they speak to Invisible Man's dilemma as if, perhaps, the end of the novel had not yet been written when the "Notes" were composed. Invisible Man has come to understand that the problem of how to figure an unfigureable audience will be solved (as much as it can be solved) only if he can "approach it through division." This contrast between the naive and mature Invisible Man provides a completion to the Trueblood episode; Invisible Man can now "sing the blues" as well as Trueblood can. His hard-fought ability to adopt the ambiguous "tragic-comic attitude adopted by folk Negroes" complements Trueblood's example of the same much earlier in the novel. As Invisible Man puts it late in the book, "in spite of myself I've learned some things" (579).

This narrative, then, in a sense, functions the same way Trueblood's ritualistic fast-turned-prayer-turned-church-song-turned-singin'-the-blues moment that moves his tale from tragic to transcendent. Recall that Trueblood says then, "All I know is I *ends up* singing' the blues. I sings me some blues that night ain't never been sang before, and while I'm singin' them blues

I makes up my mind that I ain't nobody but myself and ain't nothin' I can do but let whatever is gonna happen, happen. I made up my mind . . ." (66). This decisive moment that literally grows out of the blues mirrors this equally transcendent moment in the epilogue of *Invisible Man*:

> So now having tried to put it down I have disarmed myself in the process. You won't believe in my invisibility and you'll fail to see how any principle that applies to you could apply to me. You'll fail to see it even though death waits for both of us if you don't. Nevertheless, the very disarmament has brought me to a decision. The hibernation is over. (580)

And he readies himself to come out with full knowledge of the ambiguity he carries, saying, "invisibility has taught my nose to classify . . ." (580). While "there's still a conflict within me," he writes, "a decision has been made. I'm shaking off the old skin, and I'll leave it in the hole. I'm coming out, no less invisible without it, but coming out nevertheless" (581). Perhaps it is the word "nevertheless," both here and above, that speaks to the growth of Invisible Man. His ability to exist with ambiguity is now his strength.

This ambiguity-as-strength is what he utilizes as he speaks to the "you" in his text, a "you" I, too, read as referring to white Americans. When he projects his (white) readers as thinking "Ah, . . . so it was all a build-up to bore us with his buggy jiving. He only wanted us to listen to him rave!," he responds that such a reaction would only be "partially true" and concludes, "Being invisible and without substance, a disembodied voice, as it were, what else could I do? What else but try to tell you what was really happening when your eyes were looking through?" (581). He is saying he had no choice, that the events of the narrative were what he *could* do. In Trueblood's words, he is now determined to "let whatever is gonna happen, happen."

As such, the Trueblood episode, even though it is an embedded narrative rather than a frame narrative, cements the idea of the frame acting as model. The difference here is that the rest of the novel acts as a "close frame"; the Trueblood episode is unintelligible without it.

NOTES

1. Ross Chambers, in *Story and Situation: Narrative Seduction and the Power of Fiction* (Minneapolis: University of Minnesota Press, 1984), defines an embedded narrative as "narrative act within narrative act, narrative situation within narrative situation: it implies the representation, internally to the fictional framework, of a situation involving the major components of a communicational act (emitter-discourse-recipient)—and very frequently the mirroring within a story of the story-telling relationship itself narrator-narration-narratee" (33).

2. Susan Rubin Suleiman, *Authoritarian Fictions: The Ideological Novel As a Literary Genre* (New York: Columbia University Press, 1983), 65. All subsequent quotations are cited parenthetically in the text. I'm certain Ellison would object to my analyzing his novel with the assistance of a book which contains the term "Ideological Novel" in the subtitle, an objection I can certainly understand. He is quite explicit in "The World and the Jug": "I can only ask that my fiction be judged as art; if it fails, it fails aesthetically, not because I did or did not fight some ideological battle" (*The Collected Essays of Ralph Ellison*, John Callahan, editor, [New York: Modern Library, 1995], 182. All subsequent quotations are cited parenthetically in the text). "Ideology" is, to some, a fighting word. And yet, as Raymond Williams writes in *Marxism and Literature* (New York: Oxford University Press, 1985), "there is an obvious need for a general term to describe not only the products but the processes of all signification, including the signification of values" (70). Furthermore, Ellison himself, in "Society, Morality and the Novel," pretty much agrees with Williams (without using the word itself), when he writes,

> It is by appealing to our sense of experience and playing upon our shared assumptions that the novelist is able to reveal to us that which we do not know—that is, the unfamiliar with the familiar—and affirm that which we assume to be the truth, and to reveal to us his own hard-won vision of the truth.
>   In this sense the novel is rhetorical. Whatever else it tries to do, it must do so by persuading us to accept the novelist's projection of an experience which, on some level or mixtures of levels, we have shared with him, and through which we become empathetically involved in the illusory and plotted depiction of life we identify as fictional art. (697)

3. Perhaps the most popular definition of the blues mode comes from Ellison himself:

> The blues is an impulse to keep the painful details and episodes of a brutal experience alive in one's aching consciousness, to finger its jagged grain, and to transcend it, not by the consolation of philosophy but by squeezing from it a near-tragic, near-comic lyricism. As a form, the blues is an autobiographical chronicle of personal catastrophe expressed lyrically. (*Collected Essays* 129)

My contention here is that Trueblood's tale-as-blues is the model for Invisible Man's autobiography-as-blues, that the tale Trueblood tells is a crucial early step in Invisible Man's maturation into a bluesman who can, by the time he has finished his autobiography, deal with the ambivalence that grows out of the tragedy and absurdity of the Negro existence in America.
    4. Houston A. Baker, Jr., describes Trueblood as a bluesman in "To Move without Moving: Creativity and Commerce in Ralph Ellison's Trueblood Episode": "The main character in the Trueblood episode . . . is a country blues singer (a tenor of "crude, high, plaintively animal sounds") who is also a virtuoso prose narrator. . . . Trueblood [has a] dual manifestation as trickster and merchant, as creative and commercial man. Blues and narration, as modes of expression, conjoin and

divide in harmony with these dichotomies. And the episode in its entirety is . . . a metaexpressive commentary on the incumbencies of Afro-American artists and the effects of their distinctive modes of expression" (*Blues, Ideology and Afro-American Literature: A Vernacular Theory* [Chicago: The University of Chicago Press, 1984], 175. All subsequent quotations are cited parenthetically in the text). Other descriptions of Trueblood as a blues artist can be found in E.M. Kist, "A Langian Analysis of Blackness in Ralph Ellison's *Invisible Man*," *Studies in Black Literature* 7 (1976), 23; Raymond Olderman, "Ralph Ellison's Blues and *Invisible Man*," *Wisconsin Studies in Contemporary Literature* 7 (1966), 146; George E. Kent, "Ralph Ellison and the Afro-American Folk and Cultural Tradition," in *Ralph Ellison: A Collection of Critical Essays.* Ed. John Hersey. Englewood Cliffs, N.J.: Prentice-Hall, 1974, 45–6; and Robert G. O'Meally, *The Craft of Ralph Ellison*, Cambridge, Mass.: Harvard University Press, 1980, 86–7; Marvin F. Thomas, "Children of Legba: Musicians at the Crossroads in Ralph Ellison's *Invisible Man*," *American Literature* 68:3 (Sept 1996): 587–608.

5. Ralph Ellison, *Invisible Man* (New York: Vintage Books, 1989), 3. All subsequent quotations are cited parenthetically in the text.

6. The "source" of Trueblood's difficulties are twofold. Yes, he committed incest with his daughter, but Ellison is careful to provide the reader with a context for that intercourse by revealing the economic difficulties that prompted his sleeping in the same bed with his wife and teenage daughter. By no means does that excuse the behavior, but it does allow the space to view Trueblood as a heroic figure—not, of course, for the initial action, but for extricating himself from the position in which his actions placed him.

7. Robert Stepto, "Distrust of the Reader in Afro-American Narratives." *From Behind the Veil: A Study of Afro-American Narrative.* 2nd ed. (Urbana, Ill: University of Illinois Press, 1991), 207. All subsequent quotations are cited parenthetically in the text.

8. Henry Louis Gates, Jr. "King of Cats," *The New Yorker* (8 April 1996), 76. All subsequent quotations are cited parenthetically in the text.

9. This issue of belief is an all too common one in African-American storytelling. I discuss it in detail in my sixth chapter, below.

10. Trueblood must have altered somewhat the description of the incest act, depending on the audience before him. I cannot imagine that a man as audience-aware as Trueblood would have gone into such vivid detail describing the way Matty Lou eventually "gits to movin' herself . . . [and] grabs holt to me and holds tight" (60) while trying to calm and explain to Kate what happened that morning. The idea of Trueblood actually saying to his wife, in front of his daughter, "She didn't want me to go then—and to tell the honest-to-God truth I found out that I didn't want to go neither" [60] would, it seems to me, greatly strain credulity.

11. Wolfgang Iser, *The Implied Reader: Patterns of Communication in Prose Fiction from Bunyon to Beckett* (Baltimore: The Johns Hopkins University Press, 1974), 121. All subsequent quotations are cited parenthetically in the text.

12. Although it is easy to think of the book as existing in a linear form, it is, like *Their Eyes Were Watching God*, a circular narrative. Invisible Man writes, early in the prologue, "But that's getting too far ahead of the story, almost to the end, although the end is in the beginning and lies far ahead" (6). And in the last sentence before the epilogue, he restates, "The end was in the beginning" (571).

13. After all, as Suleiman points out, "The persuasive effect of a story of apprenticeship 'with a thesis' results from a virtual identification of the reader with the protagonist. If the protagonist evolves toward a euphoric position, the reader is incited to follow him in the right direction: the protagonists's happiness is both a proof and a guarantee of the values he affirms. If the protagonist's story 'ends badly,' his failure also serves as a lesson or proof, but this time a *contrario*: the protagonist's fate allows the reader to perceive the wrong road without following it" (73). She is saying, in essence, that where readers "live," so to speak, will determine how their identification with characters will affect them. In this particular context, it is entirely possible that while both black and white readers chiefly identify with Invisible Man, some white (and, undoubtedly, some black) readers who identified with Mr. Norton during chapter two must confront his static characterization in the epilogue.

14. Michel Fabre, "The Narrator/Narratee Relationship in *Invisible Man*." *Callaloo* (8.3 Fall, 1985), 535. All subsequent quotations are cited parenthetically in the text.

15. John S. Wright, "The Conscious Hero and the Rites of Man: Ellison's War," *New Essays on* Invisible Man, Robert O'Meally, editor (Cambridge, Mass.: Cambridge University Press, 1988), 176.

H. WILLIAM RICE

The Invisible Man in
Ralph Ellison's Invisible Man

"Who knows but that, on the lower frequencies, I speak for you?"
—Ralph Ellison, *Invisible Man*

The apocalyptic ending to Ralph Ellison's *Invisible Man* is nothing if not
startling. Still, among all of the alarming moments in this ending, there
is one that stands out for sheer absurdity. The narrator casts a spear at his
long-time nemesis Ras the Exhorter, who has recently evolved to Ras the
Destroyer. As the spear rips through both cheeks, it locks shut Ras's jaws.
The narrator describes the scene in these unforgettable terms: "I let fly the
spear and it was as though for a moment I had surrendered my life and
begun to live again, watching it catch him as he turned his head to shout,
ripping through both cheeks, and saw the surprised pause of the crowd as
Ras wrestled with the spear that locked his jaws."[1] Even a casual reader is
hard pressed to ignore the importance of this scene. The narrator seems
to gain his long-sought moment of transcendence, finds his life in losing
it, and reaches the end of his quest (the burden of his tale) in an act of
violence. But it is an act of violence that partakes of the absurd. Only in
cartoons do spears work so well or so conveniently to silence their victims,
particularly when the spear caster is in such peril. Ras has called for the
execution of the narrator: "'hang him!'" (559). Clearly, we as readers are
at an important juncture in the text: as the main character's life hangs in

From *Ralph Ellison and the Politics of the Novel.* © 2003 by Lexington Books.

the balance, a spear locking the jaws of his rival seems to set him free by creating silence.

There are many ways to read this incident. Ras is the last of a series of father figures that the narrator has had to confront, understand, and escape. M.K. Singleton, among other critics, has detailed the repeated patterns of influence and rebellion that characterize the novel.[2] Starting with Booker T. Washington, evoked in the narrator's speech at the Battle Royal and continuing through Mr. Norton, Homer Barbee, Dr. Bledsoe, Mr. Emerson, Lucious Brockway, and Brother Jack and the Brotherhood, the narrator falls under the influence of one leader after another, only to rebel. Ras is the last of these figures, the representative of African nationalism who stalks him through the streets of Harlem as a rival speaker, accusing the narrator of faithlessness to the black man, seeking to align him with the ultimate father/mother symbol: Africa. When the narrator spears Ras with a part of Ras's own outlandish outfit, he is free, having found his life by losing it. Thus, he has lived out the prophetic words of the vet from the Golden Day: "'be your own father, young man'" (156). In the prologue and the epilogue, both of which take place outside of the context of the main events of the novel, we see a narrator who has become his own father, who has shaken off the restraints of a culture that cannot see him, a narrator who has achieved at least some measure of freedom.

Despite the appeal of its symmetry, such a reading ignores two important points: the similarity between Ras and the narrator and the manner in which the narrator silences Ras. Though he has been thrown into a leadership position in the novel, the narrator has actually not consciously sought to lead politically. Rather, he has sought success in general, a way to exercise his skill as a public speaker[3] and in so doing he has been pushed into the position of political leader. Most of his speaking in Harlem has been on behalf of the Brotherhood, an organization that hopes to use, even sacrifice, the black community to further its own revolutionary agenda. Though this fact is unknown to the narrator until late in the novel, the relatively lucrative salary, clothing, and office accommodations that association with the Brotherhood brings entice the narrator into being their voice in Harlem, even to the point of allowing them to script his speaking style.[4] These traditional trappings of American success have drawn the narrator in rather than the more spiritual/political search for black identity that seems to motivate a man like Ras. The narrator has been unwittingly the instrument of manipulating the black community. Thus, garish as it is, Ras's costume is less outlandish than the invisible narrator's various embodiments as a speaker in the novel—from his bloody speech before the white men at the Battle Royal to his weeping before the audience at his first Brotherhood speech. Ras and the narrator are charlatans of the same order; they live by manipulating audiences with the oldest snake oil in the business: rhetoric. The narrator wants an American vision of success; Ras wants to return to the womb of Africa, taking his black brothers and sisters with him. But both of them are professional speakers, political candidates who seek the black vote.

Still, as Ellison's narrator tells us while ruminating on a portrait of Frederick Douglass in the Harlem office of the Brotherhood, "there was a magic in spoken words" (381). Thus, despite the fact that the narrator is drawn into the role of Brotherhood speaker out of a desire to find lucrative employment, a desire to exercise his skills as a speaker, the "magic" of language ultimately creates a relationship between him and the audiences to whom he speaks, a relationship that is transformed, perhaps even ruptured, in the spearing of Ras. In fact, after his first Brotherhood speech, the narrator feels drawn to and committed to the audience in a way quite different from how he feels drawn to and committed to the Brotherhood. His commitment to the Brotherhood is motivated by ambition, even greed: "I saw no limits, it was the one organization in the whole country in which I could reach the very top and I meant to get there" (380). But his connection to the audience is more seminal: "I felt a kind of affection for the blurred audience whose faces I had never clearly seen. They had been with me from the first word.... I had spoken for them, and they had recognized my words. I belonged to them" (353). If the narrator is opportunistic in his use of the Brotherhood (just as they are in their use of him), he is quite different in his approach to the audience. To them he feels committed, not by money or ambition, but by the intrinsic demands of truth.

Though this new reading of the scene places the issue of speech at the very center of the novel, the skeptical reader should note that in much of Ellison's mature work, speech is a vital issue. The narrator of *Invisible Man* clearly sees himself as a speaker when he alludes to "my talent for public speaking" (298) or when he describes himself in the Prologue as "an orator and a rabble rouser" (14) or when he agrees to become a professional speaker on behalf of the Brotherhood. What is more, a significant portion of the text of *Invisible Man* is devoted to describing and analyzing the narrator's speeches, which he delivers at the Battle Royal, at the eviction in Harlem, at various Brotherhood gatherings, or at Tod Clifton's funeral in Harlem. Even the speeches of others, such as that of Blind Homer Barbee, are described in great detail. Finally, in the posthumous *Juneteenth*, a portion of a book that Ellison spent much of his mature life attempting to complete, speech is also at center stage. Not only are the main characters (one a politician, the other a minister) professional speakers, but also, as in *Invisible Man*, the text of the novel itself focuses upon speeches. The opening chapters give us verbatim Senator Sunraider's speech on the floor of the Senate. Sunraider has learned to speak from Hickman, so much so that Hickman recognizes in Sunraider's congressional speech techniques that he has taught him.[5] Finally, as Hickman talks with the dying Sunraider, a sizable portion of their conversation recounts the life of an evangelist, a man who spreads God's message word by word. Certain chapters are almost entirely given over to recounting speeches: chapter two of *Juneteenth* gives us verbatim Senator Sunraider's speech on the floor of the Senate prior to his being shot. What is more, as Hickman and Sunraider uncover the past, they are consistently drawn into remembering sermons. Chapter six is a recounting of the creation story in sermon form with constant references to a famed preacher called Eatmore. Chapter seven is a recapitulation of the call and response sermon that Bliss and Hickman delivered. Thus, the emphasis on speech that we find in *Invisible Man* seems hardly unique to that novel. Given the attention that Ellison seems to grant to speech in his work as a novelist, it should not surprise us to find it at center stage in the climactic closing scene in *Invisible Man* when the narrator's spear locks the jaws of Ras, his rival speaker in Harlem. Thus, the task of understanding this scene becomes vitally important, perhaps even pivotal, in understanding the novel itself. Further, I contend that understanding the role of language, in terms of both speech and writing, plays a major role in understanding Ellison's work as a whole.

In locking the jaws of his rival, the narrator is actually locking his own jaws. By so doing, he is liberated, saved from a role that has become intolerable. "I had surrendered my life and begun to live again" (560), he tells us. Importantly, the role that has become intolerable is not only the role of Brotherhood representative but also the role of speaker. As the narrator says just before this pivotal spear hurling, "But even as I spoke I knew it was no good. I had no words and no eloquence" (558). Ironically, notwithstanding the title of the novel, speech has brought to the narrator a kind of visibility. In the context of such an understanding of the novel, the narrator's trip underground is more than an attempt to rediscover himself or finally become his own father. Rather, it is a flight from speech, which has brought him visibility, to writing, a new mode of expression, that brings with it invisibility. Ras is a very visible speaker in Harlem. With his outlandish costume, he cannot be missed. Despite the many levels on which he is invisible as a black man in a white man's world, the narrator, like Ras, is recognizable in Harlem when he speaks. In fact, even in the turmoil of a riot-torn night in Harlem, Ras sees and recognizes the narrator.

What is more, the narrator's whole career quite literally begins when he becomes visible as a speaker. Brother Jack watches him deliver an impromptu protest speech at a Harlem eviction. As he speaks for the Brotherhood, it is the organization's hope that he will be visible as a black man, thereby swaying others in their behalf. Even when he discovers late in the novel the trick of slipping into the identity of Rinehart by putting on dark glasses, he is still visible as Rinehart. Only in going underground to write does the narrator truly become the invisible man of the novel's title. Thus, invisibility is a many-faceted metaphor in this novel. The title of the novel implies that the narrator is invisible to white people because he is black. White people refuse to see black people. But I contend that in another sense only by being invisible can the narrator escape the visible embodiment of what he has become, only by the invisibility of writing can he overcome the visibility of speech. What is more, when the novel is finished, invisibility is a condition not only of the narrator but also of all people and of Ellison himself.

There is no point in *Invisible Man* when we see the narrator engaged in the act of writing. Nonetheless, in many respects the novel foregrounds the written text as a phase of the narrator's life qualitatively different from his life as a speaker, the life he describes in his story. It is the embodiment of what he becomes after the events of the novel, the fruit of the underground, the story of his life told in retrospect, from the standpoint of invisibility underground. It is quite literally the only means for him to understand and articulate his aboveground experience. The narrator's words in the prologue express this fact: "Could this compulsion to put invisibility down in black and white be thus an urge to make music of invisibility? But I am an orator, a rabble-rouser—Am? I *was*, and perhaps shall be again. Who knows?" (14). We do not know as we read the novel whether the text will be that which propels the narrator to speak again or that which substitutes for speaking. As Yonka Kristeva argues in "Chaos and Pattern in Ellison's *Invisible Man*," "Ellison focuses on a liminal state, a process of transition and becoming which is unresolved at the end of the novel."[6] We do know, however, the underground has enabled the narrator "to put invisibility down in black and white."

Several statements from Ellison himself suggest that writing has become an important part of the circle of the narrator's experience, perhaps even more important than the events the novel describes. He told one interviewer, "The epilogue was necessary to complete the action begun when he [the narrator] set out to write his memoirs."[7] At another point in the same interview. Ellison suggests that the narrator does become visible again through the vehicle of writing: "The hero comes up from underground because the act of writing and thinking necessitated it."[8] In another interview Ellison says "he comes out of the ground, and this can be seen when you realize that although *Invisible Man* is my novel, it is really his memoir."[9] Thus, the novel, or "memoir" as Ellison calls it, may be understood as the narrator's path out of the underground. Paradoxically, as irony begins to pile on irony, the very act of writing invisibly gives the narrator a way of becoming visible to an audience of readers whereas speech was done visibly but necessitated his invisibility.

Complicating the matter still further, Ellison speaks in these quotations of an event that never occurs in the novel. In actuality, the narrator never leaves the underground. He implies that he will, that it will be a part of the next phase, but in the text of the novel he never separates himself from the underground.[10] Ellison clearly assumes that he will leave and even ties that act to writing, saying, "the act of writing and thinking necessitated it" or "the epilogue was necessary to complete the action begun when he [the narrator] set out to write his memoirs." Thus, writing assumes quite a significant role. It is not only the narrator's way out of the underground, but also, in Ellison's eyes, it points toward the completion of an action that is in actuality never completed in the novel. Understanding these ironies and complications that are here unearthed forces the reader to explore writing as a facet of this novel and subsequently of Ellison's work as a whole. However, since writing is never directly a part of the action in *Invisible Man* or any other Ellison work, our best route to understanding it is to explore its relationship to its alter ego: speech. Given its prominence as a form of African-American art and the ways in which it appears and reappears in Ellison's work, speech deserves more attention than most Ellison critics have accorded it. My first task will be to address this failure. But I wish to do more than examine speakers and speeches in Ellison's work. My hope is to grasp at least some of the ways in which Ellison understood writing and his role as a black writer in twenti-eth-century America. After all, while he wrote, American life was changed forever by the speeches of Dr. Martin Luther King, Jr., a man who perfected the very art that Ellison's narrator seems at least for a time to reject. All the while, Ellison himself remained essentially invisible, working on a novel that he never finished.

Ellison is certainly not the first writer to suggest that speech is in profound ways different from writing. In fact, any careful reading of the history of rhetoric, indeed the history of Western literature and philosophy, demonstrates that speaking and writing have been understood as vastly different ways of communicating. I do not argue here that Ellison alludes in any way to the history of rhetoric or to any other specific interpretation of the differences in speech and writing. I argue only that in making his main character "an orator, a rabble rouser" who becomes a writer on the way to evolving into some new entity, Ellison invites us to consider some of the differences between the two.

Fifth-century Athens is generally known as the birthplace of rhetoric in the Western world, the place where the first serious discussions of this issue occurred. Most of the public use of language in that culture was speaking. In fact, the writing that the sophists and other teachers of rhetoric undertook was primarily to write speeches for hire or to teach students to become proficient at writing their own speeches: the assumed media of language was the spoken, not the written, word. Two of Plato's dialogues deal directly with the subject of rhetoric. In the earlier dialogue, the *Gorgias*, Socrates tells Gorgias, a well-known speaker, rhetorician, and sophist from Sicily, that rhetoric is a branch of flattery. When asked if it is a base or a fine thing, Socrates unequivocally calls it "base."[11] Even in the later dialogue, the *Phaedrus*, which scholars tend to agree is more favorable toward rhetoric,[12] Socrates makes the job of the speaker one requiring almost superhuman skill and endeavor: "He who is to be a rhetorician must know the various forms of the soul."[13] Later in the same dialogue Socrates argues that the path of rhetorical skill is a long one and should not be undertaken to please men but to please the gods: "Therefore, if the path be long, be not astonished; for it must be trodden for great end."[14] One wonders whether any mere mortal is capable of being a rhetorician if the requirements are so intense. On the other hand, in the same dialogue Socrates comes very close to ridiculing writing when he tells Phaedrus that words sown by a pen "cannot defend themselves by argument and cannot teach the truth effectively."[15] Phaedrus calls the written word "an image" of the "living and breathing word of him who knows."[16]

Much of what we are presented as speech in *Invisible Man* suggests that Ellison's narrator discovers, as Socrates argues in the *Gorgias*, that rhetoric as it is embodied in speech is "a base thing." What is more, never in the course of *Invisible Man* do we see the narrator treading the path of speaker for the great end of pleasing the gods or any other divine entity. Rather, he is interested in pleasing men, all too often the wrong men. On the other hand, contrary to Plato, Ellison seems to grant to writing a higher position, one that prefigures Jacques Derrida's rethinking of the relationship between speaking and writing in the last half of the twentieth century.

Still, important aspects of the tradition of speech and writing stand closer in time to Ellison than to Plato. Though the foundations of classical rhetoric are evident everywhere in our culture, there were no sermons in ancient Athens, and there were no novels. Each of these forms profoundly colors the perception of both speech and writing in *Invisible Man*. Ellison's own particular experience with writing and with speech clearly involved the novel and the sermon. Furthermore, by the time he wrote *Invisible Man* he had also heard many political speeches. Thus, any examination of the issues of speech and writing in Ellison's work must examine the role that these three forms play in Ellison's work. Ellison was, after all, a novelist, and a novelist who took quite seriously the task of speaking out on the role of the novel in American culture and Western history. His two collections of essays, *Shadow and Act* and *Going to the Territory*, give us ample evidence of this fact.[17] What is more, Ellison almost certainly heard more sermons and political speeches than any other types of speech. Both of these forms are reenacted in *Invisible Man* and in *Juneteenth*. Our concern here will be first to explore Ellison's use of speech in his work. Later, in a separate chapter, we will delve into the other half of the issue, namely, his understanding of and use of the role of the novel.

Ellison was named for Ralph Waldo Emerson, the grand man of American letters during the first half of the nineteenth century, who also happened to be a defrocked minister who became an essayist and a poet and arguably the most important speaker during the first half of the nineteenth century in the United States.[18] What is more, after Ellison's father (who chose the name in the hope that his son would become a poet) died when his son Ralph was only three, Ellison's mother, Ida, worked as stewardess of the Avery Chapel Afro-Methodist Episcopal church.[19] Since the minister had a home of his own, the widow and her sons even lived in the parsonage where the young Ralph Waldo read books that were left in the house by the minister.[20] It is quite likely that most of the early speeches that Ellison heard were sermons and that his understanding of speech was in large part shaped by the sermonic form. The overpowering figure of Alonzo Hickman in *Juneteenth* would certainly underscore that fact.

The speeches Ellison heard while a student at Tuskegee Institute were probably quite similar in form. Mark Busby explains in *Ralph Ellison* that Homer Barbee's speech in *Invisible Man* was likely modeled on an actual speech delivered in chapel at Tuskegee Institute while Ellison was a student. Major Robert Moton, president of the college, delivered an oration during the fall of Ellison's freshman year in which he described a dying Booker T. Washington summoning Moton to his bedside and saying "'Major, don't forget Tuskegee.'"[21] The fact that Ellison the writer remembers this incident more than ten years later, giving to his character Homer Barbee a similar incident in a fictional chapel speech, suggests that Ellison had more than a cursory understanding of the power of pulpit oratory. After all, when he heard the speech, he was not a writer at all. Rather, he was studying to be a musician.

Though Ellison might not have heard political speeches as frequently as he heard sermons, by the time he wrote *Invisible Man* he was doubtlessly quite familiar with the form. In "The Rhetoric of Anticommunism in *Invisible Man*," Barbara Foley argues that Ellison's connections to the American Communist Party during the forties were much closer than most people have assumed. In fact, she states that until the end of the war, "Ellison hewed to the Communist Party line."[22] She also contends that Ellison repudiated such stances in *Invisible Man* by indulging in what she calls anticommunist Cold War rhetoric. Such an argument (not to mention Ellison's well-known connections to Richard Wright and Ellison's writing for Communist Party publications) makes highly likely the idea that Ellison very much had the political speeches he had heard in mind when he wrote *Invisible Man*.

Critics have often tied *Invisible Man* to the rich heritage of music that Ellison knew and absorbed as a young man growing up in an African-American community, as a young man educated in music at an African-American college. Far fewer critics have tied the novel to the equally rich oral tradition that it clearly grows out of.[23] Despite this fact, there is ample evidence to support the existence of such influences not only in Ellison's past but also in the work itself. Still, before exploring the speeches we find in *Invisible Man*, we must understand some of the basic qualities of the oral traditions that Ellison explores in both of his novels.

One of the most distinctive qualities of the sermon when placed in the context of other oratory is its adherence to a particular text. George Kennedy explains this distinction in his history of rhetoric: "The classical orator had a free field in choice of a proposition and the topics for proving it. He used or invented arguments from many sources. . . . The primary function of the Christian orator, in contrast, was to interpret and bring into practice the holy word."[24] A second point is implied here. As an oratorical midwife, bringing to life scripture, the minister's role is essentially passive; as Kennedy says later in the same passage, the minister's job is to create "'a projection of the eloquence of scripture."[25] Thus, whatever eloquence may be a part of the final product should find its source in the text of scripture and not in the speaker. In his history of preaching, Yngve Brilioth attributes to Augustine's *De Doctrina Christiana* the notion that "the sermon is basically the exposition of a text."[26] What is more, calling Augustine's book the first attempt to write "a homiletics," Brilioth states that in the sermon, oratory "is the humble servant of wisdom."[27] Both of these discussions recall for us the classical distinction of the two roles of rhetoric drawn by Socrates as "a branch of flattery" and as a means for finding and conveying truth. Implicit here is the notion that the minister who sticks to the text conveys truth, and the minister who indulges in eloquence outside of that provided by the text is somehow illegitimately seeking flattery. Ministers should not seek beautiful words in themselves or as a means to impress their audiences. Rather, the minister allows the beautiful words of the text to shine through his or her sermon. Still, applying such observations wholesale to the black pulpit oratory Ellison experienced and re-creates in his novels is a tricky proposition. In fact, the distance between this classical definition of the sermon and the sermons that we see in Ellison's work illuminates for us some of the distinctive qualities of the black sermon.

In his book *The Sermon and the African American Literary Imagination* Dolan Hubbard argues that "Christian explanations" have never adequately or fully explained black oratory or the black church because they fail to account for the large impact of oral and folk traditions on the black world.[28] What is more, according to Hubbard, the black sermon is focused primarily on two effects: the proclamation of black freedom and the creation of a communal sense of catharsis, releasing the audience not only from domination by white folks but also from what Hubbard calls "the tyranny of the everyday."[29] According to Hubbard, the road to both of these effects is not rational persuasion, which he associates with the Euro-American sermon, but "authoritative proclamation and joyful celebration."[30] Implied in this explanation of black pulpit oratory is the celebration of both individuality and community. The minister proclaims the word out of his authority, his adherence to the text not only of the Bible but also of black life. But in this authoritative proclamation the minister brings to life not just the text but also the communal catharsis of his audience. It is for this reason that the "call and response" pattern of black pulpit oratory is so important. Thus, whereas in traditional pulpit oratory, the minister allows the text of scripture to speak with its own eloquence and by so doing is in many respects midwife to the sacred text which he or she had no part in constructing, in the black pulpit, the speaker is interested in giving to the audience a communal voice, in creating the possibility of self-definition through community articulation. Looking back again at Plato's discussion of rhetoric, one may conclude that the African-American sermon plays havoc with Plato's carefully honed distinction between rhetoric as a kind of flattery, a matter of sound and not sense, and rhetoric as a tool for finding and conveying truth. The black sermon conveys a kind of truth that involves not just the text or the truth, but also a kind of play with language that the call and response tradition celebrates. In fact, one might almost argue that the minister finds his text in what goes on between him or her and the audience.

When we place these distinctions into the context of Kennedy's comments quoted above concerning preaching in general, we notice another important distinction between black pulpit oratory and pulpit oratory in general. The black preacher is much more likely than the Euro-American preacher to bring the Bible to life specifically as it applies to black people. Accordingly, Hubbard argues "'Let my people go' is the most responsive mascon in the peculiar eschatology of the black church."[31] Hubbard also maintains that in the black church the minister is clearly focused on God's role in history, in particular, God's role in bringing freedom to black people. As Hubbard argues, "The Israelites victory is transformed into black victory."[32] To Hubbard, the preacher "defines freedom as the ability to articulate the self."[33] Since he stands before the audience and does this not as an individual but as a man who is collectively speaking for the whole community, he allows the audience to define itself through his articulation of its needs. The center of these needs for most of the twentieth century was the liberation of black people from the tyranny of white prejudice and the poison of white assumptions. Clearly, the black minister goes far beyond the literal text of the scripture to achieve his task while the European minister is one who simply allows the text to speak. Rather than being a kind of midwife, delivering unto the congregation the text that he or she was handed, the black minister becomes the burning center of communal transformation.

Two speeches in *Invisible Man* clearly fall into the tradition I have set forth here: the sermon the narrator dreams of in the prologue to the novel on the "Blackness of blackness" and Homer Barbee's speech in the chapel at the narrator's college. But before we can examine these speeches, we must understand the basic form of the political speeches that we encounter in *Invisible Man*. In at least some respects these speeches give us the opposite pole of speech in the novel, the speech as a tool of community conformity rather than community articulation, speech that ironically resembles Kennedy's definition of the European sermon: the delivering of a text.

Political speech is not nearly so easy to define as the sermon, for it is a much looser category. Earlier I quoted Kennedy's comments concerning the sermon: the preacher is limited to the text of the Bible or the religious tradition to prove a point, whereas the classical rhetorician has a free field of reference. Political speakers would fall in this broader category; ostensibly they adhere to no prescribed text. A political speech may be any oral presentation that sets forth a proposal of a political position, particularly one in which the speaker hopes to influence others. For example, Senator Sunraider's speech on the floor of the Senate in *Juneteenth* in which he advocates changing the name of the Cadillac to the "Coon Cage Eight" is a political speech.[34] He hopes to move those in his audience to understand his political position and even adopt it insofar as they accept and enact his proposal. In his *Rhetoric* Aristotle sets forth a category for political speech when he divides rhetoric into three groups: deliberative, forensic, and epideictic speech.[35] Political speech falls into the first category and is distinguished from the other two by its time orientation. Unlike forensic rhetoric that focuses on the past and epideictic rhetoric that focuses on the present, deliberative rhetoric focuses on the future. Its intent is always to shape policy. The speaker who uses forensic speech hopes to establish guilt or innocence in a legal setting based on examination of the past, whereas the speaker who uses epideictic speech celebrates a particular event or occasion in the here and now.

Still, Aristotle's categories are only useful insofar as they retain a kind of looseness. For example, though the sermon fits into the broad category of

celebratory or epideictic rhetoric, we may also observe that at least some sermons seek to effect policy change or even indict someone or some organization that might be antithetical to the aims of Christianity or of the Christian
community, or perhaps even the community in general. By the same token, the
political speech, which is deliberative in form, might also invoke some sort of
celebration. Dr. Martin Luther King, Jr.'s "I Have a Dream Speech" set forth a
policy agenda, but it also celebrated the American ideal of freedom as it indicted
the country as a whole for failing to live up to the opening lines of the Declaration of Independence. King's speech clearly partakes of all three of the categories that Aristotle sets forth. Hubbard's observation that "'Let my people go' is
the most responsive mascon in the peculiar eschatology of the black church"[36]
suggests a sermon form that falls somewhere between deliberation of policy
and celebration of community. It is also clearly an indictment of white America,
tying it to the image of the Egyptians in the Old Testament who enslaved
the Israelites. Despite the looseness and the mixing of these categories, this
basic distinction will be very important to our understanding of Ellison's work:
the black sermon celebrates and liberates through celebration and articulation,
whereas the political speech sets forth policy. The latter is much more a matter
of logic, while the former invokes emotion as the partner of logic. Indeed on
some occasions, emotion becomes the doorway to understanding.

Just as we see sermons in *Invisible Man*, we also see political speeches:
the narrator's attempts to speak as representative of the Brotherhood are in
every case political speeches. In fact, the narrator's first Brotherhood speech
delineates for us the distinctions set forth above between the black sermon
and the political speech. Whereas the narrator and the audience seem very
much attuned to each other in this speech, the Brotherhood finds the audience involvement troubling. During the speech itself, an audience member
screams out that the narrator is "batting .500" (345) in his speech, and the
narrator responds to the audience, "I feel, I feel suddenly ... *more human*"
(346). The narrator even weeps before the audience. But the Brotherhood
assessment of the speech attacks it on the grounds of its emotionalism, the
very grounds of what would seem to be its success. One brother describes
the speech as "wild, hysterical, politically irresponsible and dangerous," (349)
whereas another calls it "the antithesis of the scientific approach" (351).
Accordingly, the Brotherhood officially silences the narrator, so that he can
be "trained." The Brotherhood's understanding of political speech rejects the
emotionalism of the narrator's first attempt. Indeed, whatever articulation
of community needs that the Brotherhood desires is to be carefully scripted,
imposed from without rather than discovered and articulated in the give-
and-take between the audience and the speaker. It is a "text," we might conclude, to which the narrator must adhere.

I began this chapter with the image of the narrator of *Invisible Man* locking shut Ras the Destroyer's jaws with a spear. Thereby, I argued that the narrator finds new life by silencing not only Ras but also himself. "I had surrendered my life and begun to live again," (560) he tells us. In silencing himself the narrator moves from the visibility of speech to the invisibility of writing. Paradoxically, the hopes that he expresses in the prologue and epilogue suggest that writing will bring him a kind of self-definition that speech has denied him, that his novel or his "memoirs" as Ellison calls them, will ultimately allow him to step out of the underground and assume a role as a visible man influencing a visible audience.[37] Thus, it would seem that speech is rejected in *Invisible Man* as an idiom of transformation, perhaps even as a vehicle of community articulation. But as with so much else that we find in Ellison, these conclusions may be tenuous. Though the narrator of *Invisible Man* does indeed become a writer, it is as a speaker that we know him best, for that is his role in most of the story he writes. Thus, it is not quite as easy as we might expect to dismiss speech or to understand fully the transformation of the narrator. We are left with questions, with loose ends.

If speech is rejected as a mode of self or community definition in *Invisible Man*, why does Ellison put before the reader the many forms of speech that his narrator encounters? Why does the narrator hint in the prologue that he may indeed become a speaker again, claiming still to be a speaker?[38] Such devices show us that Ellison's own understanding of the culture of which he writes places speech in a position of great importance, defining not only the individual but also the community. Despite these facts, the narrator, a self-confessed "rabble rouser" with "a talent for public speaking," chooses to go underground and write, producing a document that Ellison himself would later call the "memoirs" of the narrator. In similar fashion, Ellison would define himself as a writer, even going so far in his famous written exchange with Irving Howe as to claim writing as his role in the Civil Rights movement.[39] But after the 1952 publication of *Invisible Man* Ellison was a writer who worked for the rest of his life (some forty-four years) on a novel he never finished. What is more, that novel in part chronicled the death and in some respects the life of another speaker, a political speaker who learned political speech from a black preacher, a black preacher who presides over his death. In addition, during at least a portion of this time, the very ground underneath Ellison's feet was being shifted by the sermons of Martin Luther King, Jr., and the actions that those sermons inspired, by the speeches of Malcolm X and the subsequent Black Power movement, both movements that Ellison remained aloof from in any active sense of involvement. With such a welter of images and counter images of speech and speakers, writers and writing, in both the writing and the world of Ralph Ellison, many questions come to mind. My task here will be to phrase these and with luck answer at least a few of them.

NOTES

1. Ralph Ellison, *Invisible Man*, 2nd ed. (New York: Vintage, 1995), 559–60. All references are to this edition and appear parenthetically within the text. The abbreviation *IM* only appears within the parenthetical listing if the context of the quotation does not establish to which of Ellison's novels I am referring.

2. Many articles argue this position. Among the most interesting are these: M. K. Singleton, "Leadership Mirages as Antagonists in *Invisible Man*," in *Twentieth Century Interpretations of Invisible Man*, ed. John M. Riley (Englewood Cliffs, N.J.: Prentice Hall, 1970). Robert B. Stepto, "Literacy and Hibernation: Ralph Ellison's *Invisible Man*," in *Ralph Ellison: Modern Critical Views*, ed. Harold Bloom (New Haven, Conn.: Chelsea House, 1986).

3. The narrator observes "It was, after all, a job that promised to exercise my talent for public speaking" (298).

4. The narrator initially refuses to work for Brother Jack. Then he changes his mind, seeking him out because, "if the pay was anything at all it would be more than I had now" (298). His initial reaction to his new salary is "Sixty a week!" (310). Clearly, money is an important factor in his decision.

5. Hickman observes, "Imagine, going up there to New England and using all that kind of old Southern stuff, our own stuff, which we never get a chance to use on a broad platform—and making it pay off," Ralph Ellison, *Juneteenth*, ed. John Callahan (New York: Vintage, 1999), 35.

6. Yonka Kristeva, "Chaos and Pattern in Ellison's *Invisible Man*," *Southern Literary Journal* 30, no. 4 (fall 1997): 68.

7. Ralph Ellison, "The Art of Fiction: An Interview," *TCERE*, 219.

8. Ellison, "The Art of Fiction," *TCERE*, 220.

9. Ralph Ellison, "On Initiation Rites and Power," *TCERE*, 537.

10. Understanding the narrator's comments on this matter is in itself difficult. On the last page of the novel, he states, "Thus, having tried to give pattern to the chaos which lives within the pattern of your certainties, I must come out, I must emerge. And there's still a conflict within me. With Louis Armstrong one half of me says, 'Open the window and let the foul air out,' while the other says 'It's good green corn before the harvest.' Of course Louis was kidding, *he* wouldn't have thrown old Bad Air out, because it would have broken up the music and the dance, when it was the good music that came from the bell of old Bad Air's horn that counted" (581). These words suggest at least that the underground is the only context that makes the music of the novel possible.

11. Plato, *Gorgias*, in *Readings in Classical Rhetoric*, Ed. Thomas W. Benson and Michael H. Prosser, trans. W. R. M. Lamb (Davis, Calif.: Hermagoras Press, 1988), 19.

12. Eric Segal, "Introduction," *The Dialogues of Plato* (New York: Bantam, 1986), X.

13. Plato, *Phaedrus*, in *Readings in Classical Rhetoric*, Ed. Thomas W. Benson and Michael H. Prosser, trans. H. N. Fowler (Davis, Calif.: Hermagoras Press, 1988), 35.

14. Plato, *Phaedrus*, 37.

15. Ibid., 39.

16. Ibid., 24.

17. Ellison writes: "The novel was not invented by an American, nor even for Americans, but we are a people who have perhaps most need of it—a form which can produce imaginative models of the total society if the individual writer has the imagination, and can endow each character, scene and punctuation mark with his own sense of value." Ralph Ellison, "The Novel as a Function of American Democracy," *TCERE*, 764.

18. Reverend Hickman discusses Emerson with Bliss in this passage from *Juneteenth*: "I guess it's 'bout time I started reading some Shakespeare and Emerson. Yes, it's about time. Who's Emerson? He was a preacher too, Bliss, just like you. He wrote a heap of stuff and he was what is called a *philosopher*. Main thing though is that he knew that every tub has to sit on its own bottom. Have you remembered the rest of the sermon I taught you?" Ralph Ellison, *Juneteenth*, Ed. John Callahan (New York: Vintage, 1999), 45.

19. Ellison writes in a letter to Albert Murray dated July 24, 1953, concerning a trip home, "The sad thing about it, of course, was that so many were missing: my mother and father (who I learned used to say that he was raising me for a poet! Poor man.)" Quoted from Albert Murray and John Callahan, *Trading Twelves: The Selected Letters of Ralph Ellison and Albert Murray* (New York: Modem Library, 2000), 43.

20. Lawrence Jackson, *Ralph Ellison: Emergence of Genius* (New York: John Wiley and Sons, 2001), 26.

21. Mark Busby, *Ralph Ellison* (New York: Twayne, 1991), 7.

22. Barbara Foley, "The Rhetoric of Anticommunism in Invisible Man," *College English* 59 (1997): 9.

23. Notable exceptions here would be Dolan Hubbard's discussion of *Invisible Man* in his *The Sermon and the African American Literary Tradition*.

24. George A. Kennedy, *Classical Rhetoric and Its Christian and Secular Tradition from Ancient to Modern Times* (Chapel Hill: University of North Carolina Press, 1980), 137.

25. Ibid.

26. Yngve Brilioth, *A Brief History of Preaching*, trans. Karl E. Mattson (Philadelphia: Fortress, 1965), 50.

27. Ibid.

28. Dolan Hubbard, *The Sermon and the African American Literary Imagination* (Columbia: University of Missouri Press, 1994), 19.

29. Ibid., 24.

30. Ibid., 17.

31. Ibid., 83.

32. Ibid.

33. Ibid., 5.

34. Sunraider states: "I am led to suggest, and quite seriously, that legislation be drawn up to rename it the 'Coon Cage Eight.' And not at all because of its eight super efficient cylinders, nor because of the lean springing strength and beauty of its general outlines. Not at all, but because it has now become such a common sight to see eight or more of our darker brethren crowded together enjoying its power" Ralph Ellison, *Juneteenth*, Ed. John Callahan (New York: Vintage, 1999), 23.

35. Aristotle, *The Art of Rhetoric*, trans. H. C. Lawson-Tancred (New York: Penguin, 1991), 80–81.

36. Hubbard, 83.

37. "Perhaps that's my greatest social crime, I've overstayed my hibernation, since there's a possibility that even an invisible man has a socially responsible role to play" (581).

38. "But I am an orator, a rabble rouser—Am, I was and perhaps shall be again" (14).

39. At the end of "The World and the Jug," Ellison states: "Dear Irving, I am still yakking on and there's many a thousand gone, but I assure that no Negroes are beating down my door, putting pressure on me to join the Negro Freedom Movement, for the simple reason that they realize that I am enlisted for the duration. . . . For, you see, my Negro friends recognize a certain division of labor among the members of the tribe. Their demands, like that of many whites, are that I publish more novels—and here I am remiss and vulnerable, perhaps." Ralph Ellison, "The World and the Jug," *TCERE*, 187–88.

CHRISTOPHER HANLON

Eloquence and Invisible Man

1

"It is the doctrine of the popular music-masters that whoever can speak can sing"—or so Emerson opens his essay "Eloquence," included in the 1870 volume *Society and Solitude.* As Emerson describes it near the end of his career as an orator, verbal eloquence becomes a form of musical expression, not only inasmuch as both share the formal elements of pitch, rhythm, and meter, but also to the extent that both make "instruments" of their audience. Hence, "Him we call an artist who can play on an assembly of men as a master on the keys of the piano,—who, seeing the people furious, shall soften and compose them, shall draw them, when he will, to laughter and to tears" (1903–04, 7. 65). The Emersonian speaker is a "master" of men, an Orphic wordsmith who "will have them pleased and humored as he chooses." But eloquence is for him no mere art of domination, the art of propaganda Emerson keeps in mind as he paraphrases Plato's definition of rhetoric: "the art of ruling the minds of men" (7. 64). The symphonic and harmonic dimensions of eloquence suffuse Emerson's essay of 1870, so that when he describes the eloquent speaker's art as that of "compos[ing]" "the people," he does not primarily point toward the power of the word to dominate and control un-self-reliant minds. Composing the people may involve calming them, as it did for Emerson during the opening moments of the Civil War and later, after Lincoln's Emancipation Proclamation, but it also

From *College Literature* 32, no. 4 (Fall 2005): 74–98. © 2005 by *College Literature.*

means constituting them as a group, composing them as a "social organism." But more so than either of these, Emerson thinks of eloquent composition as a process of musical collaboration that draws upon, channels, provides a conduit for energies already in circulation among "the people." "Of all the musical instruments on which men play," Emerson explains, "a popular assembly is that which has the largest compass and variety, and out of which, by genius and study, the most wonderful effects can be drawn." This is because "An audience is not a simple addition of the individuals that compose it. Their sympathy gives them a certain social organism, which fills each member, in his own degree, and most of all the orator, as a jar in a battery is charged with the whole electricity of the battery. No one can survey the face of an excited assembly, without being apprised of new opportunity for painting in fire human thought, and being agitated to agitate" (1903–04, 7. 62–63).

Emerson's model of spoken composition, proceeding from the recognition that every listener is also a potential speaker ("How many orators sit mute there below!" [1903–04, 7. 63]), also captures the most charged moments of eloquence to appear in Ralph Ellison's *Invisible Man*, a novel that measures the self-reliance of its nameless protagonist through his growing acumen as a public speaker. Midway through the novel, Ellison's narrator stands before a massive audience after his initiation into the political organization called the Brotherhood, observing that "The audience seemed to have become one, its breathing and articulation synchronized" much like the "social organism" or "battery" to which the Emersonian speaker both addresses and connects himself. The Brotherhood has hired Ellison's protagonist as a political agitator, but having achieved only measured success with past public speeches, he now approaches his first large audience with trepidation. Fumbling at the lectern and blinded by the spotlight, he makes an awkward beginning:

> The microphone was strange and unnerving. I approached it incorrectly, my voice sounding raspy and full of air, and after a few words I halted, embarrassed. I was getting off to a bad start, something had to be done. I leaned toward the vague audience closest to the platform and said, "Sorry, folks. Up to now they've kept me so far away from these shiny electric gadgets I haven't learned the technique. . . . And to tell you the truth, it looks to me like it might bite! Just look at it, it looks like the steel skull of a man! Do you think he died of dispossession?"
>
> It worked and while they laughed someone came and made an adjustment. "Don't stand too close," he advised.

"How's that?" I said, hearing my voice boom deep and vibrant
over the arena. "Is that better?"
     There was a ripple of applause.
     "You see, all I needed was a chance. You've granted it, now it's
up to me!"
     The applause grew stronger and from down front a man's far-
carrying voice called out, "We with you, Brother. You pitch 'em
we catch 'em!"
     That was all I needed, I'd made contact, and it was as though
his voice was that of them all. (Ellison 1981, 341–42)

In the end, the speech is fabulously successful; after finding his point
of "contact" within an otherwise inscrutable mass of listeners, the protagonist delivers a virtuoso spoken performance drawing its strength from the
audience's enthusiastic participation. The format of his speech is, in a way,
generic: "I had to fall back upon tradition and since it was a political meeting," the narrator explains, "I selected one of the political techniques that I'd
heard so often at home" (Ellison 1981, 342). But more than strictly "political," his chosen technique is also spiritual and musical, drawing upon a tradition of call-and-response oration that also informs the improvisational
styles of jazz composition. The anonymous point of contact in the audience becomes for the protagonist a kind of duet partner or Greek chorus,
ostensibly speaking for the audience as a whole and encouraging the spoken
composition onward. This dynamic of collaboration (wherein it becomes
difficult, as Emerson's 1870 commentary implies it might, to distinguish
between speaker and listener) finally gives way to a moment of sanctifica-
tion: as the protagonist nears the end of his speech, he finds himself at "a
natural pause [where] there was applause, but as it burst I realized that
the flow of words had stopped. What would I do when they started to
listen again?" (344) Feeling suddenly "naked, sensing that the words were
returning and that something was about to be said that I shouldn't reveal"
(345), the protagonist throws himself into the welter of coagulating phrases,
achieving as he does so a new but long-sought stature:

My shoulders were squared, my chin thrust forward and my eyes
focused straight into the light. "Something strange and miraculous
and transforming is taking place in me right now . . . as I stand here
before you!"
     I could feel the words forming themselves, slowly falling into
place. The light seemed to boil opalescently, like liquid soap
shaken gently in a bottle.

"Let me describe it. It is something odd. It's something that
I'm sure I'd never experience anywhere else in the world. I feel
your eyes upon me. I hear the pulse of your breathing. And now,
at this moment, with your black and white eyes upon me, I feel
. . . I feel. . . ."
    [. . .] "What is it son, what do you feel?" a shrill voice cried.
    My voice fell to a husky whisper, "I feel, I feel suddenly that I
have become more human." (Ellison 1981, 345–46)

There is much irony in the narrator's statement that this speech for the
Brotherhood has effected his transmogrification, has allowed him to become
more "human," especially since though the protagonist's audience recognizes
and values this moment of becoming, the Brotherhood itself largely does not.
Precisely inasmuch as the speech is steeped in the sort of community identification call-and-response engenders and the Brotherhood strives to efface,
and precisely inasmuch as the speech abandons quasi-"scientific" ratiocina-
tion in favor of emotionally charged oratory, many of the Brothers resent it
and their new fellow traveler deeply. But the speech nevertheless marks a crucial turning point for the protagonist of *Invisible Man*, whose journey along
the color line of 1930s America has up until now been a steady descent into
a hell of racist *de*-humanization. It is also, moreover, a quintessentially Emersonian moment, inasmuch as the protagonist's re-humanization is facilitated
through his re-birth as an eloquent speaker. As in Emerson's "Self-Reliance,"
where the burden of speech is precisely the burden of speaking oneself into
existence (the un-self-reliant individual, Emerson complains, "dares not say,
'I think,' 'I am'" in an elocutionary gesture of auto-genesis akin to "I am that
am"), *Invisible Man* invests the public words of its protagonist with the capacity to re-substantiate the self whose existence other selves have effaced. In this
way, Ellison's novel formulates its own ethos of spoken self-creation along
Emersonian lines. As a collaborative but also improvisational model of eloquence, the protagonist's first speech for the Brotherhood privileges spontaneous expression over rehearsed argument: its achievement is thus to commit
itself to the Emersonian challenge, "Speak what you think now in hard words
and to-morrow speak what to-morrow thinks in hard words again, though it
contradict everything you said to-day" (Emerson 1983, 265).
    At moments such as this, the protagonist of *Invisible Man* finds himself
within the context Ellison would later identify—echoing the musical metaphors of Emerson's essay on eloquence—as that of the American author,
whose audience is "a far more receptive instrument than may be dominated
through a skillful exercise of the sheerly 'rhetorical' elements—the flash and
filigree—of the artist's craft" (1995, 492). For Ellison, indeed, Emerson's sense

of spoken performance as an orchestral event carries over into a musicological understanding of written composition. Of the American writer's readership, Ellison explains that "Like a strange orchestra upon which a guest conductor would impose his artistic vision, it must be exhorted, persuaded, even wooed, at the price of its applause" (492). The American writer Ellison describes "play[s] artfully upon the audience's sense of experience and form"; his audience is that which "he is called to play as a pianist upon a piano," though "this second instrument can be most unstable in its tuning, and downright ornery in its responses," a fact that Ellison regards as "a special, most American problem" (496). Such collaborative interaction between writer and audience, Ellison explains, comprises an act of "democratic faith" entailing "an incalculable scale of possibilities for self-creation" (494).

Other commentators on *Invisible Man* have concluded that Ellison's novel mounts a sustained critique of Emersonian ethics, suggesting that Ellison rejects "Self-Reliance" as irreducible to—and also insensitive of—the powerful social forces that burdened African Americans throughout the twentieth century. Still other readers of *Invisible Man* have focused upon the novel's musicological qualities, the ways in which the narrative experimentation of the novel incorporates Ellison's early love of and expertise with music, pulling together an authorial voice that draws upon the techniques of several musical forms in order to re-invent the American novel.[1] None of these commentators, however, have considered that these two facets of *Invisible Man*— the novel's musicological commitments, on the one hand, and its struggle with the legacy of Emerson on the other—may shed light upon each other, that part of the Emersonian tradition that is Ellison's inheritance might be the musical, harmonic, and improvisational understanding of eloquence that Emerson outlines most explicitly in the 1870 essay devoted to this topic but that also circulates through much of Emerson's writing prior to this work.[2] In exploring this possibility, then, I am suggesting at least two things about Ellison's relationship with Emerson. The first is that, viewed in such a way, *Invisible Man* affiliates itself with a crucial strain of thought, running throughout Emerson's writings, that ponders the musical qualities of eloquent communication and links these qualities to a promise of speakerly rebirth. But another premise from which I proceed is that imposing, larger-than-life figures like Emerson lead a protean life in American literary and intellectual history, since the resonance of such essays as "Self-Reliance," "The American Scholar," or "The Poet" shifts in accordance with whatever desires or values a given generation of readers brings to them.[3] In *Invisible Man* particularly, the name of "Emerson" marks a site of contest and struggle where various interests compete to authorize their values through reference to an "Emersonian" tradition. In this sense, Ellison's affiliation with Emersonian values of eloquence does not come about through a simple process of "transmission" and "reception," nor even through a Bloomian *mise en scène* wherein Ellison unconsciously if productively misreads Emerson. The Emersonian strains at work in *Invisible Man* constitute a series of appropriative gestures on Ellison's part; they are deliberate, revisionary attempts at constituting an Emersonian tradition that resists other versions of "Emerson" that are largely antithetical to the sort of American intellectual history Ellison wishes to write. The Ellisonian reading of Emerson is a transformative reading, faithful to the wide-ranging ramifications of Emerson's philosophy even as it assimilates its particular components into Ellison's specific and progressive philosophical aims. This is to say that before Ellison's protagonist is able to learn the kind of improvisatory give-and-take *Invisible Man* values, Ellison himself enacts such give-and-take with Emerson as duet partner. To put it still another way, Ellison's reading of Emerson is a reading undertaken in the spirit of "Quotation and Originality," in which Emerson tells us that "Original power is usually accompanied with assimilating power ..." (1990, 433). What Henry Louis Gates, Jr., refers to as "signifyin(g)," the spoken tradition of "expressive doubleness" by means of which generations of African Americans have commandeered existing oral or written texts in order to redirect the thematics of those texts along their own lines of intent, is for Emerson the paradoxical genius of "originality" itself, since "In hours of high mental activity we sometimes do the book too much honor, reading out of it better things than the author wrote,—reading, as we say, between the lines" (435). And we might liken this stratum of meaning the Emersonian reader discerns "between the lines" to what practiced blues and jazz players call microtones—the "notes between the notes" or tonal gradations that lie unscripted, invisible, within the apparently blank spaces of the measure.[4] Ellison's metaphor for this mode of Emersonian reading, the kind of reading to which *Invisible Man* subjects Emerson himself, also emphasizes the musicological dimension of "reading ... between the lines," suggesting that only "on the lower frequencies" of any text do we find the matrix of possibilities for reconstruction and renovation.

2

As if in fulfillment of its thesis that eloquence emerges as the product of a dialogue between orator and audience, Emerson's 1870 version of "Eloquence" bears the impress of its long history of spoken delivery. Passages of the 1870 text appear in Emerson's Journal as far back as 1844; Emerson drafted the essay on his second trip to Europe in 1847; and as an address, "Eloquence" was a frequent part of Emerson's repertoire throughout the second half of his public career, during which he revised, redeveloped, and rethought the essay repeatedly. One of these revisions is especially worth noting here. Near the outset of the 1870 text, Emerson ascribes particular powers of eloquence to various regional, ethnic, and national sensibilities, describing the "Irishwoman" whose "speech flows like a river—so unconsidered, so humorous, so pathetic, such justice done to all the parts!" as well as "Our Southern people" who "are almost all speakers, and have every advantage over the New England people, whose climate is so cold that t'is said we do not like to open our mouths very wide" (1903–04, 7. 68–69). In a footnote to a later edition of *Society and Solitude*, Edward Emerson reports a second-hand anecdote concerning the essay's reception, in which "Colonel Thomas Wentworth Higginson relates that he heard Emerson speak thus in praise of Southern eloquence, to the content of students from that section, in the audience; a content that was lessened when he went on, 'The negro too is eloquent'" (1903–04, 7. 368). By 1870, Emerson had apparently decided to omit the remark.

It would be tempting to suppose that Emerson's decision to exclude the remark from his 1870 edition of *Society and Solitude*, and hence to exclude African Americans from the constellation of articulacy and ethnicity that essay charts, was more of a grudging acquiescence to the popular racism of his day than it was an indicator of Emerson's felt ambivalence over the eloquence of the "negro." Such a view is certainly implied in Edward Emerson's notes to "Eloquence." But Emerson's troubled attitudes about race necessarily bar the way to such a conclusion. While Emerson was always a monogenicist—while he never found that African Americans and Caucasian Americans were so profoundly different as to indicate ultimately disparate biological origins for each race—he long believed that the differences were significant enough to make genuine social and political equality impossible. Writing in his journal at the age of 19, attempting to argue the case in favor of slavery as a kind of thought-experiment (only months before, he had proclaimed in the same journal that "no ingenious sophistry can ever yet reconcile the unperverted mind to *slavery*"), he slipped into the required perspective rather too easily, relating that "I saw ten, twenty, a hundred large-lipped, low-browed black men in the streets who, except in the mere matter of language, did not exceed the sagacity of an elephant" (1960–82, 2. 55). In 1837, no longer writing within such a consciously constructed persona, he actually suggested that the middle passage was "only a little worse than the old sufferings. [Africans] exchange a cannibal war for a stinking hold" (5. 382). But Emerson progressed well beyond such views by the time he reached middle age. Two years after the Civil War, he wrote angrily in his Journal, "You complain that the negroes are a base class. Who makes & keeps the jew or the negro base, who but you, who exclude them from the rights which others enjoy?" (16. 55).

Emerson's liberal abolitionism, like the liberal abolitionism of many of his peers in Concord and Boston, often consisted of a paternalistic attitude toward African Americans, which in turn rested upon the assumption that Africans were less rational and more childlike than Europeans. And yet, when we consider the great premium Emerson places on autonomy, on self-reliance, and also how closely these values are tied to Emerson's sense of the self-reliant *voice*, his assumptions about the capacity of "negroes" to reach such ideals become more difficult to pin down. After hearing speeches by Toussaint L'Ouverture and Frederick Douglass in 1844, Emerson recorded his impression that

> now it seems to me that the arrival of such men as Toussaint if he is pure blood, or of Douglas [sic] if he is pure blood, outweighs all the English & American humanity. . . . Here is Man, & if you have man, black or white is an insignificance. Why at night all men are black. The intellect, that is miraculous, who has it has the talisman, his skin and bones are transparent, he is a statue of the living God: him I must love & serve & perpetually seek & desire and dream on: and who has it is not superfluous. (Emerson 1960–82, 5.63)

For Emerson, the eloquence of Douglass and L'Ouverture is the eloquence of self-reliance itself, the sort of eloquence he believed would liberate all African Americans. Offering individual exemplars of Emerson's more general sense in "Eloquence" that the successful public speech was a fundamentally musical event, orators like Douglass and L'Ouverture signaled a new "occasion of . . . jubilee" in which "the black race can begin to compete with the white; that in the great anthem of the world which we call history . . . after playing a long time a very low and subdued accompaniment they perceive the time arrived when they can strike in with force & effect & take a master's part in the music" (1960–82, 5. 63).

It is Emerson's unpatronizing accolade for such speakers as Douglass and L'Ouverture, resonant with the eventually deleted assertion from "Eloquence" ("The negro too is eloquent"), that I want to emphasize here, but in doing so I do not mean to suggest that Emerson's attitudes toward race, or indeed on self-reliance, are uncomplicated at any level. Rather, it is Emerson's very inconsistency on such issues that makes him such a contested figure for all sorts of intellectual historians, including Ellison himself. *Invisible Man*, for instance, circulates the name of Emerson in ways that question which values the name signals and for whom these values resonate. At an early point in the narrative, Mr. Norton, a white college trustee whom the young protagonist chauffeurs for the better part of an afternoon, asks the boy, "You have studied

Emerson, haven't you?" Embarrassed that he has not, the boy replies, "Not yet, sir. We haven't come to him yet."

> "No?" [Norton] said with a note of surprise. "Well, never mind. I am a New Englander, like Emerson. You must learn about him, for he was important to your people. He had a hand in shaping your destiny. Yes, perhaps that is what I mean. I had a feeling that your people were somehow connected with my destiny. That what happened to you was connected with what would happen to me...." (Ellison 1981, 41)

Later, when the protagonist promises to read Emerson, Norton describes his own sense of subjection to an abiding "destiny" or "fate," which for him seems always connected in some way to Emerson's philosophical legacy: "Very good. Self-reliance is a most worthy virtue. I shall look forward with the greatest of interest to learning your contribution to my fate" (Ellison 1981, 108). In the early chapters of the novel, however, it is Norton who shapes the fate of the protagonist. After taking Norton first to visit a local sharecropper who describes his rape of his daughter, and then to a local asylum (the "Golden Day" hospital for shell-shocked veterans, where one inmate criticizes Norton's hypocritically condescending views toward the very "Negroes" he professes to uplift), the boy is expelled from college as punishment for his role in these escapades. Norton's obliviousness to the ripple effects his words and deeds have upon the protagonist's life has led some commentators to conclude that Ellison rejects the "Emersonian" outlook Norton claims to embrace. Kun Jong Lee, for example, points to several statements from Emerson's journal—statements, like those I have already mentioned, that echo the ideologies of racial hierarchy endemic to Emerson's era—in order to argue that Ellison creates Norton as an indictment of cryptically racist facets of Emersonian philosophy. Without accusing Emerson of bigotry, Alan Nadel argues that Norton represents a parody of Emersonian idealism, which remains blind and aloof wherever mechanisms of social coercion operate; Emerson, Nadel suggests, is for Ellison an "author of false hopes" whose blithe optimism serves to obscure "the complicated form [evil] takes in the real world" (1989, 118, 116).

    In a recent answer to such charges, however, James Albrecht insists that Nadel's reading places much too high a premium on Norton's allegedly "Emersonian" evocations of self-sufficiency (as when he blithely and vaguely mentions that "Self-reliance is a most worthy virtue" for black individuals such as the protagonist). Nadel's readiness to take Norton at his word insofar as the latter aligns himself with Emerson, as Albrecht points out, already obscures what should be the first question here: are Norton's references to Emerson coherent in the first place? Whereas Norton repeatedly espouses his notion of an operative "fate" upon which his own legacy as a philanthropist depends ("I am dependent upon you to learn my fate," he explains, since "Through you and your fellow students I become, let us say, three hundred teachers, seven hundred trained mechanics, eight hundred skilled farmers, and so on" [Ellison 1981, 45]), Albrecht rightly points out that such notions concerning "fate" are antithetical to Emerson's essay of the same name, which "explicitly rejects fatalism in favor of activism" (1999, 49). Looking beyond the disjunctions Albrecht identifies, even Norton's stated appreciation for "Self-Reliance" should seem less discerning when we recall that essay's critique of the "foolish philanthropist," the "angry bigot who assumes this bountiful cause of Abolition ..." (Emerson 1983, 262). Apropos of such philanthropists as Norton, who enjoin social causes in order to prove themselves virtuous, Emerson asks, "why should I not say to him, 'Go love thy infant; love thy wood-chopper; be good-natured and modest; have that grace; and never varnish your hard, uncharitable ambition with this incredible tenderness for black folk a thousand miles off. Thy love afar is spite at home'" (262). The "tenderness" of such individuals is, for Emerson, "incredible," literally lacking in credibility, a form of false compassion—a fact that should underscore that Emerson does not belittle social activism and charitable involvement as such. Rather, what is at issue in "Self-Reliance" is precisely the sort of "philanthropy" Norton embraces, a philanthropic project grounded in "penance," what Emerson refers to as that virtuous work "done as an apology or extenuation of ... living in the world ..." (262).

In at least this sense, Norton represents the sort of individual "Self-Reliance" deplores, not the sort of individual the essay values. Norton's desire to associate himself with an Emersonian tradition he barely understands thus marks off "Emerson" as a site of interpretive dissent for Invisible Man. This is to say that in depicting Norton as a self-professed "Emersonian," Ellison does not dismiss Emersonian philosophy as impertinent to the racial and social struggles Invisible Man depicts. Rather, he includes the name of Emerson within the horizon of these struggles, contesting the various renditions of "Emerson" that have sometimes eclipsed his abiding relevance to the problem of "the color line" and the forms of self-consciousness it engenders. Norton's misreadings of Emerson are precisely what Ellison wants to contest, but the protagonist's reply to Norton's early query as to whether he has studied Emerson—"Not yet, sir. We haven't come to him yet."—comments more widely upon Emerson's posthumous reception and philosophical legacy. In certain ways, Ellison's novel suggests that we have yet to come upon Emerson—that if, "on the lower frequencies," Ellison's narrator speaks for us, then his journey toward self-emergence and self-reliance coincides with the project of extract-ing a living dimension of Emersonian thought from an ossified and nomi-nally "Emersonian" narrative. While *Invisible Man* may complicate and often challenge the idealism Emersonian philosophy represents, it does not simply discard the hopes this philosophy articulates. Rather, *Invisible Man* capital-izes upon Emersonian motifs that are more submerged than those readers such as Norton typically use as shorthand for Emersonian thought *in toto*. In other words, Ellison reads Emerson in an Emersonian way.

So if there are in fact Emersonian figures to be found in *Invisible Man*, they appear in less grandiloquent guise than Norton, and certainly not as either of the "Mr. Emersons" who enter the narrative after the protagonist's arrival in New York. It is telling that Ellison chooses here to divide his "Emerson" in two, presenting to us a young Emerson apparently wracked with Freudian angst, tyrannized by and alienated from Emerson, Sr., the absent father who never appears directly in the narrative but toward whom the novel's protago-nist has been misdirected. Young Mr. Emerson bars the protagonist's way to Emerson, Sr., but Emerson, Sr., we discover, is himself part of the conspiracy to "keep this nigger boy running": the letters of introduction with which the protagonist has been provided by his college headmaster (one of which he is now attempting to deliver to the elder Emerson) instruct their addressees to deny him assistance, since (as the letters say) he "shall never, under any cir-cumstances, be enrolled as a student here again" (Ellison 1981, 190). Having set off in search of one Emerson, the protagonist finds another; attempting to deliver a message he has not read to Emerson, Sr., he instead receives that message from Emerson, Jr. (who reveals to the protagonist the contents of the letters he has been delivering and thus enables him to begin the process of making his own way in the world). But again, this is not to say that young Mr. Emerson lives up to his surname; for one thing, he offers the protagonist little more than an un-Emersonian, nihilistic resignation as he dismisses the very notion of the self as passé: "Identity! My God! Who has any identity anymore anyway?" (187) In *Invisible Man*, Emerson's thought channels not through the characters who speak or bear Emerson's name but rather through those who speak in Emersonian fashion.

Take, for example, the character Peter Wheatstraw, the riffing and gre-garious blues man whom the protagonist meets earlier in the narrative, as the latter is on his way to keeping his appointment with Emerson. At this point in the narrative, Ellison's protagonist has placed his confidence in the plan of action supplied to him by Bledsoe, a plan of action that is founded on his let-ters of introduction and that hence masks an elaborate deception. The blues man appears at this juncture as a walking personification of the protagonist's (actual, though yet to be ascertained) situation: when the protagonist first sees Wheatstraw, the latter is pushing a cart filled with a stack of abandoned plans, blueprints that represent designs for nearly every conceivable building project—from cities to country clubs—but which never came to fruition. As Wheatstraw remarks, "I guess somebody done changed their plans" (Ellison 1981, 175).

Part of the comedy here hovers over the absurd mystery of *Wheatstraw's* plans—what, after all, does he plan on *doing* with the hundreds of rolls of paper, of which he explains he has "a coupla loads"? But though he cannot fully realize it, Wheatstraw's remarks also offer a commentary on the protagonist's de facto situation as someone whose long-nurtured plans are about to disintegrate. "Folks is always changing their plans," Wheatstraw comments, to which the protagonist responds, "Yes, that's right [. . .] but that's a mistake. You have to stick to the plan." To this, Wheatstraw appears "suddenly grave" before stating, "You kinda young, daddy-o" (Ellison 1981, 175). As someone who knows by first-hand experience that "this Harlem ain't nothing but a bear's den," Wheatstraw also presumably understands, better than the young protagonist, how early plans have a way of falling through, a lesson the protagonist will learn only too soon once he discovers the damaging statements contained in his letters of introduction. Wheatstraw's message of resilience is an Emersonian message, redressing the false confidence we tend to place in designs that may or may not turn out as we had initially hoped. Emerson's answer to this misplacement of confidence is to insist that the self-reliant individual "has not one chance, but a hundred chances"; his response to the fragility of human "plans" is to ridicule the common wisdom according to which "If the finest young genius studies at one of our colleges and is not installed in an office within one year afterwards [. . .] he is right in being disheartened and in complaining the rest of his life" (1983, 275). Wheatstraw's ironic distance toward the protagonist's faith in "the plan," however, does not issue directly from a self-consciously Emersonian philosophy of self-reliance, but rather from Wheatstraw's status as a "blues man" whose primary mode of communication draws a source of strength from what W. E. B. Du Bois recognized as the "half-despised" African American tradition of musical wordplay and improvisation. Wheatstraw embodies what Ellison described as the fundamental impulse proper to the blues, "an impulse to keep the painful details and episodes of a brutal experience alive in one's aching consciousness," "not by the consolation of philosophy, but by squeezing from it a near-tragic, near comic lyricism" (1964, 78). Explaining that "All it takes to get along in this man's town is a little shit, grit, and mother-wit," Wheatstraw performs these necessary qualities for survival—and simultaneously claims them as his own—through a spiel of spoken performance: "man, I was bawn with all three. In fact,

I'maseventhsonofaseventhsonbawnwithacauloverbotheyesandraisedonblack-
catbones-highjohntheconqueorandgreasygreens—" (1981, 176)[5]
So what precisely is Wheatstraw's place in this narrative? Though his
appearance in *Invisible Man* is brief, Wheatstraw serves as one of several sur-
rogate father figures for the narrator, who also receives paternal guidance of
varying worth from figures such as the grandfather, the vet at the Golden
Day, the yam man in New York, and Brother Tarp—and who is also subject to
the paternal tyranny of tricksters such as Bledsoe, Norton, and Brother Jack.
But what distinguishes Wheatstraw from the array of possibilities these characters represent is that he models a loquaciousness—a lingua franca of shit,
grit, and mother-wit—enacting his message of resilience at the register of
spoken performance. His eloquence is both traditional *and* improvisational;
though he addresses the narrator through a series of tropes and codes he
assumes the boy will recognize (since both are, as he points out, "from down
home"), he also deploys these codes in ways that enact the spoken equivalent
of developing one's own "plan" as one proceeds. In this sense, Wheatstraw
appears as one of a string of spoken performers in *Invisible Man*, but one who
stands out for his improvisational powers. Unlike, for instance, the Reverend
Homer A. Barbee, whose earlier speech at the protagonist's college is a tightly
rehearsed repetition of other, similar speeches (as Barbee begins his speech,
he remarks "my young friends, it is indeed a beautiful story. I'm sure you've
heard it many times" [Ellison 1981, 119]), Wheatstraw's eloquence is an off-
the-cuff, organic eloquence, an eloquence that foregrounds the possibilities of
improvisation as opposed to strict recitation.[6] To borrow a terminology once
used by Charles Mingus, Wheatstraw appears as a "spontaneous composer"
as opposed to speakers like Barbee, whose adherence to a pre-prepared script
would make him a "pencil composer." And so though Wheatstraw qualifies as
an Emersonian speaker whose wordplay blends whim with self-reliance, and
though he is also a "blues man" who sublimates his adversity into art, Wheatstraw's improvisational abilities also connect him to aesthetic principles that
formed the core of Ellison's relationship with jazz.

3

For Ellison, improvisation enabled each jazz performer's emergence as a
distinctive figure within a larger compositional group. "Each true jazz
moment," he remarked in a 1958 essay on Charlie Christian, "springs from
a contest in which each artist challenges all the rest; each solo flight, or
improvisation, represents (like the successive canvases of a painter) a definition of his identity as individual, as members of the collectivity and as a link
in the chain of tradition" (1995, 267). Ellison's commentary on jazz also
describes his own Emersonian relationship with Emerson, a relationship

that connects Ellison to a certain tradition even as it distinguishes him from that tradition. Simultaneously including the artist within a "chain of tradition" and providing an outlet by means of which this artist may distinguish him- or herself as an "individual," jazz concocts an equilibrium between the artist's sense of indebtedness and belonging, on the one hand, and this same artist's impulse to distinguish his or her own voice within that of "the collectivity," on the other. In this way, Ellison's understanding of jazz resembles T. S. Eliot's effort to mediate between individual genius and the efficacy of tradition in "Tradition and the Individual Talent," where Eliot describes literary tradition not as a monolith against which each artist must either turn his or her back or be subsumed, but rather as a form of aesthetic ground upon which the artist's idiosyncratic talents take root. Analogously, Ellison's understanding of improvisation requires that every jazz artist "learns tradition, group techniques and style" even as it affords this artist an opportunity for individuated "rebirth." "For after the jazzman has learned the fundamentals of his instrument and the traditional techniques of jazz—the intonations, the mute work, manipulation of timbre, the body of traditional styles—he must then 'find himself,' must be 'reborn,' must find, as it were, his soul," Ellison explains. "All this through achieving that subtle identification between his instrument and his deepest drives which will allow him to express his own unique ideas and his own unique voice. He must achieve, in short, his self-determined identity" (245).[7]

Ellison's connections between improvisation and the attainment of an "original" voice, an attainment coinciding with an achievement of "self-determined identity" and thus facilitating a form of "rebirth," suggest a certain correspondence with both Emerson's musicological descriptions of eloquence and his habit of attaching self-reliance to a mode of spontaneous, "impertinent" speech. Emerson's descriptions of self-reliant speech often emphasize an improvisational dimension, requiring us to "Speak today what you think now in hard words and to-morrow speak what to-morrow thinks in hard words again, though it contradict everything you said to-day" (1983, 265). Emerson gives us this advice in view of his famous insistence that "A foolish consistency is the hobgoblin of little minds"—that is, in light of his understanding that at times, the most powerful obstacle to self-reliance is indeed our tendency to imagine ourselves beholden to our past statements and formulations, to imagine that we are simply what we once were, and that only. Against the imagined rebuttal that without at least some degree of consistency in our speech we risk incoherence, Emerson reminds us that "The voyage of the best ship is a zigzag line of a hundred tacks" (266), or that though the surface of contradiction, revision, and experimentation making up the texture of self-reliant speech may appear as a broken and uneven landscape when viewed from up close, these same elements "are insignificant in the curve of the sphere" they ultimately shape (265).

So as Ellison assesses jazz improvisation as a technique for self-definition, Emerson values contradictory, revisionary, and above all spontaneous speech as the hallmark of self-reliance. This is not to lose sight of the obvious fact that Emerson's own addresses were carefully rehearsed events, culled from journal entries and often reworked over years of delivery, just as it should not be to lose sight of the fact that improvisation is only possible for musicians (jazz or otherwise) who have spent years honing their craft. Indeed for neither Emerson nor Ellison does successfully improvised performance or self-reliant speech resemble or verge upon bedlam, since neither abandons tradition so much as it expands the boundaries of tradition proper to any given moment. One of Emerson's ways of saying this is to explain that he hopes his whim is somewhat more than whim; another is to urge the self-reliant speaker to "Speak your latent conviction, and it be the universal sense" (1983, 259). The alternative to such bravado is for Emerson the elocutionary equivalent of self-dismemberment: "We but half express ourselves, and are ashamed of that divine idea which each of us represents" (260). Lacking self-reliance, our speech lacks declarative force, becoming instead derivative, formulaic, utterly non-disruptive and cautious: "I hear a preacher announce for his text and topic the expediency of one of the institutions of the church," Emerson recalls. "Do I not know beforehand that not possibly can he say a new and spontaneous word?" (264). The preacher Emerson describes becomes little more than the mouthpiece of an institution, a kind of propaganda machine that only imitates the qualities of authentically eloquent speech; but self-reliant speakers, as Emerson put it as early as *Nature*, "pierce this rotten diction" by breaking with conventional modes and mores of expression (1903–04, 1. 30).[8]

Emerson's image of the cautious, circumscribed preacher might call to mind Ellison's protagonist's eventual position as a speaker for the Brotherhood, the Marxisant organization on whose behalf the protagonist speaks fervently—and finally too eloquently—but whose leader, Brother Jack, eventually explains, "You were not hired to think" (1981, 469). But it should also remind us of what is probably the most famous episode from *Invisible Man*, where as a recent high-school graduate, Ellison's protagonist is invited to re-read his valedictory address before the white power-brokers of his small southern town. Shortly after arriving to deliver his speech, the narrator is forced to participate in a "Battle Royal," for which he is blindfolded with a handkerchief and forced to box a group of similarly-blinded black adolescents. After the boxing match, the protagonist is allowed to give his speech (remarkably, he remains eager to deliver it even throughout his humiliating ordeal), in fact a well-known passage from Booker T. Washington's Atlanta Day Exposition Address, (though Ellison seems to imply that in the diagetic reality of his novel, the boy remains the speech's true author). The satire here is bifocal. First and perhaps foremost, the outrageous conditions of the boy's speech (for which he remains clad in his boxing shorts, swallowing "blood, saliva and all" in order to pronounce every word faithfully for a group of white racists who barely listen) point up the ludicrousness of the Atlanta Day Exposition Address itself, in which Washington advanced his own accommodationist program of African American economic advancement at the expense of social equality. But in addition to initiating *Invisible Man*'s sustained critique of Washington, the sequence initiates a series of questions that will continue to pervade *Invisible Man*, questions concerning the qualities and conditions of moving, eloquent oration. This is to say that the first public speech of *Invisible Man* is not only undercut by the inappropriateness of its specific message to the specific setting of its delivery (southern blacks, the young man explains, should "cast down their buckets" in "cultivating friendly relations with the southern white man who is his neighbor," presumably southern white men like those who have subjected the protagonist to an elaborate humiliation). Washington, in other words, is not Ellison's primary target here, and to focus on the fact that the speech comes from Washington is to miss Ellison's point about the (overly) poised way in which the protagonist pitches Washington's (obtuse) social program. Reading his pre-prepared text verbatim, apparently attempting to duplicate a prior performance from his high-school graduation, the narrator recalls that he "spoke automatically and with such fervor that I did not realize that the men were still talking and laughing until my dry mouth, filling up with blood from the cut, almost strangled me. . . . The speech seemed a hundred times as long as before, but I could not leave out a single word. All had to be said, each memorized nuance considered, rendered" (30).

The speech is not simply bad because the scene of its delivery lays bare the naïve philosophy it espouse, and it's not simply bad because history had already shown Ellison upon which side of the Du Bois/Washington divide to situate himself. More primarily for Ellison, it is bad because of its unmoved and unmoving recital, because even in spite of the appearance of "fervor" the protagonist attempts to project through his inclusion of "memorized nuance[s]," such rhetorical flash only constitutes the simulation of an inspired voice. Its inept delivery is in keeping with the speech's irrelevant logic, the let's-just-all-get-along wisdom the speech offers an imagined audience of black southerners but which is now rehearsed for a set of white men who recoil from the phrase "social equality." Even as the protagonist departs from his script in uttering these disruptive words, he does not improvise so much as he is improvised upon: sensing the dangerous ground he has opened up, he quickly substitutes the words "social responsibility" and hence returns to the prudent conventions of Washingtonian segregation. And so as an address that ventriloquizes the actual speech of Washington and hence strives to mimic the tradition of oratory authorized by such figures as he—the speech is constructed of what Emerson describes as the parlance of the derivative. "We are like children," he explains, "who repeat by rote the sentences of the grandames and tutors, and, as they grow older, of the men of talents and character they chance to see—painfully recollecting the exact words they spoke" (1983, 270–71).

As an aspiring public speaker, the young protagonist of *Invisible Man* is a mnemonic impersonator of other voices, and as he later recollects the numerous speeches he gave prior to his expulsion from college, the narrator recognizes and theorizes his failures in terms of musical dissonance and cacophony. In the campus chapel, he recalls, "I too had stridden and debated, a student leader directing my voice at the highest beams and farthest rafters," but though these speeches and debates once provided the boy with self-satisfaction, in retrospect the narrator finds them "a play upon the resonances of buildings, an assault upon the temples of ears" (Ellison 1981, 112–13).

> *listen to me, the bungling bugler of words, imitating the trumpet and the trombone's timbre, playing thematic variations like a baritone horn. Hey! old connoisseur of voice sounds, of voices without messages, of newsless winds, listen to the vowel sounds and the crackling dentals, to the low harsh gutturals of empty anguish, now riding the curve of preacher's rhythm I had heard long ago in a Baptist church, stripped now of its imagery. . . . Ha! as upon a xylophone; words marching like a student band, up the campus and down again, blaring triumphant sounds empty of triumphs . . . the sound of words that were no words, counterfeit notes singing achievements yet unachieved, riding upon the wings of my voice out to you. . . .* (Ellison 1981, 113)

The narrator's memory of his own youthful and abortive eloquence extends Emerson's equation of musicality and effective oratory. Here, the narrator recalls that his prior mode of address was a mere "imitation" of eloquence that could never have engaged its audience because it directed itself away from them, "at the highest beams and farthest rafters." The result is not properly speech, for Ellison's narrator, but rather the simulation of speech, "the sound of words that were no words," mere "counterfeit notes" as opposed to genuinely musical intonations. Ellison's point here, as with his fashioning of the Battle Royal Speech, is not at all akin to a vapid bias one might

entertain against "tradition" in favor of "innovation"—his aim is not to deni-
grate "the curve of the preacher's rhythm" or to hold it liable for its hold over
the young speaker who imitates it. Rather, Ellison's stance on eloquence and
form resembles the stance of Henri Bergson regarding his concepts of *élan
vital* and *durée real*: just as the very sequentiality and orderedness entailed
in our perception of events tend to fragment otherwise irreducible living
systems, rendering the living curl a mere succession of straight lines, so to
speak, so does Ellison's young speaker witness the petrification of his own
impulse to speak (his own *élan vital*, in a way) in the forms he finds available
to him.[9] Those forms are essentially monological forms, and they result in
the same torpor that afflicts Homer Barbee and Emerson's preacher, speakers
who cannot possibly say a new or spontaneous word. In Ellison as in Emerson, the possibility of eloquence is bound to the possibility of breaking with
such forms, entering into something akin to a collaboration with one's audience, and later in *Invisible Man*, Ellison's commitment to such a possibility is
brought closer to the fore.

Midway through the novel, Ellison's protagonist finds himself adrift in
New York City, having come to the painful realization that his earlier plans—
among which was his hope of returning to college in order to finish his degree
and hopefully attain a position—have run aground. "And the more resent-
ful I became," he explains, "the more my urge to make speeches returned"
(1981, 259). Within a few pages, the protagonist in fact makes a speech, and
this speech dramatizes the sort of symbiotic, compositional qualities Emerson associates with eloquence as such. Wandering the streets of Harlem, the
protagonist comes across a mid-winter eviction of an elderly couple, and
joins a crowd of onlookers who soon begin an open debate over whether
or not to charge the armed marshals enforcing this eviction. The narrator's
response to this possibility is ambivalent, swinging between his identification
with the growing mob and his desire to avert a bloody disaster: "I knew they
were about to attack the man and I was both afraid and angry, repelled and
fascinated. I both wanted it and feared the consequences, was outraged and
angered at what I saw and yet surged with fear; not for the man or of the
consequences of an attack, but of what the sight of violence might release
in me. And beneath it all there boiled up all the shock-absorbing phrases
that I had learned all my life" (275). As if without his conscious volition, the
protagonist's sense of moral outrage begins to transform itself into words and
phrases, the sum of which now override his anxiety:

> "No, no," I heard myself yelling. "Black men! Brothers! Black
> Brothers! That's not the way. We're law-abiding. We're a law-
> abiding people and a slow-to-anger-people."

[...] They stopped, listening. Even the white man was startled.

"Yeah, but we mad now," a voice called out.

"Yes, you're right," I called back. "We're angry, but let us be wise. Let us, I mean let us not. . . . Let us learn from that great leader whose wise action was reported in the newspaper the other day. . . ."

"What mahn? Who?" a West Indian voice shouted.

[...] This was it, I thought, they're listening, eager to listen. Nobody laughed. If they laugh, I'll die! I tensed my diaphragm.

"That wise man," I said, "you read about him, who when the fugitive escaped from the mob and ran to his school for protection, that wise man who was strong enough to do the legal thing, the law-abiding thing, to turn him over to the forces of law and order . . ."

"Yeah," a voice rang out, "yeah, so they could lynch his ass."

Oh, God, this wasn't it at all. Poor technique and not at all what I intended. (Ellison 1981, 275–76)

Unlike prior speeches he has given, this speech is directed at an audience that will not constrain itself to listen quietly, that offers its own retort when provoked. Over the course of his potentially disastrous intervention, the protagonist finds himself forced to adjust his pronunciations to the temperament of the crowd; as his listeners fire back their own answers and protests in response to his various statements, they actively interfere with the trajectory of the protagonist's address, but in such a way as to tease a sort of repressed eloquence from him. Over the course of this sequence, the protagonist's audience functions as the "ornery" American audience Ellison identifies as the writer's muse; it is also, for that matter, the critical, evaluative audience Emerson describes in the essay on eloquence: "The audience is a constant meter of the orator. . . . If anything comic or coarse is spoken, you shall see the emergence of the boys and the rowdies, so loud and vivacious that you might think the house was filled with them. . . . There is also something excellent in every audience,—the capacity for virtue. They are ready to be beatified. They know so much more than the orator,—and are so just!" (1903–04, 7: 66). Regathering his powers, Ellison's protagonist continues:

"But wasn't it the human thing to do? After all, he had to protect himself because—"

"He was a handkerchief-headed rat!" a woman screamed, her voice boiling with contempt.

"Yes, you're right. He was wise and cowardly, but what about us? What are we to do?" I yelled, suddenly thrilled by the response. "Look at him," I cried.

* * *

"And look at their possessions all strewn there on the sidewalk. Just look at their possessions in the snow. How old are you sir?"

"I'm eighty-seven," the old man said, his voice low and bewildered.

[...] "Did you hear him? He's eighty-seven. Eighty-seven and look at all he's accumulated in eighty-seven years, strewn in the snow like chicken guts, and we're a law-abiding, slow-to-anger bunch of folks turning the other cheek every day of the week. What are we going to do? What would you, what would I, what would he have done? *What is to be done?* I propose we do the law-abiding thing. Just look at this junk! Should two old folks live in such junk, cooped up in a filthy room? It's a great danger, a fire hazard! Yes, yes, yes! Look at that old woman, somebody's mother, somebody's grandmother, maybe. We call them 'Big Mama' and they spoil us and—*you* know, *you* remember...."
(Ellison 1981, 276–77)

More than any other spoken performance in *Invisible Man* (I would suggest, even more so than the narrator's eventual eulogy for Tod Clifton), this speech is energized by its tempo and rhythm, its dramatic repetition (not only "Yes, yes, yes!" but also the building momentum of the ironic phrase "law-abiding") and the Ciceronian wink and nudge of ending rhymes like "turning the cheek every day of the week." So begins the protagonist's career as a public speaker, for it is this event that will draw the attention of the Brotherhood, the shadowy political organization that hires the protagonist as a political agitator and mouthpiece. The speech is finally unsuccessful as an effort to quell a burgeoning riot (at a later juncture in his speech, the protagonist is rushed by a group of men who decide to follow through on their original plans), but as an act of Emersonian auto-genesis, it is utterly successful, since over the course of this speech, the protagonist re-invents himself as a public orator. Ellison figures this reinvention as a moment of rebirth; as the protagonist flees the scene of his brief but transformational intervention, he passes a car from which he sees "a man leap out with a physician's bag."

"Hurry, Doctor," a man called from the stoop, "she's already in labor!"

"Good," the doctor called. "That's what we've been waiting
for, isn't it?"
"Yeah, but it didn't start when we expected it." (Ellison 1981,
287)

"What a time to be born," the protagonist thinks as he passes by, and
it should be clear here that the birth with which Ellison is concerned is
the protagonist's new birth as a public intellectual, a speaker whose voice
is now—as Emerson would say—"agitated to agitate."[10] In this way, the
re-birth of Ellison's narrator resembles the sort of speakerly self-creation
advocated in "Self-Reliance," where so often, Emerson describes the
affirmation of the "I" as a simultaneously elocutionary and melodic act.
"Speak your latent conviction," Emerson insists, "and it shall become
universal sense; for the inmost in due time becomes the outmost, and our
first thought is rendered back to us by the trumpets of the last judgment"
(1983, 259). In speaking before the crowd before his phrases have fully
taken shape, the protagonist initiates the process of elocutionary self-
invention that was always Emerson's truest subject matter; though this
process will ultimately end where the novel begins, in the catastrophic
revelation that "I am an invisible man," the laying-bare of selfhood Ellison describes variously as a form of "invisibility," of "hibernation," or of
"going underground" is itself presented as preliminary to some as-yet
unrealized—but newly attainable—moment of becoming. The hibernation of Ellison's protagonist is of a piece with that process Emerson
describes in *Nature*, where transcendentalist selfhood comes only at the
price of selfhood itself: "Standing on the bare ground—my head bathed
by the blithe air and uplifted into infinite space—all mean egotism vanishes. I become a transparent eyeball; I am nothing; I see all; the currents
of the Universal Being circulate through me; I am part or parcel of God"
(1903–04, 1. 10).

For his part, Ellison's protagonist witnesses something like the vanish-
ing of what Emerson calls "mean egotism" in an abandoned basement deep
under New York, where he can finally say only one thing with confidence:
"I am an invisible man." Jazz itself, though it finally conceives musical patterns that would have been impossible otherwise, only discerns these patterns by delving deep into chaos and contingency, which is why Ellison
recognized jazz aesthetics as an aesthetics of self-erasure, commenting that
"the jazzman must lose his identity in order to find it" (1995, 267). For both
Emerson and Ellison, the process of spoken self-invention entails a moment
of self-annihilation, which is why both writers are drawn to metaphors of
invisibility in the first place. Which is to say that Emerson's transparent eye

is to "the current of the Universal being" what Ellison's transparent I is to
the mellow, melodious voice that speaks for me and for you.

NOTES

Earlier versions of this essay received helpful commentary from Jeffrey Insko of
Oakland University as well as Julie Campbell, Daiva Markelis, Francine McGregor,
Dana Ringuette, Donnelle Ruwe, Martin Scott, and Angela Vietto of Eastern Illi-
nois University. I am also indebted to an anonymous reviewer for *College Literature*.

1. See, for instance, Robert O'Meally, who traces Ellison's narratological and
thematic incorporation of jazz throughout *Invisible Man*. C. W. E. Bigsby suggests that Ellison's improvisational narrative form amounts to an improvisation of
America itself, what Ellison viewed as a political and cultural gesture akin to that
of the founders, who "were improvising themselves into a nation, scraping together
a conscious culture out of the various dialects, idioms, lingos, and mythologies of
America's diverse peoples and regions" (qtd. in Bigsby 1987, 177). Houston Baker
traces the blues aesthetics of *Invisible Man* through the "Trueblood episode," which
spins its blues narrative out of the mythical phallic power of black males while also
recognizing the cultural capital of its mystique. And describing it as "the true musical idiom of modernism," Berndt Ostendorf views jazz as both synthesizing agent
and aesthetic "world" in which Ellison's anthropological, folkloric mindset comes to
terms with his Modernist sensibility (1986, 147).

2. The organic mode of composition proper to the Emersonian essay has led
some commentators to note that in certain ways, Emerson's prose is less formally
constrained (for some, more "musical") than his poetry. Mutlu Konuk Blasing, for
example, argues that "Emerson's concept of poetry as the language of law—or even
language *as* law—makes clear that his idea of poetry is much more restrictive than
what critics have termed the musical or inspired speech of his essays" (1985, 11). Less
inclined to inscribe broad aesthetic distinctions between the Emersonian essay and
the Emersonian poem, but equally attentive to the musical elements of Emerson's
eloquence, Brian Harding suggests that Emerson's writing "attempted to express an
idea of poetry that combined (through metaphor) the apparently irreconcilable qualities of architecture and music" (1985, 101).

3. Much recent scholarship on Emerson takes up some version of this thesis:
that, for instance, the resonance and meaning of Emersonian individualism has
always been contested in American culture. For examples that produce very different
accounts of Emerson's political legacies in America (swinging between "corporatist"
versions of Emerson, which see him as fundamental to a tradition of middle-class
submission, and "democratic individualist" renditions which highlight Emerson's
ethics of autonomy, see Kateb (1992), Newfield (1996), or Mitchell (1997).

4. Thanks to Martin Scott of Eastern Illinois University for alerting me to
this connection.

5. Thomas Marvin opens up an extended investigation here concerning
Wheatstraw's self-description as "the devil's son-in-law," as well as the supernatural
motifs at play in the rapid-fire, extended epithet quoted above. The blues, as Marvin reminds us, always carries with it connotations of the demonic, so that African
Americans who deploy blues themes on their own behalf also identify themselves,
at least to some extent, as what Marvin calls "children of Legba," or as magicians of
vaguely Satanic forces (1996, 591–95).

6. Similarly, Robert List sees Wheatstraw as a "bricoleur" who "saves and juxtaposes heterogenous materials" in the aesthetic tradition of Joyce or Ellison himself, "an embodiment of buoyant self-determination and of the rebelliousness of High John the Conqueror . . . [who] echoes the past and eyes the future" (1982, 200–201).

7. The history of jazz criticism in the U.S. has often been shaped by listeners who revere jazz for having "transcended" the earliest conditions of its production, for having moved past its "merely" folk origins in order to "elevate" itself as a more "universal" art form. One example of this perspective can be found in Gunther Schuller's *Musings*, which consistently measures the achievement of jazz in terms of its transformations during the 1930s and 40s, before which jazz was "sometimes hardly more than sociological manifestations of a particular American milieu . . . but in the process of maturing has gradually acquired certain intellectual proper-ties" (1986, 94). An alternative account may be found in Albert Murray, whose influential *Stomping the Blues* focuses upon the folk tradition behind jazz as the determining force *within* jazz—for Murray, jazz "is the product of the most compli-cated culture, and therefore the most complicated sensibility, in the modern world" (1970, 166); hence, the "particular American milieu" Schuller imagines jazz to have "transcended" is for Murray the very source of jazz's aesthetic power. For more on the history of jazz criticism in the United States, especially concerning the compet-ing ideologies within this critical tradition, see John Gennari's "Jazz Criticism: Its Development and Ideologies."

It is worth noting in this context that Ellison himself embraced the national culture other jazz artists and critics saw as co–opting and reductive. Against Amiri Baraka, for instance, who wrote that jazz and the blues were essentially revolutionary aesthetic forms that had been commodified and commandeered by whites (see, for instance, Baraka 1963) Ellison said simply that "The tremendous burden of sociol-ogy which [Baraka, then LeRoi Jones] would place upon this music is enough to give even the blues the blues" (1964, 249–50).

8. As Sheldon Liebman indicates, Emerson's later pronunciations concerning eloquence and speech grew out of his shifting readings in rhetoric during the late 1820s. During his years at Harvard, Emerson followed closely the advice of Hugh Blair, the eighteenth-century rhetorician whose advocacy of a measured and rational style would cause the early Emerson to exercise caution with his use of metaphor, to model his prose self-consciously upon that of figures such as Samuel Johnson, and to adopt an ornamental Latinate vocabulary. By the late 1820s, however, Emerson had begun to value spontaneity over convention, to believe that "an alehouse is a better school for eloquence than a college" (qtd. in Liebman 1969, 193). While Emerson still sought out models of eloquence in other writers, he was now drawn to those whose writing, like Carlyle and Montaigne, "draws strength and mother-wit out of a poetic use of the spoken vocabulary," whose writing was "the language of conver-sation transferred to a book" (195). For an early and still intriguing assessment of Emerson's successes and failures as public orator, see Scudder (1935).

9. Here is how Bergson puts it:

A very small element of a curve is very near being a straight line. And the smaller it is, the nearer. In the limit, it may be termed a part of the curve or a part of the straight line, as you please, for in each of its points a curve coincides with its tangent. So likewise "vitality" is tangent, at any and every point, to physical and chemical forces; but such points are, as a fact, only views taken by a mind which imagines stops at various moments of the movement that generates the curve. In reality, life is no more made of physicochemical elements than a curve is composed of straight lines. (Bergson 1911, 31)

10. In this way of course the scene fits with the larger motif of death and regeneration treated since the inception of Ellison criticism, beginning with Jonathan Baumbach's 1963 essay.

Works Cited

Albrecht, James M. 1999. "Saying Yes and Saying No: Individualist Ethics in Ellison, Burke, and Emerson." *PMLA* 114: 1 (January): 46–63.

Baker, Houston A. 1984. *Blues, Ideology, and Afro-American Literature*. Chicago: University of Chicago.

Baraka, Amiri. 1963. *Blues People: Negro Music in White America*. New York: Morrow.

Baumbach, Jonathan. 1963. "Nightmare of a Native Son: Ellison's *Invisible Man*." *Critique* 6: 1 (Spring): 48–65.

Bergson, Henri. 1911. *Creative Evolution*. Trans. Arthur Mitchell. New York: Henry Holt.

Bigsby, C. W. E. 1987. "Improvising America: Ralph Ellison and the Paradox of Form." In *Speaking For You: The Vision of Ralph Ellison*, ed. Kimberly W. Benston. Washington D.C.: Howard University Press.

Blasing, Mutlu Konuk. 1985. "Essaying the Poet: Emerson's Poetic Theory and Practice." *Modern Language Studies* 15: 2 (Spring): 9–23.

Ellison, Ralph. 1964. *Shadow and Act*. New York: Random House.

———. 1981. *Invisible Man*. 1952. Reprint. New York: Random House.

———. 1995. *The Collected Essays of Ralph Ellison*. Ed. John F. Callahan. New York: Modern Library.

Emerson, Ralph Waldo. 1903–04. *The Complete Works of Ralph Waldo Emerson*. Ed. Edward Waldo Emerson. 12 vols. Boston and New York: Houghton Mifflin.

———. 1960–82. *Journals and Miscellaneous Notebooks of Ralph Waldo Emerson*. Ed. William H. Gilman et al. 16 vols. Cambridge: Belknap.

———. 1983. *Emerson: Essays and Lectures*. Ed. Joel Porte. New York: Library of America.

———. 1990. *Ralph Waldo Emerson*. Ed. Richard Poirier. Oxford and New York: Oxford UP.

Gennari, John. 1991. "Jazz Criticism: Its Development and Ideologies." *Black American Literature Forum* 25: 3 (Autumn): 449–523.

Harding, Brian. 1985. "Frolic's Architecture: Music and Metamorphosis in Emerson's Poetry." *Nineteenth-Century American Poetry*: 100–17.

Kateb, George. 1992. *The Inner Ocean: Individualism and Democratic Culture*. Ithaca: Cornell University Press.

Lee, Kun Jong. 1992. "Ellison's Invisible Man: Emersonianism Revised." *PMLA* 107: 2 (March): 331–44.

Liebman, Sheldon. 1969. "The Development of Emerson's Theory of Rhetoric, 1821–1836." *American Literature* 41: 2 (May): 178–206.

List, Robert. 1982. *Dedalus in Harlem: The Joyce–Ellison Connection*. Washington: University Press of America.

Marvin, Thomas. "Children of Legba: Musicians at the Crossroads in Ralph Ellison's *Invisible Man*." *American Literature* 68:3: 587–608.

Mitchell, Charles E. 1997. *Individualism and its Discontents: Appropriations of Emerson, 1880–1950*. Amherst: University of Massachusetts.

Murray, Albert. 1970. *The Omni-Americans: Black Experience and American Culture*. New York: Vintage.

———. 1982. *Stomping the Blues*. 1976. Reprint. New York: Vintage.

Nadel, Alan. 1989. *Invisible Criticism: Ralph Ellison and the American Canon*. Iowa City: University of Iowa Press.

Newfield, Christopher. 1996. *The Emerson Effect: Individualism and Submission in America*. Chicago: University of Chicago Press.

O'Meally, Robert G. 1980. *The Craft of Ralph Ellison*. Cambridge: Harvard University Press.

Ostendorf, Berndt. 1986. "Anthropology, Modernism, and Jazz." In *Ralph Ellison*, ed. Harold Bloom. New York: Chelsea House.

Schuller, Gunther. 1986. *Musings*. New York: Oxford University Press.

Scudder, Townsend III. 1935. "Emerson's British Lecture Tour, 1847–1848, Part II: Emerson as a Lecturer in Britain and the reception of the Lectures." *American Literature* 7: 2 (May): 166–80.

VALERIE SWEENEY PRINCE

Keep on Moving Don't Stop: Invisible Man

Invisible Man was *par excellence* the literary extension of the blues. It was as if Ellison had taken an everyday twelve bar tune ... and scored it for an orchestra.

—Albert Murray

When I had come to New York seven years before that, I wondered about the need for such huge buildings. No one ever seemed to be in them for very long; everyone was out on the sidewalks, moving, moving, moving—and to where?

—Gloria Naylor, *Mama Day*

The title *Native Son* is clearly ironic; Bigger Thomas has no home or paternity. Yet the novel lays out three terms that sketch a blueprint for the place of home within African American literature traceable through works produced over the following three decades: the city, the kitchen, and the womb. The city dominates Bigger's landscape even as he is pressed into geographically more restrictive spaces. The kitchen is represented as the kitchenette, an abbreviated version of a more complete place; and Bigger's retreat into the basement of the Dalton house is but the initial stage of a literary retreat into the womb.

From *Burnin' Down the House: Home in African American Literature.* © 2005 by Columbia University Press.

In Ralph Ellison's masterpiece published twelve years later, *Invisible Man* (1952), the nameless protagonist goes on a journey that begins at the end, when he seems to have found "a home of sorts"—a basement apartment in an "all white" building outside Harlem. I will examine the ways that Ellison picks up and revises the theme of home that appears in *Native Son* specifically as the three geographical markers. I am interested in the changes Ellison makes in representing these sites so that they seem to yield the possibility of community fundamental to establishing home. The womb is defined more clearly in this novel, and the kitchen also plays a more significant role in *Invisible Man* than in *Native Son*. However, the city still dominates the landscape and serves as the chief concern in the narrator's quest for home.

Invisible Man augments the scenes of home found in *Native Son* as Ellison explores other possibilities of the Northern city. Numerous scenes, most within the city, provide the backdrop for the plot. Of all the settings featured in *Invisible Man*, Mary Rambo's house most reads as "home" because it contains her blues kitchen. In addition to Mary's house, only the basement apartment and the South are overtly characterized as home for the invisible man. The narrator looks over his shoulder to the South, a place to which he will never return. For a time, it guides his movements as Kansas does Dorothy's on her journey through Oz. The basement is a more overt representation of the womb than Bigger's basement in *Native Son*. In contrast to the city, which resists being configured as home, Mary's house, with its blues kitchen, and the basement apartment, a womblike place, lend themselves to being read as home. Yet something remains in place to trouble such a reading. We imagine home to be stable and therefore stabilizing, but Ellison builds upon Wright's problematization of stability as a quality of home. The impermeability of Wright's city does not prove stabilizing, despite the fact that it remains static. In contrast, Ellison focuses on the changing face of the city that refuses to be known or knowable, and thus refuses to engender the familiarity fundamental to the construct of home.

As in *Native Son*, in this novel the blues seems to be part and parcel of the black (home) place. Unlike Wright, Ellison believed music was a vital aspect of his literary aesthetic. Instead of social protest; Ellison sought to create art; and his art would be infused with the movement and cadence of the blues. Berndt Ostendorf says:

> Vernacular dance, vernacular language, and vernacular music represent for this high cultural modernist a total body of culture. And Ellison wants to translate that energy into the organized discipline of his art. . . . Jazz, dance, and language all partake of a total world view and a total way of life. Hence, one of the

harshest estimates that Ellison ever made of Richard Wright was that "he knew very little about jazz and didn't even know how to dance." (97)

Wright's inability to dance is tantamount to Bigger's inability to sing. Stereotypically, "Black folk got rhythm," if they do not have anything else. Ellison, believing that music and dance are fundamental to African American culture, suggests that for a black man, not knowing how to dance means lacking a crucial foundation. It is through understanding of these cultural practices that black people become connected with one another. Although the blues cannot mitigate all of the debilitating effects experienced at home, it provides a cadence through which some of the occupants make a culture of privation more bearable.

Womb: The Truebloods' Cabin

By the second chapter of the novel, two of the three terms have been introduced. The narrator, in the prologue, is already underground in New York City. But the novel goes back to the time when his journey began in the South. The Trueblood episode appears in the second chapter of *Invisible Man*. Jim Trueblood is a sharecropper who lives with his family near the campus of the college the narrator attends briefly. The narrator inadvertently escorts Mr. Norton, a wealthy white trustee, to the Truebloods' cabin. Initially Mr. Norton is struck by the age and style of the structure: "It was an old cabin with its chinks filled with chalk-white clay, with bright new shingles patching its roof" (46). He notices the cabins first, then, "looking across the bare, hard stretch of yard . . . two women dressed in new blue-and-white checked ginghams," both of whom "moved with the weary, full-fronted motions of far-gone pregnancy" (47). Filled with wonder that the buildings have lasted since slavery, Mr. Norton exclaims, "The human stock goes on, even though it degenerates. But these cabins!" (47). Mr. Norton expects the "human stock" to continue despite its degeneration but he is full of wide-eyed amazement that the man-made cabins endure so well. From his perspective, the pregnant black woman is part of an old scene of the black South. These structures and the women working in the yard, he intimates, are enduring evidence of a more wholesome past.

The narrator is mortified by his own impropriety, having stumbled upon the Truebloods without forethought. Jim Trueblood is a disgrace to the local black community, particularly the petit bourgeoisie at the college. He has brought shame to everyone by impregnating both his wife, Kate, and his eldest daughter, Matty Lou. These are the two women dressed alike and bearing the weight of pregnancy, like twins, working together in the yard. In introducing Mr. Norton to Jim Trueblood, the narrator discloses the dark underbelly of the poverty of black domestic life. The pregnant womb is necessarily part of this construction because, as even Mr. Norton recognizes in his pejorative understanding of African Americans, home is built around family. Patriarchy relies upon the woman as the kin source, and men operating under this philosophy look to women to bring forth the next generation. While no home place can be constructed around gender without some inherent conflict, the terrain of the black (home) place of the sharecropper pictured here is made even more treacherous by poverty, racism, and the imbalance of power between the genders.

Mr. Norton is attracted to the Truebloods' tale as if by a force beyond his control. He demands that the narrator stop and let him speak to Trueblood himself. Trueblood willingly narrates his woeful tale to the Northern, white, liberal philanthropist. Unable to afford coal, the family conserves body heat by sleeping together in two pallets on the floor. The younger children are in one and Matty Lou between her parents in the other. Trueblood recounts his thoughts, which include reminiscing about a past love and fending off a current suitor interested in Matty Lou, but he places responsibility for his behavior on a "dream-sin": he awakened from a dream to discover he was having intercourse with his daughter.

Initially, Ellison describes the setting as "dark, plum black. Black as the middle of a bucket of tar" (54). In this black place, he lays out the dynamics of home at work in this novel. The Truebloods' log cabin is a remnant of slavery. This part of the material landscape has hardly been altered since prior to the Civil War. This black (home) place that began in racist Southern oppression and poverty ends in the same shack with a mother and daughter impregnated by the same man. Although Mr. Norton hardly can be credited with recognizing the nuances of these sophisticated racial dynamics, he is correct in that, indeed, one incestuous seed "degenerates." Kate and Matty Lou bear the tragedy of home literally in their bodies. The two pregnant women, mother and daughter, signify the privation out of which Trueblood's blues are created.

At first, the narrator is baffled by his confrontation with Trueblood, but the sharecropper contributes one of the most profound lessons the unnamed protagonist receives in his long journey. Trueblood's blues are characterized by John S. Wright as the "creative will to transcendence" (176). Upon awakening from his nightmarish dream and recognizing his quagmire (that he is having intercourse with his daughter while his wife is lying next to them in bed), Trueblood explains, "Once a man gits hisself into a tight spot like that there ain't much he can do. It ain't up to him no longer. There I was, tryin' to git away with all my might, yet having to move without movin'. I flew in but

I had to walk out. I had to move without movin'" (59). Trueblood is caught within a situation that inflicts terrible pain upon himself as well as his family; at the same moment he experiences pleasure great enough to create an unresolvable predicament. Movement is both the problem and the solution. The narrator himself will come to accept Trueblood's quintessential blues paradox: having to arrive at the result without ever performing the action. As John S. Wright explains, "In his full awareness, then, of the irredeemable cost of freedom from sin and the attendant consequences of freely sinning, Trueblood gives eloquent testimony to his own tragic sense of life and to that need for transcendence he finally satisfies only in the resolving poetry of the blues" (176).

Incest is not the shocking new ground Mr. Norton discovers that hot afternoon as he listens to the tale. Instead, he ventures into "new territory" when he stumbles upon Trueblood's yard and encounters the black (home) place and the blues. What confounds him even more than the fact of incest is the fact that Jim Trueblood seems to have escaped judgment: "You did and are unharmed!" (51). It seems Trueblood has found a resolution to his personal dilemma. He can move without moving, as Norton demonstrates by rewarding his performance. Along with so many other guilt-ridden, wealthy white men, Norton is moved by Trueblood's tale while Trueblood, as blues performer, does not have to move at all.

The sharecropper's home, which had been threatened by poverty, the mock charity of Northern liberals, and the racial pragmatism of the black college, is now maintained by Jim Trueblood's retellings of his story. He transforms his own painful experience into a blues performance. Already known for his singing and storytelling, Trueblood has polished his tale, reconfiguring tragic circumstances to make his life more livable. His family is clad in new clothing, his roof patched with new shingles bought with money garnered from patrons of his art. Trueblood is an agent of the blues. In contrast, the women are not heard. The mark left on Jim's face from Kate's swing of an ax is the sole evidence of her resistance. Matty Lou is just silenced; she "won't speak a word to nobody" (67).

Rape is a high price for Matty Lou to pay in order for her father to be rewarded as an agent of the blues. And as Ann du Cille, Hortense Spillers, and other African American feminist critics have emphasized, care must be taken not to reduce her to an object of patriarchy.[1] She does not get to narrate her own tale; that authority is given (quite naturally) to her father, who, even after violating the (natural) rights of his daughter, retains his domestic dominance (as evidenced by the failure of his wife's attempt to kill him). To deny the horror of the scene and only acknowledge the blues expression that emerges from it risks, as Ann du Cille suggests in a critique of

Houston Baker's reading of the episode, reducing race to rape. Rape is the means through which Trueblood gains his power, at the expense of Kate and, most notably, Matty Lou. His role as father is doubly confirmed by the two pregnant women. In this household, as opposed to that of Bigger Thomas, paternity is clear—all too clear.

Kitchen: Mary Rambo's Blues Kitchen

While Bigger is unable to discover a safe place to roost in the course of his desperate flight, that is precisely what the invisible man unwittingly finds in Mary Rambo's house. The novel actually begins "underground," in the basement of an apartment in New York City, as the invisible man recites the story of how his journey to that point began. He has been propelled from place to place by a series of events that makes it impossible for him to have the comfort of a stable home. After arriving in New York, he must come to understand the naïveté of the hope that he will be allowed to return to the deep South (somehow improved by his experiences). Still reeling from yet another sudden shift in place, the narrator emerges from a subway and finds himself ushered into Mary Rambo's house.

Mary meets the visibly ailing narrator on the street, and with some assistance from another passerby, helps him into her home. This house, more than any other in the novel, manifests the mythic possibilities of home that must be constructed, at least partially, around the familiarity fostered by the past. Yet it too is part of urban blues culture and reflects the tension of blues vernacular. The blues speak of a dialectic created in the opposition of privation, poverty, and racism with privilege, wealth, and liberty. Mary's position as caregiver is well known within the community, and she expects the residents to be familiar with her reputation. She reassures the ailing protagonist, "*You take it easy, I'll take care of you like I done a heap of others, my name's Mary Rambo, everybody knows me round this part of Harlem*" (252). Mary ushers the protagonist into his next venue as she compels him to take refuge in her home.

Mary allows him to reside in her house without fear of eviction or of the social elitism that is so pervasive at the Men's House—from which he has just been banished for pouring a spittoon over the head of a reverend, whom he has mistaken for Dr. Bledsoe. Bledsoe is the Southern administrator who betrayed him by sending him to work in New York in the futile hope of returning to school. At Mary's house, he finds the comfort of good company, rest, and food. He explains his relationship with her in this way, "Other than Mary I had no friends and desired none. Nor did I think of Mary as a 'friend': she was something more—a force, a stable, familiar force like something out of my past which kept me from whirling off into some unknown which I dared not face" (258).

Friends have become obsolete in the narrator's world after Bledsoe's betrayal. Mary does not serve as "friend"; rather, she is an anchor of sorts that rescues him from an unfamiliar, and therefore terrifying, abyss of urban Northern life. The greater the "unknown," the more familiar and stabilizing is Mary. The "unknown" that the narrator so fears is not an identifiable place. Instead, it is an expanse of unencoded space that would consume him, were it not for the grounding Mary provides. The expanse feels threatening when set within the context of Harlem, the city that refuses to be constant for the invisible man. Mary's house offers the consolation of a definite site sheltered from the city, which only exacerbates the perceived chaos.

The expanse of the Northern city had seduced the protagonist and left him sick and stumbling up from the subway. Mary's "familiarity" contrasts with this large strangeness. But the narrator has difficulty articulating Mary's relationship to him. Like music, she is beyond words. Her house becomes "the South right in the middle of Manhattan" that Farah Griffin describes in *"Who Set You Flowin'?" The African American Migration Narrative*. Like the atmosphere created by the blues performance Griffin describes, Mary embodies not the South so much as "home." She becomes a metaplace that exists as a locale in the abstract. As such, Mary suggests the familiarity of Southern ritual culture without actually materializing the South. In her house, the narrator is able to find the solace of Southern practices without leaving town. She opens her doors selflessly to this man who could be categorized as a "stranger." The dichotomies inherent in the construct of home, which operate to make Mary recognizable inside the strangeness of the city, conversely function to make the protagonist known, or at least not a stranger, to her. In this way Mary and her guest develop a relationship that is not contingent upon knowing the personal details of each other's life. Mary is familiar to him because of the cultural values she represents; consequently, her house reads as "home." The blues performance that makes "the South right in the middle of Manhattan" is a musical configuration. Hence, Mary is reconfigured in this way as well.

The musical value system she embodies is made up of blue notes that begin with a man sick and stumbling into the arms of a caretaker. The narrator explains, "When I came out of the subway, Lenox Avenue seemed to career away from me at a drunken angle, and I focused upon the teetering scene with wild, infant's eyes, my head throbbing" (251). Here again the underground is a womblike place. Coming out of the subway station is like being reborn and given to a new mother. Mary shelters the narrator without concern for how his presence might impact her own well-being. When she is low on food and money, she serves cabbage instead of complaining or refusing to feed someone. What she demands in return appears as a benign pressure to perform "some act of leadership, some noteworthy achievement" (258).

The underlying tension in Mary's house is reflected by this pressure and the cabbage—suggesting the permeability of home and its potential to be infiltrated by larger forces like economics associated with maintaining such places. In another sense, the circumstances at Mary's house demonstrate the flexibility of the blues. Within the context of the blues, strangers can be allied unproblematically with each other, as are Mary and the protagonist. Further, the blues creates a space where circumstances like poverty can be integrated into the structure of home, Mary's house, without complete ruin.[2] While contemplating the meaning of the cabbage and the pressure in his room, the narrator hears Mary in the kitchen: "Then from down the hall I could hear Mary singing, her voice clear and untroubled, though she sang a troubled song. It was the 'Back Water Blues.' I lay listening as the sound flowed to and around me, bringing me a calm sense of my indebtedness" (297).

The blues serves Mary as a repository into which she can pour her pain and negative emotion. Mary's blues kitchen emerges as part of a larger cultural practice of establishing "home ground." The blues becomes a metaphorical bottle tree that is constructed to guard the home and protect its occupants by containing the evil.[3] Mary's blues, in effect, seeks to capture the evil "spirit" that troubles her home. The blues kitchen helps her negotiate the conflict between her home as a safe space and poverty as a threat to that perceived serenity—and the song brings order and meaning to her guest's experience.

The narrator's sense of indebtedness to Mary motivates the invisible man to accept a job with a political organization known as the Brotherhood so that he can repay her. Ironically, this job requires him to move. On his last day at Mary's home, the invisible man is awakened by a jarring sound. The cacophony has a very different effect on him than the blues tones of Mary's kitchen. The disembodied sound of metal striking against the metal of the radiator pipes reverberates throughout the building and infuriates the protagonist. He expresses hostility toward the people behind this commotion by looking for a weapon with which to contribute his own noisy blows to the pipe:

> Then near the door I saw something which I'd never noticed there before: the cast-iron figure of a very black, red-lipped and wide-mouthed Negro, whose white eyes stared up at me before his chest. It was a bank, a piece of early Americana, the kind of bank which, if a coin is placed in the hand a lever pressed upon the back, will raise

its arm and flip the coin into the grinning mouth. For a second I stopped, grabbed it, suddenly as enraged by the tolerance or lack of discrimination, or whatever, that allowed Mary to keep such a self-mocking image around, as by the knocking. (319)

Mary wonders at the racket caused by the numerous tenants throughout the building, and her bewilderment is expressed in her characteristic blues idiom, "They know when the heat don't come up that the super's drunk or done walked off the job looking for his woman, or something. Why don't folks act according to what they know?" (320). This kind of expressiveness is what allows the potential for pleasure to coexist with the likelihood of pain, and contrasts with the narrator's cacophony. Her vernacular gives voice to the rage that he so vehemently desires to articulate through his attack upon the pipe. It seems appropriate to him to use the bank that he finds so offensive. But Mary is puzzled by the self-centeredness of a response that focuses on one's own feelings of discomfort rather than recognizing the interconnectedness of human beings in the struggle to endure.

Mary identifies with the super's position as another expression of need, akin to her own. She has the unusual ability to recognize and, further, to validate another person's pain. This is significant precisely because it is a difficult thing to do, as Elaine Scarry describes:

For the person in pain, so incontestably and unnegotiably present is it that "having pain" may come to be thought of as the most vibrant example of what it is to "have certainty," while for the other person it is so elusive that "hearing about pain" may exist as the primary model of what it is "to have doubt." Thus pain comes unsharably into our midst as at once that which cannot be denied and that which cannot be confirmed. (4)

Mary bridges the chasm between the certainty embodied by her own experience of pain and the doubt about another's. Through her blues vernacular, she correlates her own experiences with the actions of those around her (even as their actions further inconvenience her), incorporating new circumstances into her blues vocabulary as they arise. In contrast, the narrator cannot handle the disruption and has trouble identifying with the figure that he finds so offensive. Yet he is able to note the pain in the bank's expression, which "seemed more of a strangulation than a grin" (312). The bank's visage shows the classic paradox of blues expressiveness that balances between pain and pleasure. This face both "grins and lies" in the way that Paul Laurence Dunbar describes in his poem "We Wear the Mask":

We wear the mask that grins and lies,
It hides our cheeks and shades our eyes,—
This debt we pay to human guile;
With torn and bleeding hearts we smile,
And mouth with myriad subtleties.

The "subtleties" of the expression are key to understanding a complex history.

Mask wearing is inseparable from the African American historical experience; no amount of shame or anger can erase the past. African Americans have been forced to contort their sorrow into laughter, anger into a grin. As Wright states in *12 Million Black Voices*, "The ridiculousness and sublimity of love are captured in our blues, those sad-happy songs that laugh and weep in one breath, those mocking tender utterances of a folk imprisoned in steel and stone" (128). The "steel and stone" framework of the city promotes the contradictory impulses that began centuries earlier, in the Middle Passage, the smiling through tears. The bank is a blues artifact that could anchor the invisible man's profound history of pain, resistance, fortitude, and pride. Yet the narrator is so angry about the stereotype it represents that he refuses to identify with the pain inherent in its expression.

He quickly dismisses the observations that might help him identify with the hidden pain (and Scarry suggests that pain is always concealed if it is not experienced personally); hence, he misses the lessons that might be learned by empathizing with others and sharing their grief. As Griffin notes, his judgment is impaired by his inability to comprehend the multifaceted layers of his experiences:

> This question, "What does it mean?" is Invisible Man's constant refrain. He is ambitious and somewhat pretentious. He feels that in order to reach his goal of leadership, he must shun those elements that bind him to a racial past. While he seeks to lead black people, it is an empty aspiration that fails to recognize the value of racial wisdom. Nowhere is this contradiction more evident than in his relationship with Mary. (131)

For the narrator to empathize with and share the grief expressed by the bank, he would have to be willing to ally himself with the collectivity the figure represents. The blues ethos that permits this kind of identification is, after all, a vernacular expression. But he is not yet ready to make the conscious choice to identify with this segment of his racial community. He dismisses his observation of the "strangulation" and the awareness it might bring. Instead, he uses the bank as a weapon to unleash his anger upon the unseen forces. Not surprisingly, in the process he smashes the head apart; and that which he hoped to destroy, he will not be permitted to discard.

City: Dispossession

Ellison assigns value to Mary's house by juxtaposing it with a scene of an eviction (one potential effect of that "unknown" space that the narrator fears) involving an old black couple. The narrator uses Mary as the point of contrast by which he assigns meaning to the city. The metropolis is large; Mary is small. While her house is not large enough to accommodate the invisible man's needs, she is an invaluable resource for him as he comes to understand his place within the urban territory.

Like the sense of homelessness found in *Native Son*, dispossession illustrates the relationship certain people have with the places they occupy. At the first eviction the narrator has ever witnessed, he makes an impassioned speech in an attempt to subdue an angry crowd, trying to explain the meaning of "dispossession." He expounds:

> "'Dispossess,' eighty-seven years and dispossessed of what? They ain't *got* nothing, they can't *get* nothing, they never *had* nothing. So who was dispossessed?" I growled. "We're law abiding. So who's being dispossessed? Can it be us? These old ones are out in the snow, but we're here with them. Look at their stuff, not a pit to hiss in, nor a window to shout the news and us right with them. Look at them, not a shack *to* pray in or an alley to sing the blues! (279)

After eighty-seven years, the elderly couple has little of material value, and their condition presages the state of the entire community. Ellison draws upon William Faulkner's use of the dispossession theme in *Go Down, Moses*, where Ike struggles with the idea when he inherits land because the rightful heir, Lucas Beauchamp, is black. Ike dispossesses his cousin, Lucas, of the land (only to repudiate it later). Ike laments, "Dispossessed of Eden. Dispossessed of Canaan, and those who dispossessed him dispossessed him dispossessed" (247). Ellison recasts this literary theme from Faulkner's Mississippi within the setting of the Northern city. Dispossession is an active condition enforced upon the community by officials with orders such as those who block the old couple's door. The narrator captures in his speech the sense of transience and indeterminacy that residents, recast as travelers, experience in city life.

When we meet the invisible man in the prologue, he has taken up residence in the basement of an apartment building. He has lit it with 1,369 light bulbs illuminated by unregulated electricity. The protagonist uses the lights to establish this territory as his home. Marking territory in this way can be situated within the African American practice of establishing "home ground." Anthropologist Grey Gundaker claims that such practices exist within the context of African America from coast to coast in both urban and rural settings: "Scale varies, but the claim, I am here, stays the same" (1). In this gesture, the narrator declares, "I am here," but with much less emphasis on the "here" than on the "I am." One reason is that place, within the context of the novel, continues to be unstable, as tenuous a construct as any seemingly fixed identity.

In fact, Monopolated Light & Power, the electric company responsible for distribution of current for the area, believes that "a lot of free current is disappearing somewhere into the jungle of Harlem" (5). The power company is, of course, a faceless white corporation whose primary goal is to serve its own interests (which may overlap with the interests of the larger white community), presumably without considering the interests of the black community. The company is quick to place blame for the loss of current on the African American community. Harlem is a black place. It is indisputably the section of New York City reserved for African Americans, so the reference to it as a "jungle" carries racist connotations. Harlem is read here as a barbaric wilderness, an untamed expanse that is far too frightening and free to be conquered. From the white perspective represented by ML&P, at best such a place can only be contained.

The invisible man exploits the image of Harlem as jungle to avoid the possibility of being discovered. Harlem during the 1920s was the scene of a great rebirth of African American culture; the contemporary Harlem pictured here contrasts with the image of that era.[4] The protagonist explains, "The joke, of course, is that I don't live in Harlem" (5). This is part of the irony. ML&P's expectation that a power drainage must come from inside the "jungle" is so restrictive that no one with this perspective could imagine that the drainage is coming from elsewhere—let alone an "all white" building *outside* of Harlem. Yet the lines delineating Harlem from the rest of Manhattan are more permeable than ML&P wishes to admit. As Gloria Anzaldúa writes, "Borders are set up to define the places that are safe and unsafe, to distinguish us from *them*. A border is a dividing line, a narrow strip along a steep edge. A borderland is a vague and undetermined place created by the emotional residue of an unnatural boundary. It is in a constant state of transition" (3). Borders, as Anzaldúa defines them, are a type of threshold that is constantly in flux. In the prologue, the invisible man has made this basement into a borderland home of sorts. If he embraces the border as his home, we might expect that he is also embracing the idea of change and mixtures. The despotism of one culture over another, of the power company's monopoly over Harlem, is challenged by the metaphor of in-betweenness. So the invisible man finds comfort in this retreat: "The point now is that I found a home—or a hole in the ground, as you will" (5).

The basement hideaway may be read as a transitional space between what is characterized as the "jungle"—representing the African American ghetto—and civilization, the white city. According to the logic employed by ML&P, a black man should not reside outside the "jungle" of Harlem and no white person in this apartment building would be siphoning electricity. But having recently come to the awareness that his identity is more precisely fixed as an *invisible* man than a *black* man, the narrator is able to orchestrate this ruse and manipulate the power structure into deceiving itself. He manages this scam because of society's insistence upon classifying places as well as people in the ways that Anzaldúa illuminates—according to race, gender, nationality, etc. It is important to ML&P and the culture associated with the corporation to be able to delineate its boundaries of power in order to maneuver the opposition (either real or imagined) onto a plane that operates under its authority. As Doreen Massey articulates:

> Two points seem clear. First, and very obviously, the way in which we characterize places is fundamentally political. But second, and far less obviously perhaps, the politics lie not just in the particular characteristics assigned to places (whether they include racist or sexist features, to which social class they are assigned) but in the very way in which the image of place is constructed. (114)

The division that demarcates the jungle and separates it from the rest of the city draws a line of safety with which the white community is able to assuage their fears of an African American threat. Identifying the territory of the jungle and African Americans as its occupants allows the whites to blindly insist upon the truth of its boundaries.

Perhaps the narrator turns on 1,369 bulbs in order to shed light on the intangibility of the barriers between the races. He then contradicts the authority of these boundaries through his tale. The reader, aware from the prologue of the narrator's true location, is not deceived by the apartment building's claim of being "all white." Hegemony's borders are not hard and fast. Instead it is the very permeability of those delineations that allows the structure to endure.

By the time the invisible man has gone through the Brotherhood and encountered Tod Clifton and Ras the Destroyer, he has come to accept the movement that compels him from place to place as a part of the African

American collective condition. As he is moved, he is forced to receive both material and psychological signs that connect him to the collective experience. His briefcase is now full of indicators of his travels, and he has the potential to identify himself as part of a larger community of racialized people and sites. But that community still refuses to yield itself to the invisible man's needs. The Harlem riot is one of the last venues depicted in the novel. During the riot the illusion of stability ordinarily associated with place gives way to chaos. In the midst of this extreme disorder, the narrator again longs for home.

The portrait of Mary surfaces as a maternal, stable, and ordering figure that comes to be read overtly as home: "It was not a decision of thought but something I realized suddenly while running over puddles of milk in the black street, stopping to swing the heavy brief case and the leg chain, slipping and sliding out of their hands" (551). Those signs of his journey—the case heavy with the weight of the coins, the bank he broke at Mary's house, and the leg chain given to him earlier by Tarp—become the physical manifestations of the vernacular blues expressiveness inherent in black experiences, which have the potential to defend him against hostile enemies. Although the physical weight of the metal blues artifacts protects him during the upheaval of the riot, like Bigger in his doomed flight, the narrator is searching for a safe place to roost. He is trying to reach Mary's house, but he is running the wrong way. He cannot go back to Mary's—the maternal imagery is rendered useless as the milk already wasted upon the ground.

The past is not available to the protagonist because of the laws of physics, regardless of social, cultural, or personal history. Further, as Doreen Massey suggests, "There is no one essential past about which to get nostalgic. This is true in the sense that there has never been a historical movement untouched by the world beyond" (116). Time is the inevitably corrupting presence that complicates the ability to construct home as an ideal in the present. The knowledge required to construct home as a perfected shelter is predicated upon experience that comes through living over time. The invisible man cannot go home to Mary's because of the impossibility of returning through time and space with the knowledge he has acquired through the act of moving away. He is, indeed, moving in the wrong direction if he is trying to go home, because Mary's house becomes home for him only after he leaves. The challenge facing the invisible man is to use the tools available to him to create a home in the present. In the midst of this confusion, he suddenly finds himself falling to safety underground.

Womb: "A Home of Sorts" in the City

The narrator finds himself below ground after falling through an open manhole: "I was never to reach Mary's, and I was over-optimistic about removing the steel cap in the morning. . . . I tried to find the usual ladder that leads out of such holes, but there was none" (567). Falling underground, into a womblike place, in effect represents an impossible return. The serendipitous event parallels the desire to deliberately return to an originary moment while drawing upon the knowledge accumulated in his journey away from that very place. The narrator is able to use the things he has carried with him from his past as fuel. He burns the combustible objects in his briefcase in order to light his way out of the hole. Just as the leg chain and bank became pragmatic tools for his survival, these other things literally are able to help him survive.[5] This moment represents the culmination of past events as he tries to create a livable future out of the tools he has acquired.

The characterization of a place is, as Massey argues, "fundamentally political" because it is how societal institutions are able to sustain control over areas that otherwise would not belong to them. Although the characterizations may be presented as "natural," or unchanging essences already determined by the very existence of particular locations, they are dynamic rather than fixed. Consequently, Harlem is read as "jungle," not to determine accurately who is illegally pilfering power from ML&P, but to maintain the illusion of definitive boundaries and therefore the semblance of absolute control through the metaphor of containment. "Very often," Massey writes, "moreover, that intrinsic nature [of place] is seen as eternal, unchanging. And even where change is acknowledged, this approach often views the 'essence of place' as having evolved through a history which is read as a sense, an internal history" (11). If the narrator is African American and he lives outside the "jungle," then he challenges the logic embodied in the establishment of boundaries. However, it is the narrator's claim to invisibility that sets the ruse into action.

Motion is, of course, the primary directive of the novel: "Keep that nigger boy running." This directive sets the narrator in motion. Jerry Gafio Watts quotes Albert Murray saying, "'Improvisation,' Murray tells us 'is the ultimate human (i.e. heroic) endowment.' The blues-oriented hero is a matter of improvisation" (58). The narrator is such a blues hero, although the characterization is conflicted. By the end of the novel, he is claiming, "I would have to move them [Harlem] without myself being moved" (507). This sentiment echoes one he heard earlier from Jim Trueblood—"I had to move without movin'" (59). The narrator returns to that sentiment, derived from Trueblood's immoral rape and impregnation of his daughter alongside the legitimate impregnation of his wife. He tries to employ the sharecropper's blues logic in the environment of the ever-changing city. But the narrator cannot perform his way out of the blues paradox of the Harlem riot. His world has become one of sight, not invisibility, which illuminates rather than obscures the mechanisms that operate to maintain place. So Trueblood's solution to his perverse situation is thwarted in the narrator's relationship to Harlem. He cannot employ the blues strategy, so he is both physically and emotionally moved.

Another aspect of the home life captured in this revision of Trueblood's blues must not be overlooked. Jim Trueblood's blues reappear in the language of the protagonist, sanitized of the female body, that reminds us of the high stakes involved in blues production. Kate and Matty Lou are not accommodated by the narrator's blues sentiment, or more precisely, they are used and discarded. The black (home) place is subsumed within the more attractive figure of the pregnant black woman even as the woman is effaced by her womb. The slave cabin does not endure in the narrator's revision of Trueblood's blues—it has fallen away during the migration to the Northern city—and the "human stock ... degenerates." From the outset, the narrator has been trying to get home—first back to the South, then to Mary's—and finally he finds himself underground. "I was in strange territory now and someone, for some reason, had removed the manhole cover and I felt myself plunge down, down ... and I lay in the black dark ... no longer running, hiding or concerned" (565). The womb reappears as a manhole, in Baker's terminology, "an irresistible attractive force" drawing all things into itself. This is indeed a black hole: "I tried to reach above me but found only space, unbroken and impenetrable" (567).

It would be nearly twenty years before Toni Morrison offered another vantage from which to view this impoverished black (home) place and its impact upon family life by introducing Pecola Breedlove in *The Bluest Eye*. In *Inspiriting Influences*, Michael Awkward reads Pecola, who suffers rape by her father, as a feminist revision of Matty Lou. I will discuss Pecola and the relationship incest has to the place of home further in the next chapter. The external specter of the city that haunts the migrants' early encounters in Wright's and Ellison's works is not the focus for Morrison in *The Bluest Eye*. While the male authors choose to focus on the confrontation between races that implicates the city, paying little deliberate attention to gender, home for this female author tends to read more specifically as the built physical structure. Yet, even as Morrison looks to the dynamics of a more intimate sphere, she records evidence of a devastating conflict that has the potential to destroy the quality of her characters' lives. The protagonist is threatened by directives issued from home that characterize human action and behavior as either legitimate or illegitimate. The city seems to fall away as we move further inside the built structure of home. Kitchens become the focal point in *The Bluest Eye*, before we again are pulled tragically into the womb.

Notes

1. Baker's reading of this scene in *Blues Ideology* ignited a firestorm among African American feminist critics because he suggests:

Only the Trueblood encounter reveals the phallus as producing Afro-American generations rather than wasting its seed upon the water. The cosmic force of the phallus thus becomes, in the ritual action of the Trueblood episode, symbolic of a type of royal paternity, an aristocratic procreativity turned inward to ensure the royalty (the "truth," "legitimacy," or "authenticity") of an enduring black line of descent (183).

Baker argues that Trueblood's union with his daughter produces a royal lineage, and thus Matty Lou becomes the source who ensures a black line through the act of rape by her own father. The phallus is supreme and compassion for the daughter is sublimated by the dominance of patrimony.

2. John Bardi of Pennsylvania State University, Mont Alto, performed a witty, philosophical interpretation of three musical forms at the "Blues Traditions: Memory, Criticism, and Pedagogy" conference at Pennsylvania State University in June 2000. His performance on electric guitar read music as a metaphor for political systems. He presented a baroque piece as "exclusive"—any notes from outside the classical scale are banished from the "kingdom" by the resolution of the piece. An avant-garde piece represented a chaotic and unstable government, while the blues successfully presented a system that afforded both order and inclusiveness.

3. Such practices can be seen throughout the American landscape as African Americans lay claim to the territory and structures they inhabit. Containers like gourds, jugs, and bottles are often hung from trees or set on porches near doorways to both guard and mark the home. The blues is another such container. Like the bottle trees that appear as a distinctly African American aesthetic practice, the blues plays a significant role in maintaining Mary's home ground. Robert Farris Thompson explains such cultural practices in "Bighearted Power: Kongo Presence in the Landscape and Art of Black America" (in Grey Gundaker, ed., *Keep Your Head to the Sky: Interpreting African American Home Ground* [Charlottesville: University Press of Virginia, 1998]):

> The *nkisi* tradition, brought to the United States from Kongo and Angola by Gullah Jack and other legendary healers, was a matter of embedding spirits in earths, keeping the spirit in a container to concentrate its power, and including with these earths material signs which told the spirit what to do. The gist of those expressions are seemingly regained in a creole art wherein the house guards the spirit of the owner and the icons in the yard guard or enhance that spirit with gestures of protection and enrichment.

A collection of *minkinsi* figures were featured in an exhibition at the Smithsonian as an introduction to a show featuring art by sculptor Renee Stout. At the entrance to the exhibition were these figures and a prominent sign explaining their presence and significance. The sign explained that the English language has no direct parallel for the word "*minkinsi.*" "*Minkinsi* are fabricated things, yet they can be invoked to produce desired effects, they have a will of their own, and they may willfully command the behavior of human beings . . . people depend on *minkinsi* to do things for them, even to make life itself possible" (quoted in Wyatt Macaffey and Michael D. Harris, *Astonishment and Power: The Eyes of Understanding and the Art of Renee Stout* [Washington, D.C.: The Smithsonian Institution Press, 1993], 13).

4. For a comprehensive examination of the image of Harlem in literature
see James De Jongh, *Vicious Modernism: Black Harlem and the Literary Imagination*
(Cambridge: Cambridge University Press, 1990).

5. Ellison romanticizes this site by imagining a disembodied womb wherein
his protagonist can hibernate only to emerge, some time later, renewed. In chapter
4, "She's a Brick House," about *Corregidora*, I deal with the futility of the gesture as
well as some of its gendered implications.

Works Cited

Anzaldúa, Gloria. *Borderlands/La Frontera: The New Mestiza*. San Francisco: Spinters-Aunt
    Lute, 1987.
Faulkner, William. *Go Down, Moses*. New York: Vintage, 1940.
Gundaker, Grey, ed. *Keep Your Head to the Sky: Interpreting African American Home Ground*.
    Charlottesville: University Press of Virginia, 1999.
Griffin, Farah. *"Who Set You Flowin'?": The African-American Migration Narrative*. New York:
    Oxford University Press, 1995.
Massey, Doreen. "Double Articulation: A Place in the World." In Angelika Bammer, ed.,
    Displacements: Cultural Identities in Question. Bloomington: Indiana University Press,
    1994, 110–21.
Ostendorf, Berndt. "Ralph Waldo Ellison: Anthropology, Modernism, and Jazz." In Robert
    O'Meally, ed., *New Essays on* Invisible Man. New York: Cambridge University Press,
    1988, 95–121.
Scarry, Elaine. *The Body in Pain: The Making and the Unmaking of the World*. New York:
    Oxford University Press, 1985.
Watts, Jerry Gafio. *Heroism and the Black Intellectual: Ralph Ellison, Politics, and Afro-American
    Intellectual Life*. Chapel Hill: University of North Carolina Press, 1994.
Wright, John S. "The Conscious Hero and the Rites of Man: Ellison's War." In Robert
    O'Meally, ed., *New Essays on* Invisible Man. New York: Cambridge University Press,
    1988, 157–86.
Wright, Richard. *12 Million Black Voices*. New York: Thunder's Mouth Press, 1941.

TUIRE VALKEAKARI

Secular Riffs on the Sacred: Ralph Ellison's Mock-Messianic Discourse in Invisible Man

I am come a light into the world. . . . I am the way, the truth, and the life.
John 12:46; 14:6

The truth is the light and light is the truth.
Ralph Ellison, *Invisible Man*

[T]hat's allusion, that's riffing. . . . Placed in the right context and at the optimum stage of an action, it vibrates and becomes symbolically eloquent.
Ralph Ellison, "The Essential Ellison"

Ralph Ellison's unfinished second novel, *Juneteenth*—his notoriously prolonged work-in-progress that was finally published posthumously, in heavily edited form, in 1999—highlights the role of Christianity and religious discourse in his literary imagination. Before *Juneteenth*'s publication, commenting on religion in Ellison's fiction tended to elicit the reaction, "What religion?" (to echo Claudia Tate's sardonic 1987 remark that early analyses of women in Ellison's first novel, *Invisible Man*, were typically greeted with the response, "What women?").[1] *Juneteenth*, with its cultural context, is likely to revive critical interest in Ellison's creative use of religious idiom and imagery.[2] Drawing on the rhetoric and practices of black Baptist communities, the novel recounts the story of the brief reunion of a prodigal son—a

From *Religious Idiom and the African American Novel, 1952–1998.* ©2007 by Tuire Valkeakari.

173

conservative, black-baiting New England senator—with his adopted father, an African American preacher who raised the white-looking boy (of indefinite racial origin) in the black South. The social and cultural matrix of black Baptist Christianity frames and informs the two protagonists' respective processes of remembrance as they reconstruct their individual and shared histories during their difficult but necessary encounter after a separation of several decades.

This chapter responds to the powerful presence of black Christianity in *Juneteenth* by showing that religious idiom also plays an intriguing role in *Invisible Man* (1952), a secular novel that investigates the complex interrelationships between black identity, responsibility, self-empowerment, and (self-) sacrifice in the 1930s/40s United States (particularly in the urban North) and explores the interconnectedness of black and white American lives and destinies. *Invisible Man* contains a number of intertextual networks that Ellison wove into his text to enhance both the tragic power and the hilarious playfulness of his narrative. One aspect of this allusive play consists of evoking religious images and tropes, of rearranging them into new patterns, and of using them for purposes of social commentary and artistic innovation. In most instances, Ellison's religious references are quick and brief. His passing (but recurring) riffs on religious idiom and imagery in *Invisible Man* may therefore initially seem to resist any kind of logic, mundane or mythical. Yet, they are ultimately part of his more comprehensive project of "improvising America"[3]—here, of composing a jazz-influenced blues narrative about "America" and "race."

In connection with Ellison, such concepts as "improvisation" and "riffing" immediately bring to mind jazz aesthetics. Inspired by Ellison's comment on allusiveness as riffing (quoted in the third epigraph to this chapter), the literary critic Mark Busby writes: "Riffing is a jazz technique where an artist improvises upon another artist's musical leitmotif until it takes new shapes and creates new sounds. In this way the artist achieves the presentness of the past."[4] Busby's concise and insightful definition of riffing closely resembles Henry Louis Gates Jr.'s discussion of the term "Signifyin(g)" (addressed in the prologue to this book), a concept elaborating on the nature of African American literary intertextuality. The kinship between riffing and Signifyin(g) hardly comes as a surprise; most creators, performers, and students of African American music know intimately the concepts (or, in any case, the actual phenomena) of signifying and Signifyin(g). Gates indicates as much when he refers, in *The Signifying Monkey*, to such jazz compositions as Count Basie's "Signify" and Oscar Peterson's "Signifying," both of which are "structured around the idea of formal revision and implication."[5] In *The Power of Black Music* (1995), the musicologist Samuel A. Floyd Jr. aptly translates Signifyin(g) as "commenting."[6] Floyd's translation, simple as it is, captures the quintessential—as does his longer definition, which addresses music but fully applies to literary Signifyin(g) as well:

> [M]usical Signifyin(g) is troping: the transformation of preexisting musical material by trifling with it, teasing it, or censuring it. Musical Signifyin(g) is the rhetorical use of preexisting material as a means of demonstrating respect for or poking fun at a musical style, process, or practice through parody, pastiche, implication, indirection, humor, tone play or word play, the illusion of speech or narration, or other troping mechanisms.[7]

In *Invisible Man*, Ellison plays with Judeo-Christian idiom in ways suggested by Gates's and Floyd's definitions of Signifyin(g). Ellison was a writer deeply immersed in the world of music, and the Signifyin(g) strategies characterizing his first novel echo improvisation and modification techniques used in jazz and the blues. Musically inspired (simultaneously free and controlled) improvisation informs Ellison's play with Judeo-Christian imagery as he riffs on religion, or Signifies on the sacred, in *Invisible Man*, a secular novel about the complexity of socially and individually responsible black action in the pre–civil rights United States.

The Tropes of the Scapegoat and the Messiah/Christ

Among the Judeo-Christian elements on which Ellison riffs in *Invisible Man* are the tropes of the scapegoat and, relatedly, the Messiah/Christ. While by no means solely an African American device, the subversion of messianic and christological discourse is one of the most prevalent ways of bending religious idiom in black American literature. One only needs to think, for example, of early-twentieth-century African American writers' development of the Black Christ trope (discussed in chapter 1), the miraculous ending of Bukka Doopeyduk's three-day suffering on the third day's night in Ishmael Reed's *The Freelance Pallbearers* (1967), the Christic transformation of a sacrificed pig in Paule Marshall's *The Chosen Place, the Timeless People* (1969), the frequent surfacings of christological images in Toni Morrison's novels, the birth of the young Ethiopian Mariams child at the end of Gloria Naylor's *Bailey's Cafe* (1992), or Senator Sunraider's cry, "Lord, LAWD, WHY HAST THOU . . . ?" in Ellison's *Juneteenth*.

The frequent use of the christological trope in African American literature can be explained, at least in part, by the historical connection between the ancient Hebrew scapegoat rite and Christian messianism/christology. The original scapegoat rite—the celebration of the Day of Atonement, or Yom

Kippur, described in Leviticus 16—consisted of two stages: the sins of the salvation-seeking community were at first ritually projected onto a sacrificial goat, and the "sin-laden" animal was then expelled from the midst of those thus delivered from their sins. In other words, the scapegoat bore the community's burden of guilt and was then killed or driven away. Christians know this logic very well, because the idea of sacrificial scapegoating was later famously revived and reinterpreted in the Christian doctrine of the vicarious sacrifice of Christ. The Christian view of the Messiah/Christ not only as a mighty savior and a leader of his people but also as a suffering scapegoat has particular resonance for African Americans, who are all too familiar with what Ellison calls "the [sociocultural] designation of the Negro as national scapegoat."[8] While the scapegoating of black Americans has historically found its most violent manifestations in racially motivated lynchings,[9] the presence of this phenomenon continues to be felt in the sociopolitical climate of the United States in subtler, more modified ways.[10]

Invisible Man, a fiercely ironic and parodic text, makes use of both aspects of the duality inherent in messianic imagery: the novel portrays scapegoats, including lynchees, as well as ironically evokes the notion of messianic leadership. True, not every single one of Ellison's "Messiahs" is both a leader and a scapegoat, nor do all of his scapegoats represent pure examples of the two-phased process of scapegoating described above; yet, his play with these tropes in his modern(ist) migration narrative clearly reveals his familiarity with their ancient origins. In Invisible Man, Ellison harnesses the culturally powerful discourses of messianism and scapegoating for his own purposes, in order to enhance the literary and political force of his secular blues narrative about the complex dialectic of hope and disillusionment in the life of a young southern black migrant (hereafter called "the narrator") in New York City in the era/wake of the Great Depression.

A Crowd of Messiahs

Invisible Man's first six-and-a-half chapters, the prologue excluded, take place in the South, where the narrator, a scholarship grantee, attends a black college. One of the novel's "Messiahs" is the college's Founder, who, as critics have observed, resembles Booker T. Washington as much as the campus resembles Tuskegee. (Neither is an exact copy of the original, and the narrative explicitly distinguishes the Founder from Washington; yet, the disguises are thin.) The Founder's legend and legacy are kept alive in the school through a determinedly cultivated oral tradition that blends Christian devotion with secular hero worship. When the Reverend Homer Barbee, a revered African American preacher from Chicago, visits the campus and delivers a speech at a "Founders' Day" celebration, he fittingly calls the school a "shrine" (*IM* 93). At the narrative's parodic level, this seemingly innocent shorthand for a "shrine of knowledge" suggests a shrine dedicated to the excessive worship of the Founder. The school tradition projects the Founder as a semi-God, a Messiah who rescued his people from the darkness of ignorance. When Barbee addresses his audience—faculty, students, and patrons—in the college chapel, he, accordingly, not only presents the Founder as a "black Aristotle" and a Moses but also calls him "a humble prophet, lowly like the humble carpenter of Nazareth," and refers to his death as the "setting of this glorious *son* of the morning" (*IM* 92, 93, 96; italics added).[11] Christological allusions do not end here; the eloquent orator unabashedly goes as far as to apply the New Testament exhortation that Christians identify with Christ (in particular, with his suffering and resurrection) to the identification with the Founder expected of the "congregation" (*IM* 94–95). Barbee openly manipulates his listeners' emotions and cleverly justifies his calculating stagecraft by pointing out that the Founder, the adored role model, also used to "hold[] the audience within the gentle palm of his eloquence, rocking it, soothing it, instructing it" while giving public speeches (*IM* 96).

However, although Barbee may know, as Hortense Spillers writes, how to play with "both a generalized poetic diction and the prose of King James,"[12] such oratorical skills do not save his christological commemoration of the Founder from becoming a tragicomic (and, in the final analysis, a pathetic) spectacle. The homily is "mocked by time and reality in the very process," as Ellison mentions in his private working notes,[13] because Barbee so hyperbolically attributes divine qualities to a mortal being during his cult-like attempt to put the audience into a Founder-adoring trance. Rather than endorsing this oratorical extravaganza, the narrative ironically portrays Barbee as going totally overboard: at the end of his speech, he literally falls from the speaker's platform—and from grace. At its most immediate level, the fall is caused by the pompous orator's physical blindness, as befits Ellison's mock-Homeric portrait of *Homer* Barbee. Ultimately, this imagery—focusing on a covered but all the more acute lack of (in)sight and direction—accentuates Tuskegee-educated Ellison's criticism of the accommodationist aspects of the pedagogical and political thought of the real-life Booker T. Washington.[14]

However, merciless as his assessment of the cult of the Founder may be, Ellison also carefully includes in his portrait of the college a crucially complicating factor: the accountability of the African American professors and administrators to a host of powerful white cofounders and trustees. This configuration of dependence, from which the black pedagogues cannot opt out without bankrupting the school, inevitably affects their policies and severely limits their options. It is no coincidence that another "Savior," in addition to the Founder, whom the reader encounters in the novel's early chapters, is the wealthy Bostonian liberal Mr. Norton, one of the college's chief benefactors, "forty years a bearer of the white man's burden" (*IM* 29).

In the spring of the narrator's junior year, the "Messiah" Norton makes a parodic journey to the underworld that begins with his descent from North to South for the same Founders' Day celebration during which Barbee delivers his memorable speech. The narrator acts as Norton's guide and driver on a sightseeing tour to the countryside. A penniless student, the inexperienced young man sees the pink-faced, wealthy donor as a St. Nicholas figure, a saint-like provider of presents (although his retrospective narration, of course, ridicules this initial perception). The narrator's boundless eagerness to please the influential patron during the trip is motivated by a hope of gifts—"Perhaps he'd give me a large tip, or a suit, or a scholarship next year" (*IM* 30)— or, to echo the same chapter's later mock-messianic discourse, by a hope of "redemption" in the form of deliverance from financial distress.

Although the narrator's project of calculated adulation begins promisingly, his luck soon starts to turn sour. Norton, a classic imperialistic explorer of the exotic, wants to stop at what used to be a slave quarter—an old, run-down cabin in a poverty-ridden area that contrasts sharply with the idyllic campus. There Norton initiates a discussion with Trueblood, a sexually errant black sharecropper whose wife *and* teenage daughter both are, as all locals seem to know, pregnant by him. While the famous Trueblood episode primarily ridicules Norton's self-righteous "slumming," it also provides a rich example of Ellison's ironic riffing on biblically derived images—that is, of his strategy of evoking ancient tropes to offer sharp social and political commentary on the contemporary. Trueblood, most pivotally, epitomizes the trope of the scapegoat and, at the same time, represents a highly parodic modification of it:[15] in the local constellation of black–white relations, Trueblood's role is to embody whites' traditional negative expectations of poverty-ridden African Americans—to be a "confirmer of their [whites'] misconceptions," as the narrator later says of himself (*IM* 384). In the novel's South, those holding such misconceptions project the "first cause" of black poverty on African Americans themselves, rather than wanting to look into the racially configured history, power structures, and economic organization of the United States. Trueblood fulfills his prescribed role (his function as a modified scapegoat who "deserves" the blame projected on him) so splendidly that the white community, in return, rewards his performance generously, instead of expelling him from the locality. As Trueblood himself "innocently" says in a passage where Ellison's racial/social irony cuts particularly deep: "That's what I don't understand. I done the worse thing a man could ever do in his family and instead of chasin' me out of the county, they gimme more help than they ever give any other colored man, no matter how good a nigguh he was" (*IM* 52). Trueblood's presence in the margins of the dominant community helps the local whites to preserve the conceptual categories that enable them to define themselves as superior, whereas the college-affiliated black professionals implicitly challenge those categories and thus "need" to be kept in their place through Washingtonian accommodationism. It is therefore only logical that the whites reward Trueblood for his behavior—the scapegoat rite being, after all, a strategy whereby a community maintains or restores the status quo and asserts the continuity of its way of life.

The exchange between Trueblood and Norton offers an excellent example of Ellison's parodic play with the logic of sacred rites in *Invisible Man*. A religious ritual can generally be described as a symbolic repetition of, and participation in, an "original event." At the core of the "rite" portrayed in the Trueblood episode is Norton's involuntary, yet all the more intense, vicarious participation in Trueblood's incestuous transgression (here, the "original event") that resulted in his young daughter's pregnancy. While listening to the sharecropper's uninhibited confession of his "sinnin'" (*IM* 46), Norton, too, loses control (just as Trueblood once did), albeit in a modified manner: entranced by Trueblood's folkloric storytelling performance (a verbal variation of the blues, as Houston A. Baker Jr. has famously stressed),[16] Norton finds himself descending into the depths of his own illegitimate and repressed sexual craving, namely, his forbidden desire for his own late, adored daughter.[17] Invisible as this vicarious "act" is, Norton's total exhaustion after the story reflects (in keeping with the ritualistic logic of participation) his "postcoital" fatigue. Moreover, his weariness discloses his shocked recognition that he is, in fact, a secret sharer in Trueblood's crime. Although the blue-veined Bostonian's racially, regionally, and economically configured worldview prevents him from placing himself on the same moral footing with a poverty-ridden black southern sharecropper, Norton nevertheless gradually realizes, as the blues confession unfolds, that at some level he is listening to a story about himself; hence his paralyzing panic attack. A mirror has been placed in front of him, and suddenly his white self and the black Other no longer seem separate (or different, or split) the way they, in his view, should.

As Norton unsuccessfully attempts to cope with this cognitive dissonance, the exchange between the two men develops into Trueblood's "blues ministry"—his act of officiating at a peculiar, carnivalesque rite that momentarily reverses, in Rabelaisian fashion, the social and racial power relations that would normally prevail between the two men and determine their interaction. While reciting the story of his past loss of control, the relaxed and self-confident Trueblood (who, aware of the power dynamics of the situation, is thoroughly enjoying the moment) exercises total control over his white listener. During the ceremony, the confessor Trueblood becomes, parodically speaking, a cantor or priest. As he performs his rehearsed and routined canticle/oration, his voice "tak[es] on a deep, incantatory quality," and when he finishes, his call initiates a response: "Out in the yard a woman's hoarse contralto intoned a hymn" (*IM* 42, 52). Confronted with a baffling blend of the unknown and the all too familiar, the Savior Norton totally loses his script. The blues priest Trueblood retains his strength, whereas the confused and stunned Messiah Norton is drained of all vitality; there is no "true blood" in the wealthy Bostonian, aristocratic as his blood lineage may be, Ellison's narrative implies.

A witness to the white patron's psychological breakdown and defeat, the perplexed and frightened narrator becomes anxious about the consequences of this unexpected turn of events for himself. He drives the fatigued Norton to a local bar for a drink, desperately trying to make up for the "damage" done at Trueblood's cabin. (As Ellison explains in his working notes, "The boy would appease the gods; it costs him much pain to discover that he can satisfy the gods only by rebelling against them.")[18] He is, however, out of luck: the bar, named the Golden Day, happens to be crowded with shell-shocked African American veterans of World War I—patients of a nearby mental asylum. The events that follow, further developing the Trueblood episode's carnivalesque reversal of prevailing power relations, are torture for the protagonist but hilarious for the reader. The Golden Day becomes the setting for an explicit and public (mock-)recognition of Norton as Messiah, portrayed as a casual nonevent in a chaotic world where rules of normalcy do not apply: at a tragicomically anticlimactic key moment, one of the veterans brings the pale and practically unconscious Norton a chair, saying, "Here's a chair for the Messiah" (*IM* 60). The absurd humor of the scene lies in the down-to-earth ease with which the veteran receives his "savior," kindly offering the totally helpless Norton a seat in a setting that serves, not insignificantly, as a symbol for religion's decline: the building (originally a church, a sacred space) was first transformed into a bank, then a restaurant and gambling house, at one point possibly even a prison, and finally a bar and brothel (*IM* 61–62).

After this memorable reception, the black southern veterans—forgotten and invisible men in the eyes of the mainstream society—mercilessly and perceptively disclose the self-serving motives that underlie the "noble" white northerner's philanthropy. One of the men, a seasoned observer of how a racialized society works, without hesitation articulates the true nature of the relationship between narrator and Norton, deliberately verbalizing his observations in front of the younger black man who is temporarily dazzled by his personal encounter with white privilege and wealth: "To you [Norton] he [the narrator] is a mark on the score-card of your achievement, a thing and not a man" (*IM* 73). At the same time, this veteran recognizes that the actions of the narrator, an inexperienced youth eager to please, are motivated by an opportunistic desire for material gain and reward: "And you [Norton], for all your power, are not a man to him [the narrator], but a God, a force—" (*IM* 73). Though one of the allegedly "insane," this veteran is one of the few who utter true words of wisdom in a novel that utilizes empty, manipulative speechifying as one of its most pivotal narrative devices. The man sees, without difficulty, that societally imposed and individually internalized power relations overdetermine the interaction between the white "benefactor" and the black college student and cause each to perceive the other as an exploitable object. Blind to this logic, Norton is a false Messiah, despite his status as an incarnation of "the Great Traditions" (*IM* 29). Since Norton also functions as a significant link in the chain of people and events that eventually render the narrator invisible, the infamous "offending eye" that Norton initially wants to attribute to Trueblood is ultimately his own (*IM* 40; Mark 9:47).

When Norton and the narrator eventually return to campus, the school administration forces the narrator into the classic role of a scapegoat and subjects him to the two-phased scapegoating rite: all blame for the "failed" excursion and Norton's slight injury is projected onto the young man, and he is then expelled from the college. The executor of this "rite," the college president Dr. Bledsoe, ostensibly performs an act of personal sacrifice by letting one of his star students go in order to save the college's good reputation. However, the hypocrisy of the Janus-faced leader is inscribed in his very name, which suggests implausible excess—"bled so."[19]

Purged from the midst of the "righteous" (as the logic of the original scapegoat rite would have it, "righteous" meaning, among other things, "sinless"), the narrator moves north and ends up in Harlem. Mock-christological figures continue to people the narrative: in New York City, the narrator encounters black Messiahs who constitute a peculiar reaction to the challenges of African American urbanization and modernization. Milton Sernett notes that the "absence of a Moses at the head of the refugee column during the Great Migration" led black migrants to "gravitate[] toward new messiahs in the North";[20] he quotes Ira De A. Reid's estimate that in 1926 black Harlem was home to more than 140 churches.[21] By the time Ellison's fictional narrator moves to New York, the figure has become even more impressive: *Invisible Man* mentions Harlem's "two hundred churches" (*IM* 344). These numbers point to the intense religious turmoil, tension, and spiritual enterprise characterizing the black metropolis that Ellison's novel portrays.

The rebellious and violent activities of Ras the Exhorter/Destroyer are *Invisible Man*'s most obvious example of what Ellison once, less than respectfully, called "hysterical [that is, cultlike] forms of religion."[22] Ras is a West

Indian religious leader inclined to rebellion and violence, an urban Messiah who identifies with the messianic thought of Ethiopianism,[23] whereas the protean Rinehart—who skillfully and successfully alternates between the roles of "Rine the runner and Rine the gambler and Rine the briber and Rine the lover and Rinehart the Reverend" (IM 376)—is a different example of a self-styled black Messiah. In "Change the Joke and Slip the Yoke" (1958), Ellison ironically associates the following messianic images with Rinehart: "[H]e is godlike, in that he brings new techniques—electric guitars etc.—to the service of God, and in that there are many men in his image while he is himself unseen; . . . as a numbers runner he is a bringer of manna and a worker of miracles, in that he transforms (for winners, of course) pennies into dollars, and thus he feeds (and feeds on) the poor."[24] As Ellison's irony implies, the movement that Rinehart leads is a fake church—an opportunistic project exploiting black migrants from the rural South who have, in a modern urban environment, lost the "semblance of metaphysical wholeness" previously provided by the "old time religion."[25] Craving for a sense of security, belonging, and purpose, some of these first-generation Harlemites turn to Rinehart, seduced by his apparent ability to mix the "authentic" old with the exciting new—only to eventually find out, after dutifully paying their tithes for a shorter or longer period of time, that his church represents a variety of spirituality that is mere "rind" without a "heart" (see IM 376).

Most importantly, the fluid, ever-changing Rinehart epitomizes Invisible Man's exploration of the elusive concept of African American identity. The novel is set at a time when, in Ellison's phrase, black American life's "tempo of development from the feudal-folk forms of the South to the industrial urban forms of the North is so rapid that it throws up personalities as fluid and changeable as molten metal rendered iridescent from the effect of cooling air."[26] No wonder then that the narrator—a young, chronically perplexed migrant searching for a viable way of life in the simultaneously attractive and intimidating New York City—temporarily finds Rinehart an appealing role model. Although the narrator effortlessly deems the violent example of the fanatic Ras undesirable, Rinehart—a constant fitter of new masks and, in Ellison's words, an "American virtuoso of identity who thrives on chaos and swift change"[27]—momentarily offers him a revelation-like insight into how he could follow his late grandfather's advice and overcome the powerful whites of his new environment by "yessing" them to death (IM 388). Ultimately, however, Rinehart's example of a multiple masquerade and endless plotting results, for the narrator, in yet another failed attempt at social salvation (understood here as a meaningful and implementable interpretation of "social responsibility"). Even after his decision to "do a Rinehart" (IM 383), the narrator's life continues to be one long actualization of his pre-college nightmare in which mainstream society always kept him "running" (*IM* 26)—that is, in a constant state of flight and fear.

In addition to portraying the Founder, Norton, Ras, and Rinehart as (mock-)messianic figures, Ellison also inserts christological allusions into his characterization of Tod Clifton.[28] Tod—a Black Christ figure whom even Ras once calls, in a reluctantly admiring tone, a "king" and "prince" (*IM* 281)—becomes a victim of racial violence, shot dead by the police in broad daylight in Harlem. His funeral evolves into a mass event attended by a large crowd of Harlemites who are shocked and outraged by his violent death. At the funeral, the narrator (at this point of the novel, a seasoned public speaker) gives a speech—an embittered oration delivered by a skeptic to a group of disappointed and confused disciples. His unexpectedly uninspiring antisermon reveals his growing frustration with messianic configurations: the narrator attempts to dissociate Tod's dead body from any scene of social messianism and sardonically disparages the audience's need to see Tod (German for "death," as critics have been quick to note) as "our hope" (*IM* 340). Like Homer Barbee in an earlier scene, the narrator here evokes the image of Christians being buried with Christ, but this time the disillusioned and directionless orator empties this biblically charged language of any hope of resurrection:

> His name was Clifton, Tod Clifton, and, like any man, he was born of woman to live awhile and fall and die [cf. Job 14:1]. So that's his tale to the minute. His name was Clifton and for a while he lived among us and aroused a few hopes in the young manhood of man, and we who knew him loved him and he died. . . . Now he's in this box with the bolts tightened down. *He's in the box and we're in there with him,* and when I've told you this you can go. It's dark in this box and it's crowded. . . . In a few hours Tod Clifton will be cold bones in the ground. And don't be fooled, for *these bones shall not rise again. You and I will still be in the box.* (*IM* 344, 346; italics added)

Yet, frustrated as he is with the determined desire of Tod's mourners to grieve over a dead savior, the narrator cannot but acknowledge, however mockingly, Tod's posthumous significance for the black community of New York City when he sees Harlem in flames during the violent race riot that follows the funeral. A modified profession of "faith" flashes through the narrator's brain as he witnesses how a group of Harlemites "cast down their buckets where they are" in a manner that he could never have envisioned when he, at the novel's beginning, delivered his very first "Atlanta

Compromise"—echoing speech: as he now watches rioters fill zinc buckets with kerosene and use the oil to start a fire in a dilapidated tenement building unsuitable for human habitation, the narrator sarcastically thinks to himself: "A holy holiday for Clifton" (*IM* 411). This mock-recognition of Tod's "holiness" or "divinity," prompted by a violent chaos, alludes to the centurion's acknowledgment of the divinity of Jesus in Matthew 27:54, where the Roman commander's profession of faith is inspired by violent and terrifying events in the aftermath of Jesus' death. In the biblical passage, however, the aftermath consists of "acts of God," such as an earthquake, instead of human activity. In Ellison's novel, the decisive acts are emphatically human—and, humanly enough, they totally spin out of anyone's control as black urban disaffection manifests itself on the streets of Harlem in the wake of a Black Christ's death at the hands of white authorities.

In *Invisible Man*, Tod epitomizes the problems and illusions inherent in elevating a single individual to the status of an incarnation of the promise of social salvation. The aftermath of Tod's death therefore leads, even at the level of the plot, to a thorough and explicit discussion of manipulation, leadership, victimization, and the meaning of "sacrifice" (see below). That discussion focuses on the narrator's person and personae and thus implies that mock-messianic references also inform Ellison's design of the narrator-protagonist, not just of such figures as the Founder, Norton, Ras, Rinehart, and Tod.[29] Indeed, while recounting the story of his life, the narrator not only retrospectively ridicules his narrative's *other* messianic candidates but also applies mock-christological language to *himself*. In the prologue, for example, he riffs on such statements of Jesus as "I am the light of the world" and "I am the way, the truth, and the life"—sarcastically playing with the words "light" and "truth" (as this chapter's first two epigraphs show) while preparing his readers for the story of his complex search for identity and community.[30] Mock-messianic rhetoric also flavors his discourse as he describes his transformation from an orator—a "Messiah" who is a public speaker and attracts crowds with his oratorical skills—to an author, a retiree from public life who writes his "memoir" (Ellison's term) underground.[31] The rest of this chapter amplifies these points by reconstructing the narrator's mock-messianic self-portrait and by showing how this portrait links up with his conversion from orator to author.

The Narrator as Messiah

When the narrator leaves the South after being expelled from the college, he sees a snake that signifies his (a parodic new Adam's) tragic expulsion from Eden.[32] However, although he has recently seen an apple on Trueblood's doorstep (*IM* 42) and has involuntarily tasted "forbidden" social knowledge

while giving Norton a tour of the college's surroundings, he is not yet genuinely free of prelapsarian innocence and ignorance. His encounter with the
white patron, with all its ramifications, should have been an eye-opening
experience, but the young man still gullibly believes that the seven sealed
letters of reference from Dr. Bledsoe will guarantee him a glorious future in
the North. Boldly presuming that he will need no further allies from down
home, the narrator (a future "Messiah") in a tragicomic reversal of a biblical pattern even arrogantly denies "Peter" (namely, Pete Wheatstraw, who
epitomizes folklore and the rural blues and thus makes the narrator uncomfortably aware of his own "premodern" roots) on one of his first, euphoric
days in New York City. However, his naive faith in the magic of the sealed
envelopes soon proves misguided. Once the seventh seal is broken, the narrator faces a private apocalypse, a revelation of his true condition: he is on
his own in a hostile environment where, despite city life's apparent focus on
the present, recommendations from the past dictate one's future.

The narrator's optimistic ascent to the North is followed by a humiliating
odyssey into the underworld, a nightmarish paint factory resembling the hell-
ish workplace in Charlie Chaplin's *Modern Times*.[33] As Mark Busby writes,
"By having the narrator go down deep into the bowels of Liberty Paints . . . ,
Ellison foreshadows the end of the novel when the narrator will descend
to his underground hole and then arise with Christ-like knowledge."[34] The
novel is indeed structured, as Busby and several other critics have observed, on
patterns of descent and ascent, death and rebirth, and sleep/hibernation and
wakefulness: Ellison both complements and contests his frequent use of the
motif of ascent/rebirth/wakefulness by a dynamic dialectic with its opposite.
This means that in *Invisible Man* every new beginning is pregnant with the
possibility of a new fall, or of a new lapse into a previous—undesirable, unfortunate, or misguided—mode of existence. For example, after his symbolical
rebirth in the factory hospital (ascent), the narrator leaves the factory for good
and enters the subway (descent). One of the first things he sees underground
is "a young platinum blonde nibbl[ing] at a red Delicious apple" (*IM* 190);
the motif of the forbidden fruit prophetically and proleptically suggests the
possibility of another fall and another, deeper descent into the underworld.
(Yet, ambiguity being a crucial component of Ellison's art, the apple motif at
the same time paradoxically suggests that knowledge is desirable and necessary, even if its acquisition may lead to expulsion from Eden—which may not,
after all, be the paradise that one initially anticipated.)

After his rebirth and his train ride underground, the narrator emerges
from the subway dizzy and wobbly, and sees the world through "wild, infant's
eyes" (*IM* 191). The newborn future Messiah (who, like a toddler, can hardly
walk) finds refuge with a woman who is named, as scholars have noted, after

the mother of Christ. The maternal Mary takes the narrator into her motherly care, unselfishly nurtures him back to health, and equips him for the next stage of his journey.

After the narrator has passed through his "messianic" infancy, his search for identity is increasingly depicted through parodic modifications of the King James transcription of the Tetragrammaton (YHWH), "I AM THAT I AM" (Exod. 3:14), interpreted by Jewish and Christian theologies as (being or symbolizing) the name of God.[35] Since this enigmatic divine self-appellation denotes, in Kimberly W. Benston's interpretive translation, "*namelessness, or that which cannot be named,*"[36] it is only fitting that the narrator repeatedly evokes this name—or this anti-name, as it were—to portray his search for a new personal and cultural identity that he is not yet able to define or articulate. Significantly, the narrator appears not only invisible but also nameless to the reader: none of his names is ever revealed to us, as agrees with the processual nature of his individual identity and with the fluidity and elusiveness of African American cultural identity writ large in his new milieu.

True, during his nostalgic yam-eating in Harlem the narrator experiences a temporary—a simultaneously melancholic and affirmative—resurgence of his southern rural selfhood; he articulates this sentiment through a hilarious subversion of the Tetragrammaton, "I yam what I am!" (*IM* 201), which comically echoes the spinach-loving cartoon character Popeye's motto, "I yam what I yam."[37] However, this parodic "self-revelation" only gives the narrator a very short break from the laborious work of pursuing a new self-definition: the last yam he eats is frostbitten and leaves a bad taste in his mouth. In *Invisible Man*, nostalgia, as this anticlimax demonstrates, repeatedly falls short in the face of the challenges of the modern era.

The play with the divine name continues in the eviction scene (discussed in chapter 1) and anticipates the approaching advent of messianic responsibilities in the narrator's life. Here, the narrator's reply to a bystander's inquiry about his name, "Never mind, I am who I am" (*IM* 204), takes on the function of a (mock-)divine self-designation that precedes his first public speech in the North—an appeal supporting the evicted couple's right to be allowed "fifteen minutes of Jesus" in the vacated apartment (*IM* 211). The speech is a success: after some initial caution, the crowd starts to respond to the young speaker's (secularly motivated) call, "as though answering a preacher in a church" (*IM* 210).

Having made a successful debut as a public speaker, the narrator receives a *vocatio externa*: the Brotherhood, a predominantly white leftist organization, persuades him to assume the role of a black Messiah, a proclaimer of the organization's good news in Harlem. Blissfully intoxicated by his success as a public orator, he becomes the political group's loyal member—a Brother with no past and with a new name. While elaborating and bolstering his new identity, he at times suspects, however, that existentially and ideologically he may be, as Benston puts it, "the narrated, not the narrator,"[38] the defined rather than the definer. The version that he now creates of the Tetragrammaton, "I am what they think I am" (*IM* 286), expresses his dawning realization that during his effort to manipulate others for their own "good," he, too, has been manipulated—although it takes him a long time to act on this discovery.

A seed of doubt about the Brotherhood's theory and praxis is initially planted in the narrator's mind at Tod Clifton's funeral, where an old man's spontaneous act of leadership suggests to the younger leader that what he searches and longs for may lie in a connection with history that neither religious nor political organizations can, in themselves, establish (*IM* 342). The actual turning point, however, comes after the funeral, during the heated discussion that Brother Hambro[39] and the narrator have about responsibility, leadership, and sacrifice (*IM* 378–82). Having just encountered (Tod's) death and visited Rinehart's fake church, the narrator—who converted to the Brotherhood's political philosophy after classifying religion as a survival technique of the past—is particularly alert to, and wary of, concepts with religious overtones, such as "sacrifice." Unaware of this circumstance, Hambro bluntly informs him of the Brotherhood's decision to sacrifice its Harlem branch "for the good of the whole" (*IM* 379). The narrator's shock reveals that he managed for a long time to suppress an early warning sign, Brother Jack's remark at his and Jack's first meeting that individuals "don't count" (*IM* 220).

Hambro can only respond to the narrator's stunned objections by posing a patronizing and arrogant rhetorical question: "Would you like to resurrect God to take responsibility?" (*IM* 381). This sarcasm miserably fails to convince the narrator of the "scientific objectivity" of the Brotherhood's decision regarding the fate of its Harlem district. In this scene, which reflects Ellison's disappointment with the American Communism of his day, the narrator begins to conclude that the Brotherhood's message (or at least its contemporary mode of existence and organization) is void of "saving" potential—that is, of the ability to bring about true social change and racial equality. This disillusionment with the Brotherhood in many ways parallels the narrator's earlier disenchantment with religion.

Outraged by the Brotherhood's prioritization of political abstractions over flesh-and-blood Harlemites, the narrator rebels against Hambro's insistence on the alleged necessity of sacrifice by replying, in his capacity as the Harlem branch spokesman, that the black district demands "equality of sacrifice" (*IM* 379).[40] Hambro's revealing response, "some must make greater sacrifices than others," serves as an eye-opener for the narrator: "Here I had thought they accepted me because they felt that color made no difference, when in reality it made no difference because they didn't see either color or men" (*IM* 384). At this key moment, the narrator recognizes his invisibility, his state of not being seen by white society, as his allusive riff on Hamlet demonstrates: "Well, I *was* and yet I was invisible, that was the fundamental contradiction" (*IM* 383; italics in original).

One reason why Hambro's vision is incompatible with the narrator's experience is the white ideologue's scant interest in considering the relationship between leadership and sacrifice from an African American point of view. Hambro fails to recognize the unbearable pressure that his model places on the narrator, a black leader who is expected to be both oppressor and martyr at the same time. In the narrator's words, which articulate the double role of a (parodied) Messiah: "Sacrifice and leadership, I thought. For him it was simple. For *them* it was simple. But hell, I was both. Both sacrificer and victim" (*IM* 382; italics in original).

After taking his leave of Hambro, the disillusioned narrator decides to change his strategy and become an independent agent: motivated by the black cause and his concern for Harlem, he opts for a Rinehartian masquerade whereby he "would hide [his] anger and lull [the Brotherhood's leaders] to sleep" (*IM* 385). He settles, in other words, for acting as a "spy in the enemy's country" (*IM* 13) by making an identity of invisibility and by attempting to see through others while himself remaining unseen.[41] Soon after Tod's funeral, however, the events escalate into a chaotic race riot in which the narrator finds himself performing a role that he did not design. As he feverishly tries to determine what his role in the events leading to the riot has been, he realizes that even his masquerade—ultimately requiring him to sacrifice his personal integrity and to ignore his "sense of violated responsibility" (*IM* 388)—has failed to "save" him from becoming an instrument in the power games of others. This terrifying realization resonates with his late fellow comrade Tod's similar experience of having been, as a Brother, both manipulator and manipulated, both violator and violated, both sacrificer and sacrificed. Shortly before his death, Tod expressed this devastating insight through a tragic (though ostensibly entertaining) street performance that, while saturated with ironic self-loathing, at the same time pointed to the underlying white racist control. Tod's show featured a black Sambo puppet on a black string (a black victim of black manipulation) that Tod himself (a black manipulator) pulled in order to force the doll to dance. Significantly, the string had "a loop tied in the end" (*IM* 337) like a hangman's halter—an allusion to lynching (a most repulsive form of scapegoating and sacrifice) and hence, indirectly, to the white control and "supervision" of black manipulation of black people.

Having reached an absolute dead end, the narrator abandons the imposed, though in many ways attractive, messianic vocation and withdraws from public life in the riot's wake. His true search for social responsibility can only begin when he finally resists the temptation to be a "Messiah," a public speaker who attracts crowds with his oratorical skills. For Jesus, the Messiah of Christianity, "temptation" meant the temptation to leave behind the vocation of the Savior; for the narrator, by contrast, the concept means just the opposite—the temptation to *be* a Messiah, an "orator, a rabble rouser" loved by the public (*IM* 11). During his messianic phase, the narrator manipulated crowds without a convincing message of salvation or hope, offering (not unlike Tod through his Sambo shows) empty performances without a "salvific" content. A retreat into solitude therefore eventually becomes necessary for the manipulated manipulator: he needs time to reflect on his past experiences, to reinvent himself on his own terms, and to create a new, meaningful content for any possible future "performances" in the realm of public life. During his "hibernation," the narrator stops "running," retires to a private space, and writes his memoir. (An explicit mention of the writing process is embedded in the phrase, "So why do I write, torturing myself to put it down?" [*IM* 437].) As he clarifies his identity for himself and his future readers through writing, the narrator thoroughly reevaluates his past actions. Personal and social responsibility, which can be singled out as the novel's key concepts, merge in his (Dostoyevskian) act of writing "notes from underground." By transforming his experiences into a text, the narrator not only undergoes a personal change but also performs an inherently social and political act.

Hibernation, History, Blues Aesthetics, and Resurrection

The mock-messianic aspects of the narrator's self-portrait function, in other words, as an introduction to one of *Invisible Man*'s main themes—the "birth" of an author, or Invisible Man's growth into authorship, or the transformation of a (fictitious) African American orator into a (fictitious) African American writer. As Robert B. Steno points out in *From Behind the Veil* (1979), the narrator "f[i]nd[s] himself in a hole partly as a result of over-privileging the spoken word"; he realizes during his underground existence that "he can extract himself from his circumstance by *writing* himself out of it—perhaps *only* by writing out of it."[42] Yet, crucial as this autobiographical venture is for the reinvention of his individual identity, the narrator nevertheless experiences the writing process as an emotionally cumbersome act of "torturing [him]self" (*IM* 437), because his "authorial" enterprise is not just a private therapeutic effort toward personal healing but also a laborious social commitment. While he previously considered himself as one of the "transitory ones . . . who write no novels, histories or other books" (*IM* 332), the narrator now labors underground to make the African American voice heard through the written word, hoping that his work would at some point lead to social action. "Without the possibility of action," he writes in the epilogue, "all knowledge comes to one labeled 'file and forget'" (IM 437).

The narrator himself "can neither file nor forget" (IM 437). To fully grasp the significance of this phrase for the novel as a whole, it is vital to note that Ellison's thematization of writing in Invisible Man is inextricably linked with his (subtle and brief) thematization of African American repression, far from uncommon in the era depicted in the novel, of the painful history of slavery. In Invisible Man, this repression results not only from the understandable emotional difficulty among African Americans of re-evoking and processing the horrors and humiliations of the past but also, underlyingly, from white underestimation of the significance and magnitude of the centuries-long black contribution to building "America," and from white denial of the persistent presence of slavery-induced racism and racialism in American society. These issues have later been tackled more explicitly by such novels as Toni Morrison's Beloved, but they are also present in Invisible Man—informing, for example, the narrator's ambivalence toward Brother Tarp's leg iron, a reminder of Tarp's nineteen years in a chain gang. Busy creating a new life for himself in a new environment, the narrator wants to focus on the present rather than look for connections between African American history and his own condition. The leg iron, however, a closed link "twisted open and forced partly back into place" (IM 293)—a metaphor for Emancipation and the failure of Reconstruction, as well as for the psychological implications of the two—is an invitation to pursue such connections.[43] The narrator initially considers this gift that he receives from Tarp to be a nuisance; later, however, while fighting Ras and his men during the race riot, he finds himself using the leg chain as a weapon that, together with his briefcase, literally saves his life. The entire novel centers on the logic embedded in this symbolism: while Ellison shows little appreciation for cheap nostalgia (understood here as idealizing and romanticizing the past without integrating it into the present), he at the same time stresses that the narrator acutely needs a consciously processed understanding of the past in order to survive the present and (co)create a future.

The briefcase is another of Invisible Man's pivotal symbols related to history and historiography. Before the narrator can write himself into being, he must destroy all documents accumulated in the briefcase—the papers symbolizing the earlier (trans)formative phases and rites of passage during which others have imposed their definitions of blackness, black masculinity, and black political awareness on him. The burning of the documents places the narrator outside institutions, but not outside either history or the possibility of individual agency. Ellison's narrator (unlike the protagonist of Richard Wright's 1942 story, "The Man Who Lived Underground") is a survivor who will not be destroyed by his experience of underground existence: after the initial shock, he takes control of the space that he occupies in a forgotten basement on the edge of Harlem. As he "illuminate[s] the blackness of [his] invisibility" (*IM* 11) by illegally exploiting New York's electrical power system, he takes dominion of the (white/light) power that was used against him through an electric rug during the battle royal and through electric shocks in the factory hospital where he underwent his violent urban rebirth. Preparing himself for future action, he deliberately and determinedly strengthens his personal and social agency while "hibernating."

This mode of existence continues the process that began when the narrator's deep disappointment with Hambro opened up a new perspective that led the disillusioned black leader into a dialogue with his personal and social past: "All past humiliations became precious parts of my experience, and for the first time . . . I began to accept my past and, as I accepted it, I felt memories welling up within me" (*IM* 383). The narrator's gradual discovery that he is inevitably situated in history is vital for the novel's representation of the quest for responsible action. Significantly, the common denominator between *Invisible Man*'s various false Messiahs is precisely their problematic relationship to history and the past. Both the Founder and Tod Clifton were transformed into incarnations of "Black History" by individuals who considered such monumentalizing, idealizing acts useful for themselves or their interest groups. The novel consistently critiques such creation of messianic icons, be the worshiped great figures, and the simplistically glorified histories they represent, black or white. The "Great [white] Traditions" represented by the "Messiah" Norton (a canon of knowledge and culture based on a Eurocentric interpretation of the history of human civilization) do not touch black lives in any relevant ways in *Invisible Man*. For Ras, in turn, history signifies an idealized African past that is temporally and geographically distant, and has never really existed in the utopian and unified form that he sees in his mind's eye. Rinehart, yet another black Messiah, financially exploits religious believers' nostalgia for the past and their fear of the present, instead of attempting to relate to their personal or social histories. And for the members of the Brotherhood, (black) individuals, including messianic leaders, ultimately "don't count" and can be sacrificed at the altar of the "good of the whole" when "true" and "meaningful" history is created.

After abandoning his (mock-)messianic role, the narrator, by contrast, begins to integrate his present into his personal past and into his understanding of social history. In Ralph Waldo Emerson's "Self-Reliance," which is explicitly evoked in *Invisible Man*, Ellison's namesake exhorts men to accept "the connection of events."[44] During his invisibility the narrator begins to *see*, even if not necessarily accept, the "connection of events" (that is, history), as his ironic testimony, "now I see"—parodically echoing "Amazing Grace"—suggests in the prologue. For Ellison, history inherently includes American slavery and the failure of Reconstruction; it is no coincidence that the narrator explicitly refers to the "birth of a nation"—that is, ironically riffs on the title of the notoriously racist Ku Klux Klan-glorifying movie directed by D. W. Griffith (*IM* 394)—as he undergoes his own birth into authorship. This riff is significant, because the birth of an author that takes place within *Invisible Man*'s narrative framework ultimately speaks of the need for a "rebirth" of the American nation: the novel's frame emphasizes that African American history needs to be written into the national narrative of the United States. *Invisible Man* itself, albeit fiction rather than academic historiography, actively participates in that project.

While thematizing the written word and writing, *Invisible Man* also highlights the importance of music and oral folklore for African American identity and history. The novel is permeated with musical rhythms, styles, echoes, and motifs—for example, as scholars have observed, Louis Armstrong's expression of the dilemma of being "black and blue," the song about "poor Robin" that articulates the narrator's experience of being outsmarted and exploited, Pete Wheatstraw's morning blues, and the resurgent strains of spirituals that thematize the issue of (re)memory versus repression. Most importantly, *Invisible Man* is a blues novel—according to the critic Mary Ellison, "the ultimate blues novel," in which the narrator "sing[s] his own blues as he tells his tale."[45]

For Ralph Ellison, the blues, as a form, was "an autobiographical chronicle of personal catastrophe expressed lyrically."[46] As if improvising on this definition, Mary Ellison highlights the hope and optimism that ultimately characterize the blues:

> [T]he blues push black people to defy despair, to hope and seek for better things. The blues don't usually accept defeat; they just note the set-backs. Usually, however, is not always and a few blues are permeated with a sense of drowning desolation, of omnipresent evil.... But finally the blues never succumb to this pessimism; renewing themselves endlessly, they somehow manage to assert that a belief in some value involves man in painful but necessary conflict. The bluesman in his song gives us a humanistic response to a tragic vision as strong and beautiful as any in our century.[47]

In a similar vein, Ralph Ellison also emphasizes this blues attitude of "defy[ing] despair" in his essay "Flamenco" (1954), in which he eloquently links the (secularized) Christian resurrection motif with the essence of the blues voice: "[T]he blues voice . . . mocks the despair stated explicitly in the lyric, and it expresses the great human joke directed against the universe, that joke which is the secret of all folklore and myth: that *though we be dismembered daily we shall always rise up again*" (italics added).[48] In *Invisible Man*, it is this kind of blues voice that ultimately sings the narrative and its invisible narrator into being. Invisible Man's "notes from underground" are both written notes and blue(s) notes. They chronicle personal catastrophe but, at the same time, actively seek a way out of it by giving lyrical expression to a dream of "resurrection" and political freedom.

In *Invisible Man*, the prologue and the epilogue together form the novel's narrative/blues frame, and that frame is rich in religious reference. When, in the end-foreshadowing prologue, the narrator ponders his past role as orator, he again alludes to Yahweh's enigmatic self-appellation in the burning bush ("I Am That I Am") and links it to the Book of Revelation's repetition of God's name (that is, his Being) in the past, present, and future tenses (1:8): "Am? I *was*, and perhaps shall be again" (*IM* 11; italics in original). As this phrase implies, the narrator actively reaches toward the future while reflecting on his past. In wondering what the future will bring with it, he also signifies on John 11:4, in which Jesus prepares to resurrect his friend Lazarus from death: "Who knows? *All sickness is not unto death*, neither is invisibility" (*IM* 11; italics added). In and through his "memoir," the narrator evokes the hope of a secular resurrection, a return from hibernation to active life, society, and visibility. His hibernation is "a covert preparation for a more overt action"(*IM* 11)—not "a resignation from society but an attempt to come back and be useful," as Ellison explained in an interview.[49] Although the narrator at times ridicules his past "messianic" aspirations, he nevertheless prepares himself for a second coming. Hope is embedded in the content and form of *Invisible Man*, but the ending is left open, because the narrator's future will necessarily take place in dialogue with the memoir's reception by those for whom he speaks "on the lower frequencies" (*IM* 439).

Notes

In notes to this chapter, "Ellison" refers to the novelist Ralph Ellison, and "M. Ellison" to the critic Mary Ellison.

1. Tate, "Notes on the Invisible Women," 163.

2. Previous scholarship has not completely ignored Ellison's use of religious idiom in *Invisible Man*. Robert G. O'Meally's *The Craft of Ralph Ellison* gives an overview of *Invisible Man*'s allusions to the Bible, spirituals, and gospel music (92–98). Several critics have touched upon the Reverend Homer A. Barbee's speech as well as Tod Clifton's funeral. For analyses of religious allusions in other scenes, see, for example, Melvin Dixon, "O, Mary Rambo, Don't You Weep"; Douglas

Robinson, "Call Me Jonah"; Kimberly W. Benston, *Performing Blackness*, 7–12; and Houston A. Baker Jr., *Blues, Ideology, and Afro-American Literature*, 172–88. Dixon analyzes religious echoes in Ellison's portrayal of the character Mary Rambo (101–4), Robinson reads *Invisible Man* in light of the prologue's reference to the Old Testament story of Jonah, and Benston focuses on the ways in which the prologue's sermon (which, as Benston notes, plays intertextually with Father Mapple's oration in *Moby-Dick*'s chapter 9) illustrates the performative foundation of African American expressivity. Baker's commentary on the Trueblood episode, in turn, insightfully discusses the "virtual parodies of the notions of sin and sacrifice" (184) that Trueblood composes and performs in response to Norton's appalled question about the "need to cast out the offending eye" (*IM* 40). The contributions of Baker, Mark Busby, Alan Nadel, and Wilson Jeremiah Moses will be evoked later in this chapter, as will Benston's 1982 analysis of Ellison's modification of the Tetragrammaton in *Invisible Man*. Bethel Louise Eddy's doctoral dissertation, "The Rites of Identity," provides yet another intriguing perspective on the study of religion and religious discourse in *Invisible Man*: structuring her analysis on the concepts of piety, sacrifice, and the comic, Eddy examines Kenneth Burke's influence on Ellison, situating both men in "an American tradition of religious naturalism indebted to George Santayana and Ralph Waldo Emerson" (iii). On the whole, however, it is symptomatic of the limits of recent critical approaches to Ellison's use of religious idiom and imagery that the anthology named *Cultural Contexts for Ralph Ellison's Invisible Man*, ed. Eric J. Sundquist, discusses religion in *Invisible Man* only in terms of spirituals (125–26), which are an important aspect, but nevertheless only one aspect, of the novel's religious matrix.

3. I borrow the phrase from Bigsby, "Improvising America: Ralph Ellison and the Paradox of Form," 173, 182.

4. Busby, *Ralph Ellison*, 82. Ellison's comment on allusiveness as riffing is taken from Ellison, "The Essential Ellison," 373.

5. Gates, *The Signifying Monkey*, 123.

6. Floyd, *The Power of Black Music*, 7.

7. Ibid., 8.

8. Ellison, "Change the Joke," 104.

9. For a more detailed reflection on the connection between lynching and scapegoating, see Harris, *Exorcising Blackness*, 11–19. In *Rituals of Blood*, Patterson gives Ellison credit for being "among the few Americans to have recognized the stark fact that lynching was human sacrifice, laden with religious and political significance for his culture" (173).

10. In the African American theologian Delores S. Williams's angry and frustrated 1993 phrase, "The media makes the Black individual into the national symbol of everything wrong in this country—crime, overdependence on welfare, decaying urban neighborhoods, even the high national illiteracy rate" (D. S. Williams, "Christian Scapegoating," 43). In addition to evoking the long history of scapegoating African Americans in the United States, Williams's piece—a nonacademic column rather than a research article—demonstrates the crisis that the discovery of the link between the ancient scapegoat rite, christology, and the psychological mechanism of scapegoating can trigger in religious thought: Williams wonders whether African American churches' adoption of the classic Christian doctrine of the salvific power of Jesus' suffering on the cross "inadvertently teach[es] Black people to accept their own status as scapegoats" (44). The article, radical when considered against the

backdrop of traditional Christian interpretations of the doctrine of atonement, concludes by inviting African American churches to "devise images for our Christian religion that devalue scapegoating in any form or context" (44).

11. Larry Neal also briefly notes Barbee's evocation of Moses, Aristotle, and Jesus ("Ellison's Zoot Suit," 118).

12. Spillers, "Ellison's 'Usable Past,'" 153. See also Benston, "Introduction: The Masks of Ralph Ellison" 5.

13. Ellison, "Working Notes," 345.

14. While critical of Washington's accommodationism, Ellison often spoke appreciatively of Tuskegee's library resources and the musical education he received there. See, for example, Ellison, interview by Richard Kostelanetz, 88–89, and Ellison, "The Little Man at Chehaw Station," 489–92.

15. In terms of personal guilt, the classic Judeo-Christian scapegoat is either neutral (an animal, a goat) or innocent (Christ). Trueblood fails to conform to this pattern, but his crime is committed under circumstances largely dictated by a factor beyond his control—namely, his poverty, which forces the entire Trueblood family to sleep in the same bed. See, for example, M. Ellison, *Extensions of the Blues*, 179–80.

16. Baker, *Blues, Ideology, and Afro-American Literature*, 175.

17. See also Baumbach, "Nightmare of a Native Son," 16–17.

18. Ellison, "Working Notes," 344.

19. For this transcription of Bledsoe's name, see also Busby, *Ralph Ellison*, 61.

20. Sernett, "Re-Readings," 450.

21. Ibid.

22. Ellison, "Harlem Is Nowhere," 323.

23. For a longer discussion of Ras and Ethiopianism, see Moses, *Black Messiahs and Uncle Toms*, 196–97. The narrative alludes to Ethiopianism as early as the Golden Day episode, where one of the black veterans mixes the biblical verse of "Ethiopia shall soon stretch forth her hands unto God," from Ps. 68:31, with his Vichian, cyclical view of history. Ellison confirms the reference to Giambattista Vico in his 1972 interview by John O'Brien: "Vico, whom Joyce used in his great novels, described history as circling" (231). In *Invisible Man*, Ellison's (and the narrator's) primary metaphor for history is, by contrast, a boomerang: "I described [history] as a boomerang because a boomerang moves in a parabola. It goes and it comes. It is never the same thing. There is implicit in the image the old idea that those who do not learn from history are doomed to repeat its mistakes. History comes back and hits you" (ibid., 231). This commentary explains why the narrator says in the prologue: "Beware of those who speak of the *spiral* of history; they are preparing a boomerang. Keep a steel helmet handy" (*IM* 5; italics in original).

24. Ellison, "Change the Joke," 110.

25. See Ellison, "Harlem Is Nowhere," 324.

26. Ellison, "Working Notes," 343.

27. Ellison, "Change the Joke," 110. The initials "B. P." in the name of the multifaced Rinehart stand for "Proteus" and "Bliss." "Bliss" (also the name of one of the two main characters of *Juneteenth*) refers not only to Rinehart's role as a minister but also to the motivation for his multiple masquerade—"the sheer bliss of impersonation," besides the financial gain ("Change the Joke," 110). "Proteus," evoking the Greek sea god who could assume whatever form he pleased, is a particularly appropriate name for Rinehart.

28. See Nadel, *Invisible Criticism*, 63–84.

29. Although Alan Nadel notes this fact in passing (ibid., 82), he mainly confines his analysis of *Invisible Man*'s "Messiahs" to the christological characterization of Tod, and even seems somewhat uncomfortable with the notion that *both* Tod *and* the narrator could share messianic traits. Wilson Jeremiah Moses, by contrast, points out that "the narrator himself . . . is caught up in millennial myths concerning his sense of duty and racial mission" (*Black Messiahs and Uncle Toms*, 197). Moses also observes that by the end of the novel the narrator, while still adhering to the concept of racial responsibility, has rejected "mythical racial messianism" (ibid., 206). My reading supports and amplifies Moses's observations.

30. John 8:12; 14:6; italics added. See, for example, *IM* 6: "The truth is the light and light is the truth." Ellison is familiar with the religious origins of the Manichean language of darkness and light/whiteness ("Change the Joke," 102), but in *Invisible Man* he allows this symbolism to find a life of its own, one related to race rather than to religion.

31. For the term "memoir," see Ellison, interview by Allen Geller, 76. On the narrator's transformation from orator to author, see Ellison, "Change the Joke": "The final act of *Invisible Man* is . . . that of a voice issuing its little wisdom out of the substance of its own inwardness—after having undergone a transformation from ranter to writer" (111). See also Stepto, *From Behind the Veil*, 172; and Callahan, "Frequencies of Eloquence," 86–88.

32. See also Busby, *Ralph Ellison*, 50.

33. For Ellison's allusions to Chaplin's *Modern Times* in his 1944 story "King of the Bingo Game," see Busby, *Ralph Ellison*, 38.

34. Ibid., 52.

35. Yahweh's revelation of his name/himself in the burning bush on Mount Sinai is also evoked in the Founders' Day scene, in which Barbee refers to the Founder as a "fire that burned without consuming" (*IM* 95). Benston suggests, moreover, that even Trueblood's arrival at an empowering self-understanding—"I ain't nobody but myself" (*IM* 51)—echoes "God's unnaming self-naming" (Benston, "I Yam What I Am," 8).

36. Benston, "I Yam What I Am," 4; italics in original.

37. Busby also notes the allusion to Popeye (*Ralph Ellison*, 95).

38. Benston, "I Yam What I Am," 7.

39. Hambro's name stands, ironically, for "Ham's Brother," as Eddy ("The Rites of Identity," 222) and Busby (*Ralph Ellison*, 61) observe. Ellison explicitly discusses Ham in "The World and the Jug," 157, 165. In Genesis 9:25–27, Noah places a curse on Ham's son Canaan, condemning him to slavery while praying that Ham's brothers, Shem and Japheth, will prosper in freedom.

40. The phrase ironically echoes the narrator's memorable slip of the tongue in the battle royal scene—his substitution of "social equality" for "social responsibility."

41. In a sense, Invisible Man reproduces this strategy as narrator by occasionally resorting to his ability to be, in Ellison's playful words, "something of a liar, if you ask me" (Author's Note," 243). *Invisible Man* provides Ellison with an excellent site for playing with instances of the narrator's unreliability because the narrator-protagonist ironically laughs both at himself and at others while writing his "memoir." The extent of Invisible Man's un/reliability as narrator is ultimately

for the reader to determine in the game between author and reader that comes into being in the act of reading.

42. Stepto, *From Behind the Veil*, xi.

43. The closed, opened, and partly reclosed link also serves as a reference to Tarp's condition before, during, and after his escape from South to North.

44. Emerson, "Self-Reliance," 47.

45. M. Ellison, *Extensions of the Blues*, 177, 178.

46. Ellison, "Richard Wright's Blues," 129.

47. M. Ellison, *Extensions of the Blues*, 12.

48. Ellison, "Flamenco," 10–11. A flamenco aficionado, Ellison viewed this form of music and dance as spiritually akin to the blues and exalted its creators for celebrating the fundamental unity of the temporal (particularly the physical and corporeal) and the sacred. He especially praised what he regarded as the earthiness permeating their christology: "The gypsies, like the slaves, are an outcast though undefeated people who have never lost their awareness of the physical source of man's most spiritual moments; even their Christ is a man of flesh and bone who suffered and bled before his apotheosis" (10). For connections between flamenco and the blues, see also Flaherty, *The Blues Alive*, 14–15.

49. Ellison, interview by Allen Geller, 76.

ROBERT PENN WARREN

The Unity of Experience

Even if Ralph Ellison were not the author of *Invisible Man*, his recent collection of essays, *Shadow and Act*, would be a very significant work. There are astute commentaries on literature, music, and society, and the commentaries are enriched and validated by an underlying sense of a life being lived with energy, sympathy, and joy. But Ralph Ellison is the author of *Invisible Man* and of an impending novel which, if we are to judge from excerpts, promises to illustrate new powers and to extend his fame; and this fact inevitably imputes a further significance to the essays. Here we can see how, over more than a score of years, in another dimension, the mind and sensibility of Ellison have been working, and we can hope to see some enlightening relations between that dimension and the dimension of his fiction.

In the preface to *Shadow and Act*, Ellison says of his struggle to become a writer:

> I found the greatest difficulty for a Negro writer was the problem of revealing what he truly felt, rather than serving up what Negroes were supposed to feel, and were encouraged to feel. And linked to this was the difficulty, based upon our long habit of deception and evasion, of depicting what really happened within our areas of American life, and putting down with honesty and without bowing

Commentary (May 1965): pp.91-96. © Robert Penn Warren

to ideological expediencies the attitudes and values which give Negro
American life its sense of wholeness and which renders it bearable
and human and, when measured by our own terms, desirable.

In other words, the moral effort to see and recognize the truth of the self
and of the world, and the artistic effort to say the truth are regarded as aspects
of the same process. This interfusion of the moral and the artistic is, for Ralph
Ellison, a central fact and a fact that involves far more than his literary views:
for if "truth" moves into "art," so "art" can move backward (and forward) into
"truth." Art can, in other words, move into life. Not merely, Ellison would
have it, by opening our eyes to life, not merely by giving us models of action
and response, but by, quite literally, creating us. For him, the high function of
technique is "the task of creating value," and in this task we create the self.
This process is a life-process—a way of knowing and experiencing in which is
growth: a growth in integrity, literally a unifying of the self, of the random or
discrepant possibilities and temptations of experience.

* * *

Now, "ideological expediency" would have Ralph Ellison formulate his
"difficulty" somewhat differently. It would prompt him to slant things so
that the special problems of the Negro writer would be read as one aspect
of the Negro's victimization by the white man. A very good case—in one
perspective, a perfect case—can be made out for that interpretation. But
Ellison refuses that gambit of the alibi. In various ways, he repudiates the
"Negro alibi" for the Negro writer. For instance, in the essay "The World
and the Jug," he says: ". . . when the work of Negro writers has been rejected
they have all too often protected their egos by blaming racial discrimination, while turning away from the fairly obvious fact that good art—and
Negro musicians are present to demonstrate this—commands attention
to itself. . . . And they forget that publishers will publish almost anything
which is written with even a minimum of competency."

Ellison is, in other words, more concerned with the way a man confronts
his individual doom than with the derivation of that doom; not pathos, but
power, in its deepest inner sense, is what concerns him. He is willing, pride-
fully, to head into responsibility. But in the last sentence of the above quotation from the preface to *Shadow and Act*. Ellison flouts even more violently
"ideological expediencies" which dictate that the Negro advertise the blankness, bleakness, and misery of his life. Instead, Ellison refers to its "wholeness," its desirability, and elsewhere in the same preface he refers to "the areas

of life and personality which claimed my mind beyond any limitations *apparently* imposed by my racial identity."

* * *

This attitude, which permeates Ellison's work, comes to focus in two essays which are probably destined to become a classic statement; they were written as a reply to Irving Howe's essay "Black Boys and Native Sons." Howe's piece takes Richard Wright's work to be the fundamental expression of the Negro genius. The day *Native Son* appeared, he says, "American culture was changed forever. . . . A blow at the white man, the novel forced him to recognize himself as an oppressor. A blow at the black man, the novel forced him to recognize the cost of his submission." Though Howe admires the performance of both Baldwin and Ellison, he sees them as having rejected the naturalism and straight protest of Wright, as traitors to the cause of "clenched militancy"; and then, to quote Ellison, Howe, "appearing suddenly in black face," demands: "What, then, was the experience of a man with a black skin, what *could* it be here in this country? How could a Negro put pen to paper, how could he so much as think or breathe, without some impulsion to protest . . . ?" And he goes on to say that the Negro's very existence "forms a constant pressure on his literary work . . . with a pain and ferocity that nothing could remove."

This, to Ellison, is the "ideological proposition that what whites think of the Negro's reality is more important than what Negroes themselves know it to be"; and this, to Ellison, is Howe's "white liberal version of the white Southern myth of absolute separation of the races." That is, the critic picks out the Negro's place (i.e. his feelings and his appropriate function) and then puts him in it. "I fear the implications of Howe's ideas concerning the Negro writer's role as actionist more than I do the State of Mississippi," Ellison writes. Howe's view is another example of a situation that "is not unusual for a Negro to experience," as Ellison says in a review of Myrdal's *An American Dilemma*, "a sensation that he does not exist in the real world at all—only in the nightmarish fantasy of the white American mind." That is a violation of "the basic unity of human experience," undertaken in the "interest of specious political and philosophical conceits":

> Prefabricated Negroes are sketched on sheets of paper and superimposed upon the Negro community; then when someone thrusts his head through the page and yells, "Watch out there, Jack, there's people living under here," they are shocked and indignant.

We must not fall into the same error and take his attack on the white liberal's picture of the Negro to be Ellison's concealed version of the common notion that no white man can "know" a Negro. By his theory of the "basic unity of human experience," which we shall come to presently, and by his theory of the moral force of the imagination, such a view—except in the provisional, limited way that common sense dictates—would be untenable. What Ellison would reject is the violation of the density of life by an easy abstract formulation. Even militancy, if taken merely as a formula, can violate the density of life. For instance, in "The World and the Jug," he says: " . . . what an easy con game for ambitious, publicity-hungry Negroes this stance of 'militancy' has become." He is as ready to attack a Negro on this point as a white man. In a review of LeRoi Jones's study of Negro music, *Blues People*, he says that Jones "attempts to impose an ideology upon this cultural complexity" and that even when a Negro treats this subject "the critical intelligence must perform the difficult task which only it can perform."

The basic unity of human experience—that is what Ellison asserts; and he sets the richness of his own experience and that of many Negroes he has known, and his own early capacity to absorb the general values of Western culture, over against what Wright called "the essential bleakness of black life in America." What he is saying here is not that "bleakness" does not exist, and exist for many, but that it has not been the key fact of his own experience, and that his own experience is part of the story. It must be reckoned with, too:

> For even as his life toughens the Negro, even as it brutalizes him, sensitizes him, dulls him, goads him to anger, moves him to irony, sometimes fracturing and sometimes affirming his hopes . . . it *conditions* him to deal with his life and with himself. Because it is *his* life, and no mere abstraction in somebody's head.

Not only the basic unity, but the rich variety, of life is what concerns him; and this fact is connected with his personal vision of the opportunity in being an American: "The diversity of American life is often painful, frequently burdensome and always a source of conflict, but in it lies our fate and our hope." In many places, Ellison insists on his love of diversity and a pluralistic society. For instance, in "That Same Pain, That Same Pleasure": "I believe in diversity, and I think that the real death of the United States will come when everyone is just alike." The appreciation of this variety is, in itself, a school for the imagination and moral sympathy. And, for Ellison, being a "Negro American" has to do with this appreciation, not only of the Negro past in America, but with the complex fluidity of the present:

It has to do with a special perspective on the national ideals and the national conduct, and with a tragicomic attitude toward the universe. It has to do with special emotions evoked by the details of cities and countrysides, with forms of labor and with forms of pleasure; with sex and with love, with food and with drink, with machines and with animals; with climates and with dwellings, with places of worship and places of entertainment; with garments and dreams and idioms of speech; with manners and customs, with religion and art, with life styles and hoping, and with that special sense of predicament and fate which gives direction and resonance to the Freedom Movement. It involves a rugged initiation into the mysteries and rites of color which makes it possible for Negro Americans to suffer the injustice which race and color are used to excuse without losing sight of either the humanity of those who inflict that injustice or the motives, rational or irrational, out of which they act. It imposes the uneasy burden and occasional joy of a complex double vision, a fluid, ambivalent response to men and events which represents, at its finest, a profoundly civilized adjustment to the cost of being human in this modern world.

Out of this view of the life of the "Negro American"—which is a view of *life*—it is no wonder that Ellison does not accept a distinction between the novel as "protest" and the novel as "art"—or rather, sees this distinction as a merely superficial one, not to be trusted. His own approach is twofold. On the one hand, he says "protest is an element of all art," but he would not limit protest to the social or political objection. In one sense, it might be a "technical assault" on earlier styles—but we know that Ellison regards "techniques" as moral vision, and a way of creating the self. In another sense, the protest may be, as in *Oedipus Rex* or *The Trial*, "against the limitation of human life itself." In yet another sense, it may be—and I take it that Ellison assumes that it always is—a protest against some aspect of a personal fate:

... that intensity of personal anguish which compels the artist to seek relief by projecting it into the world in conjunction with other things; that anguish might take the form of an acute sense of inferiority for one [person], homosexuality for another, an overwhelming sense of the absurdity of human life for still another ... the experience that might be caused by humiliation, by a harelip, by a stutter, by epilepsy—indeed, by any and everything in life which plunges the talented individual into solitude while leaving him the will to transcend his condition through art.

And the last words of this preceding quotation bring us to the second idea in his twofold approach to the distinction between the novel as protest and the novel as art: the ideal of the novel is a transmutation of protest into art. In speaking of Howe's evaluation of his own novel, Ellison says:

> If *Invisible Man* is even "apparently" free from "the ideological and emotional penalties suffered by Negroes in this country," it is because I tried to the best of my ability to transform these elements into art. My goal was not to escape, or hold back, but to work through; to transcend, as the blues transcend the painful conditions with which they deal.

And he relates this impulse toward transcendence into art to a stoical American Negro tradition which teaches one to master and contain pain; "which abhors as obscene any trading on one's own anguish for gain or sympathy"; which deals with the harshness of existence "as men at their best have always done." And he summarizes the relevance of this tradition: "It takes fortitude to be a man and no less to be an artist."

In other words, to be an artist partakes, in its special way, of the moral force of being a man. And with this we come again, in a new perspective, to Ellison's view of the "basic unity of experience." If there is anguish, there is also the possibility of the transmutation of anguish, "the occasional joy of a complex double vision."

For in this "double vision" the "basic unity" can be received, and life can be celebrated. "I believe," he says to Howe, "that true novels, even when most pessimistic and bitter, arise out of an impulse to celebrate human life, and therefore are ritualistic and ceremonial at their core." The celebration of life—that is what Ellison sees as the final nature of his fiction, or of any art. And in this "double vision" and the celebration which it permits—no, entails—we find, even, the reconciliation possible in recognizing "the humanity of those who inflict injustice." And with this Ellison has arrived, I take it, at his own secular version of Martin Luther King's conception of *agapé*.

* * *

If, in pursuing this line of thought about Ralph Ellison, I have made him seem unaware of the plight of the Negro American in the past or the present, I have done him a grave wrong. He is fully aware of the blankness of the fate of many Negroes, and the last thing to be found in him is any trace of that cruel complacency of some who have, they think, mastered fate. If he emphasizes the values of challenge in the plight of the Negro, he would not use this to justify that plight; and if he applauds the disciplines induced by that plight, he does so in no spirit of self-congratulation, but in a spirit of pride in being numbered with those people.

No one has made more unrelenting statements of the dehumanizing pressures that have been put upon the Negro. And *Invisible Man* is, I should say, the most powerful artistic representation we have of the Negro under these dehumanizing conditions; and, at the same time, a statement of the human triumph over those conditions.

JOSEPH F. TRIMMER

Ralph Ellison's "Flying Home"

Ralph Ellison is known chiefly for his single novel, *Invisible Man*, for which he won the National Book Award for Fiction in 1952, and for his collection of essays, *Shadow and Act*, published in 1964. It is not widely acknowledged, however, that Ellison is also a master of the short story. This ignorance or neglect of Ellison's short fiction is due mainly to two facts—his stories have appeared in relatively obscure journals, and to date they have remained uncollected. Recently, anthology editors have discovered this wealth of material, and slowly but surely Ellison's short stories are being reprinted. But despite this increased exposure, the stories remain neglected by critics. Marcus Klein, in *After Alienation: American Novels in Mid-Century* (New York: World, 1964), discusses some of the stories in his chapter on Ellison; but since his purpose was to trace the thematic concerns that eventually surfaced in *Invisible Man*, his treatment of individual stories was necessarily abbreviated. Yet his brief treatment of Ellison's stories is still the only one in print. What is needed is a detailed and systematic evaluation of all of Ellison's stories. I intend to begin that evaluation by examining a story that is readily available for inspection, "Flying Home."

As Klein has pointed out, "Flying Home" has its beginnings in a political issue: "A Negro air school had been established at Tuskegee during the war, apparently as a sap to civil libertarians. Its pilots never got out of training.

Studies in Short Fiction 9.2 (Spring 1972): pp.175-182. © Newberry College

The school became a sufficient issue for Judge Hostie to resign from the War Department in protest over it. . . ." Ellison commented on this issue in "Editorial Comment," *Negro Quarterly*, 1 (Winter-Spring 1943). He also indicated to Rochelle Girson in their interview in "Sidelights on Invisibility," *Saturday Review*, March 14, 1953, that "he had intended after the war to write a novel about a flyer. This story would seem to be its beginning."

The plot of the story is relatively simple: Todd, a young black pilot on a training mission, crashes his plane on an Alabama farm where he is saved from the white racist owner, Dabney Graves, by a black "peasant" named Jefferson. What is not so simple is the symbolic patterns that permeate the story. As with all vintage Ellison, these patterns proceed simultaneously on at least two levels, racial and mythic. On the racial level, the story gives us a parable of the complex interrelationship between the individual black man and his racial community; on the mythic level, the story refashions the Daedalus myth. The two levels are connected symbolicially by implied parallels to three other related sources—the myth of the Phoenix, the Christian doctrine of *felix culpa*, or fortunate fall, and the story of the prodigal son.

Todd's basic problem is what W. E. B. DuBois [in *Souls of Black Folk*] called the problem of "double-consciousness": "It is a peculiar sensation, this double-consciousness, this sense of always looking at one's self through the eyes of others, of measuring one's soul by the tape of a world that looks on in amused contempt and pity. One ever feels his twoness,—an American, a Negro; two souls, two thoughts, two unreconciled strivings; two warring ideals in one dark body, whose dogged strength alone keeps it from being torn asunder." Todd aspires to be a flyer, but everyone tells him that planes and flying are for white men. Thus Todd's desire to fly seems to be a desire to fly away from his Black identity and supposed inferiority and toward white acceptance and supposed fulfillment. The problem is that Todd is ambivalent. He wants to please the old black men who come to see him train at the air field, but they do not really understand his skill: "He felt cut off from them by age, by understanding, by sensibility, by technology and by his need to measure himself against the mirror of other men's appreciation." Yet he could never be certain what his white officers really thought of him. So "between ignorant black men and condescending whites, his course of flight seemed mapped by the nature of things away from all needed and natural landmarks."

Todd's relationship to the black community is communicated more enigmatically in a series of allusions relating to buzzards and horses. Todd's girl friend has written to him that he should not be bothered by the old allegation of intellectual inferiority: "they keep beating that dead horse because they don't want to say why you boys are not yet fighting." It is to escape that "dead horse" that Todd flies. But as he manipulates his "advanced trainer" he spots a kite below him, like the ones he flew as a boy. In an attempt to "find the boy at the end of the invisible cord . . . [he flies] too high and too fast. . . . And one of the first rules you learn is that if the angle of thrust is too steep the plane goes into a spin. And then, instead of pulling out of it and going into a dive you let a buzzard panic you. A lousy buzzard."The plane then falls out of the sky, "like a pitchin' hoss," onto a field. When Todd recovers consciousness he discovers that he has broken his ankle. While a Negro boy, Teddy, goes for help, Todd is attended by an "old buzzard" named Jefferson. When he is asked about the blood on the plane, Todd tells Jefferson about the buzzard. Jefferson acknowledges that buzzards are "bad luck," and that they are only after "dead things." In fact, "Teddy's got a name for 'em, calls 'em jimcrows.". Jefferson then offers the following cryptic fable: "Once I seen a hoss all stretched out like he was sick, you know. So I hollers, `Gid up from there, such! Just to make sho! An' doggone, son, if I don't see two ole jimcrows come flying right up outa that hoss's insides! Yessuh! The sun was shinin' on 'em and they couldn't a been no greasier if they'd been eating barbecue." Todd's stomach convulses at this picture and he protests that Jefferson "made that up." But Jefferson says "Nawsuh! Saw him just like I see you."

The changing identities of horse and buzzard become delightfully confusing as "Todd-plane-bird-hoss" is seen as being knocked out of the sky by "Jefferson-buzzard-dead horse-jimcrow." But what is clear in Jefferson's parable is that the dead horse of Negro inferiority provides the nourishment for the white society that enforces Jim Crow ethics, and for those "talented tenth buzzards" like Todd who wish to fly away from a sense of identification with "dead horse buzzards" like old Jefferson. Todd complains that he can never be simply himself but lsquo;most always be seen by whites as being "part of this old black ignorant man." It is this prideful aspiration away from "home," which precipitates his fall, his "flying home."

While Todd speculates on the meaning of his fall, he sees a black spot in the sky. He expects to see a plane from the airbase coming to pick him up, but sees instead a buzzard glide into the woods: "Why did they make them so disgusting and yet teach them to fly so well?" Jefferson's second fable, his experiences as an angel in heaven, follows this question, and reinforces the meaning of Todd's experience from a different perspective. Jefferson says that when he was in heaven he wanted to "let eve'ybody know that old Jefferson could fly as good as anybody else." But the "colored angels" had to "wear a special kin' a harness when we flew." Jefferson, like Todd, was not bothered by the harness, the second class status of advanced trainee, and tried to fly like everybody else. He flew so well that he was warned by Saint Peter that his "speedin' is a danger to the heavenly community." When Jefferson continues to speed, despite these warnings, Saint Peter must punish him: "If I was to let you keep on flyin', heaven wouldn't be nothin' but uproar. Jeff, you got to go!" The white angels rush Jefferson to the pearly gates, give him a parachute and a map of Alabama. But before he falls, Jefferson is allowed to say a few words: "Well, you done took my wings. And you puttin' me out. You got charge of things so's I can't do nothin' about it. But you got to admit just this: While I was up here I was the flyinest sonofabitch what ever hit heaven!"

While Jefferson's first fable seemed to say that those who aspired to fly did so at the expense of others and were therefore ultimately to be properly humbled, this second fable suggests that aspirations of flight are not bad but are simply limited by the existing power structure. Todd responds to Jefferson's second fable in much the same way that he responded to the first: he senses that Jefferson is mocking him. Todd then connects the two stories by protesting against what each seems to be implying about his desire to fly: "Maybe we are a bunch of buzzards feeding on a dead horse, but we can hope to be eagles can't we?" This question leads Todd to a series of reminiscences about his boyhood—he traces the invisible line from the kite back to the boy who desired to fly.

Todd remembers that he became fascinated with flight when he saw a model airplane "suspended from the ceiling of the automobile exhibit at the State Fair." But his mother tells him that it is a white boy's toy and that he should not only not expect to ever have one but that to even cultivate the desire for one would only lead to frustration: "Airplane. Boy, is you crazy? How many times I have to tell you to stop that foolishness. . . . I bet I'm gon' wham the living daylight out of you if you don't quit worrying me 'bout them things!" But Todd does not listen; and when he sees a real airplane flying in the sky, he thinks a "little white boy's plane's done flew away and all I got to do is stretch out my hands and it'll be mine!" He climbs over the screen and reaches for the plane and feels "the world grow warm with promise." But the plane files on and as he reaches after it he falls. Todd's mother asks the doctor if her son is crazy, and Ellison has Todd's grandmother quote the opening lines of James Weldon Johnson's "Prodigal Son":

Young man, young man
Yo' arms too short
To box with God.

Todd's third childhood experience with a plane came when he and his mother were walking through the Negro slum. A plane flies over the neighborhood, showering the streets with white cards. In expectation, Todd grabs one only to see on the card a picture of a Klansman's white hood, resembling the face of death, and the caption: "Niggers Stay From Polls."

Todd's childhood experiences certainly *seem* to reinforce the sense of Jefferson's fables. He is wrong to want to fly because it makes him aspire toward something that is an illusion and which will ultimately occasion his fall. He is also wrong to want to fly because it makes him desire to participate in an activity that is ultimately designed to cause death and destruction to his people: the godlike white man seems to have charge of things, and Todd's arms are too short to box with him.

That the white man is an agent of death and destruction is indicated in Jefferson's characterization of the man who owns the farm, Dabney Graves: "Everybody knows 'bout Dabney Graves, especially the colored. He done killed enough of us." When Todd asks what the "colored" had done to cause their murder, Jefferson says "though they was men." Todd is appalled and asks why, if this is the condition under which Jefferson is forced to live, he remains. Jefferson says simply that all black men, including Todd, "have to come by white folks" because Dabney Graves owns "this land." Todd continues to protest mainly because he still aspires to fly away from the stigma of blackness and the apparent limits that the identity places on his destiny. But "the closer I spin toward the earth the blacker I become."

At this point Todd spots three men moving across the field. The men are dressed in white, and sensing that they are doctors come to save him, Todd feels immense relief. But Todd's "vision" is again significantly in error. The men are the attendants from the "crazy house"; they have been looking for an escaped patient, Dabney's nephew, but at Dabney's insistence they settle instead for Todd. They put him in a "white straight jacket" because as Graves says, "You all know you can't let the nigguh git up that high without his going crazy. The nigguh brain ain't built right for high altitudes...." The men put Todd on a stretcher; but when they begin to carry him away, Todd protests: "Don't put your hands on me!" What follows is a predictable act of repression: Graves stomps on Todd's chest. Todd, in the midst of horrible pain, responds with laughter which for some reason reminds him of Jefferson's laughter. He looks toward Jefferson "as though somehow he [Jefferson] had become his sole salvation in an insane world of outrage and humiliation." Jefferson does come to Todd's rescue by diverting Graves's attention to the problem of the airplane. Graves is willing to let the airplane stay in his field but "you take this here black eagle over to the nigguh airfield and leave him."

The story ends as Teddy and Jefferson lift the stretcher and carry Todd across the field. Todd feels a "new current of communication . . . between the man and boy and himself." He feels that he has been "lifted out of his isolation, back into the world of men." As they continue to move across the field, Todd hears a mockingbird. He looks up only to see a buzzard. The whole afternoon then "seemed suspended and he waited for the horror to seize him again." Instead, Teddy begins to hum a song, in symbolic counterpoint to the mockingbird, and Todd "saw the dark bird glide into the sun and glow like a bird of flaming gold."

This transformation of the buzzard into the "bird of flaming gold" ties together the various symbolic patterns which have been at work in the story. Todd, like Icarus, has tried to fly too close to the sun, and his fall has taught him his conceit. But like Adam's, Todd's fall can be seen as fortunate for it eventually occasions his salvation. The Daedalus figure, Jefferson, has taught his "son" the error of his ways. That error is not so much in aspiration—the story certainly does not counsel acceptance of jimcrow—but in the method and motive of aspiration. Todd cannot box with God alone, and, like the Prodigal Son, he cannot expect to find salvation in Babylon. To expect fulfillment from the white world is an illusion since that world is designed to make "Niggers Stay From Polls." The tragic consequence of such an illusion is that it makes Todd deny not only Jefferson but himself: to fly for white approval is not a way to fulfillment but a way to psychic suicide.

Todd's ambivalent position as a black flyer, straight-jacketed and harnessed by white officers and by his own desire for white approval, has placed him in a world of isolation. His fall has brought him back home from Babylon, back to a sense of who he is. Once he accepts that identity, once he accepts the fact that he and Jefferson are part of each other, then he is resurrected, "lifted out of his isolation, back into the world of men." The myth of the Phoenix suggests a similar pattern: the fabulous bird lives from five hundred to a thousand years; then at the close of this period, he sings a melodious dirge, flaps his wings to set fire to his nest and is consumed only to come forth with a new life. Todd has crashed, but in the process he has destroyed the harness of his white aspiration, the plane, and has been resurrected by a song of communal acceptance. Once he accepts this community identity, Todd, the buzzard-jimcrow, is transformed into the bird of flaming gold. Like the Prodigal Son, Todd was dead and is now alive again and is ready to begin his flight home.

SANFORD PINSKER

America, Race, and Ralph Ellison

"All men are Jews," Bernard Malamud once (presumably) declared, and
he then added an important coda: "except they don't know it." For better
or worse, what stuck were his first words rather than his last five, and this
includes even those with deep suspicions that the oft-quoted sentiment was
in fact apocryphal. I mention this because among the notes that John F.
Callahan, Ralph Ellison's literary executor and editor of the posthumously
published *Juneteenth*, included is this one: "Bliss symbolizes for Hickman
an American solution as well as a religious possibility. Hickman thinks of
Negroes as the embodiment of American democratic promises, as the last
who are fated to become the first, the downtrodden who shall be exalted."
As the vagaries of race play themselves out in *Juneteenth*, one begins to hear
echoes of Malamud's manifesto—this time rendered as All Americans are
black, except they don't know it.

Ellison's lifelong preoccupation was racial identity. What paralyzed
others energized him, both as abiding subject and omnipresent muse. In his
modernist masterpiece, *Invisible Man* (1952), in his essays on the complicated
intertwining elements of American culture, and now in the posthumous *Juneteenth*, he explores what it means to be an individual amidst the chaos of
social definition. Small wonder, then, that his protagonists tend to be rootless
men, people who, in Ellison's words, have "turned upon [their] loneliness and

Sewanee Review, Vol. 108, Issue 2 (Spring 2000) © University of the South.

twisted it into spite and opportunism." Here he is surely describing Bliss, a character of uncertain parentage who metamorphoses himself from an ersatz black preacher to a race-baiting northern senator.

Bliss is, in this sense, a version of the tragic mulatto as William Faulkner describes the phenomenon in novels such as Light in August. There is a significant difference: whereas Joe Christmas comes to life as a character who finds himself caught between racial uncertainty and the various religious pathologies that surround him, Bliss largely remains an enigma. We learn about him as through a glass darkly. There are scenic units filled with dazzling writing (e.g., Bliss at the circus), but one's overall sense is that he lacks the brio of nearly any character in *Invisible Man*. What *Juneteenth* has in abundance, however, is a set of ideas about race and America that have made Ellison's essays a national treasure. The result is a better novel to talk about than to reread.

Part of the reason for this is that key pieces of *Juneteenth's* plot have been (systematically?) omitted. For example Bliss is not rendered dramatically. We learn little about his life from the fateful moment when a crazed white woman publicly announces that she is his mother and Bliss responds by shucking off his blackness and heading north. Fortunately the same thing cannot be said of Hickman. As large-hearted as he is large, Hickman comes alive on the page: "We know where we are by the way we walk. We know where we are by the way we talk. We know where we are by the way we sing. We know where we are by the way we dance. We know where we are by the way we praise the Lord on high. We know where we are because we hear a different tune in our minds and in our hearts." Hickman is given to, well, preaching, and that is what he tends to do most of the time. As a result he (and Ellison) tell when they should show.

Nor do the problems stop there. *Juneteenth* begins as Hickman and a group from his congregation converge on Washington, D.C., to warn Senator Adam Sunraider (the former Bliss) that he is in great danger. We are never told what the precise danger is, much less how Hickman found out about it. Suffice it to say that the group never manages to get an audience with Sunraider, and that they watch as he is shot on the Senate floor. I am told that there is a good deal of information about the gunman in the boxes of *Juneteenth* material, but on this matter the novel itself is mute, just as it is largely silent about how the light-skinned Sunraider (yet another in the long string of Ellison's allegorical/mythic names) became a senator in the first place.

What we do know, however, is that politics and religion remain prominent features of Ellison's moral-aesthetic landscape. Reading the truncated history of Sunraider's regrets (he insists on sharing them with one person: Hickman), one thinks of the contrast with Robert Penn Warren's *All the*

King's Men and the way a dying Willie Stark tries to convince Jack Burden, his cynical political operative, that it all "might have been different"—that is, if there were only world enough and time. The fallen governor's speech comes at the end of a novel that pits his acceptance (and manipulation) of man's corruptibility against Warren's tragic sense that, like Oedipus, the villain Stark is looking for is none other than himself.

By contrast Ellison's novel begins with an assassination plot and goes on to chronicle the Hickman-Bliss relationship backward. We cannot say with certainty if the senator in fact dies, but he has surely absorbed enough bullets to make this a strong possibility; and as for the way Ellison unrolls the long tangled process of memories within-memories, there is a section about moviemaking that resonates well beyond its immediate circumstances. When asked what the story will be "about," the novel's filmmaker replies this way: "I haven't decided yet . . . but I'm working on it." And when his skeptical questioner wonders why the film crew is "taking pictures all over the place," he offers up this explanation: "they're just chasing shadows, shooting scenes for background. Later on when we start working we'll use them, splice them in. Pictures aren't made in a straight line. We take a little bit of this and a little of that and then it's all looked at and selected and made into a whole."

The words are those of a character, but one gets the shivery feeling that they speak for Ellison as well, especially in a novel he wrestled with to make "whole." Whatever *Juneteenth* might have become had Ellison been able to shape it, it would not have been configured in a "straight line." My hunch is that Ellison sees the tragedy of those caught in the nets of an ill-defined identity as a function of whites who do not realize that a significant part of their being is black. The dramatic tension this position unleashes must necessarily be fused to a form ambitious enough to cover a multitude of possibilities. A straight-ahead chronological narrative is not adequate to the task.

Invisible Man worked on quite different premises, not only in terms of its protagonist moving from one disillusionment to another, but also in Ellison's belief that politics (at least as represented by the Brotherhood) can never coexist with love. Add the insistence that America's founding principles were always better than those individuals who betrayed the dream, and it is hardly surprising that, "on lower frequencies," the struggle that the invisible man chronicled turns out to be a very American story.

There is, in short, much to praise where *Invisible Man* is concerned—the rich textures of a style that effectively yokes realism with myth—but what strikes me at each successive reading is the full force of Ellison's humanity. His characters not only cover the wide range of black experience, from jazz men and storefront preachers, con men and those, like the protean Rinehart, who find freedom in shapeshifting identities, but they also become the onion skins that his unnamed character must peel off if he is to earn his true identity as an artist. That, after all, is the only "socially responsible" role he can possibly play after he leaves his underground lair.

Juneteenth, on the other hand, seems more an extended tone poem than a coherent novel. No doubt part of the problem rests with Callahan's decision to pare down some 2,000 manuscript pages to a more manageable (that is publishable) size. Ellison himself preferred to think of his baggy monster, the result of some forty years of agonizing, anguished work, as eventually coming out in three thick volumes. That, of course, was not to be, because in 1994, when Death stopped for Ralph Ellison, he was still unsure about the overall shape his ambitious novel should take. Callahan, however, worked on the principle that there was a reasonably coherent novel in the slice he offers up as *Juneteenth* (his title rather than Ellison's), and that Ellison's "notes" would supply whatever ancillary information might be required. There are any number of reasons to feel that Callahan was in a hopeless situation from the beginning, but surely the most pertinent of these was his decision to turn a postmodernist epic into a (relatively) old-fashioned novel. Callahan promises to follow the *Juneteeth* that we have now with a "scholar's edition," one that will exhaustively document how and why he selected certain passages and omitted others. But even this well-meaning effort will be but the tip of the iceberg because Callahan found himself with such an embarrassment of riches (multiple drafts, copious notes, and random jottings) that the full story of his edition will only come out when scholar-critics are able to visit the full Ellison archives. Until then they can only speculate.

In one of the eerier coincidences of modern literary life, the summer of 1999 saw the posthumous publication of *Juneteenth* and Ernest Hemingway's *True at First Light*. In both eases, the authors had made it clear that they were not happy with the work at hand (Ellison because he labored under the large shadow of *Invisible Man*'s extraordinary success, and Hemingway because he may have realized that the vaunted Hemingway "style" had turned flabby and, worse, self-parodic), but when publishers see a cash cow they invariably milk it. But, this much said, my hunch is that no one will be interested in reading full text of Hemingway's "fictional memoir," but surely some will want to compare *Juneteenth* with the longer, unshaped version Ellison left us.

Chronology

1914	Ralph Waldo Ellison is born March 1 in Oklahoma City. His father, Lewis Alfred Ellison, is a former soldier and restaurant operator who had come from Tennessee in 1911 as a construction foreman. He hoped to raise his son as a poet. His mother, Ida Millsap Ellison, had grown up on a farm in Georgia.
1917	Father dies. Mother takes work as a domestic, custodian, and cook to support herself, Ralph, and a younger son, Herbert. She would also work to enlist blacks in the Socialist Party.
1920	Enters Frederick Douglass School in Oklahoma City.
1931	Graduates from Douglass High School. Had been the first-chair trumpet player in the school band and was student conductor. During high school, he hears many well-known jazz musicians and attends rehearsals of the Blue Devils jazz band, forerunner of Count Basie's band.
1933	Enters Tuskegee Institute in Alabama on a scholarship to study music and music theory.
1935	Reads and is influenced by T.S. Eliot's *The Waste Land*; begins serious study of modern fiction and poetry; begins writing poetry.
1936	Moves to New York City to study sculpture and to find work as a musician to pay for his last year at Tuskegee. Decides to

remain in New York; employed at the Harlem YMCA, as a receptionist and file clerk, and also as a factory worker.

1937   After mother's funeral in Dayton, Ohio, remains there with his brother for seven months. Returns to New York and meets Richard Wright through Langston Hughes. Publishes his first book review in *New Challenge*, a magazine edited by Wright, and writes his first short story.

1938   Begins four years of employment with the New York City branch of the Federal Writers' Project. Through 1941, publishes essays and reviews in the *New Masses* and other radical periodicals.

1939   Publishes his first short story, "Slick Gotta Learn"; through 1944, publishes seven more stories.

1942   Becomes managing editor of the *Negro Quarterly*.

1943   Joins the U.S. Merchant Marine and serves two years as a cook.

1944   Awarded a Rosenwald Foundation fellowship to write a novel.

1945   Begins *Invisible Man* while on sick leave from Merchant Marine.

1946   Marries Fanny McConnell. She helps support them during the seven years he writes *Invisible Man*.

1952   *Invisible Man* is published.

1953   *Invisible Man* wins a National Book Award.

1955   Through 1957, works on his second novel in Rome, as guest of the American Academy of Arts and Letters.

1958   Instructor of Russian and American literature at Bard College, through 1961.

1962   Teaches creative writing at Rutgers University through 1964.

1963   Eight excerpts from the work-in-progress published in periodicals between 1960 and 1977.

1964   Publishes *Shadow and Act*, twenty years of essays, reviews, and interviews concerning literature and folklore, jazz and the blues, and race relations. Teaches at Rutgers and Yale universities.

1967   Fire destroys his summer home and the manuscript of his second novel.

1969   Awarded a Medal of Freedom, America's highest civilian honor, by Lyndon Johnson.

1970   Albert Schweitzer Professor of Humanities at New York University, through 1980.

1975   Elected to American Academy of Arts and Letters. Speaks at the opening of the Ralph Ellison Public Library in Oklahoma City.

1986   *Going to the Territory*—collected essays, addresses, and reviews—is published.

1994   Dies of pancreatic cancer on April 16.

1995   *The Collected Essays of Ralph Ellison* is published.

1996   *Flying Home and Other Stories* is published.

1999   *Juneteenth*, a novel, is published.

Contributors

HAROLD BLOOM is Sterling Professor of the Humanities at Yale University. He is the author of 30 books, including *Shelley's Mythmaking, The Visionary Company, Blake's Apocalypse, Yeats, A Map of Misreading, Kabbalah and Criticism, Agon: Toward a Theory of Revisionism, The American Religion, The Western Canon,* and *Omens of Millennium: The Gnosis of Angels, Dreams, and Resurrection. The Anxiety of Influence* sets forth Professor Bloom's provocative theory of the literary relationships between the great writers and their predecessors. His most recent books include *Shakespeare: The Invention of the Human,* a 1998 National Book Award finalist, *How to Read and Why, Genius: A Mosaic of One Hundred Exemplary Creative Minds, Hamlet: Poem Unlimited, Where Shall Wisdom Be Found?,* and *Jesus and Yahweh: The Names Divine.* In 1999, Professor Bloom received the prestigious American Academy of Arts and Letters Gold Medal for Criticism. He has also received the International Prize of Catalonia, the Alfonso Reyes Prize of Mexico, and the Hans Christian Andersen Bicentennial Prize of Denmark.

ALAN NADEL has been a professor in the language, literature, and communication department at Rensselaer Polytechnic Institute. He is the author of *Television in Black and White America: Race and National Identity.*

ANDREW HOBEREK is an associate professor and director of graduate studies at the University of Missouri. He is the author of *Twilight of the Middle Class: Post–World War II Fiction and White-Collar Work.*

MORRIS DICKSTEIN is Distinguished Professor of English at the City University of New York Graduate Center. He is a literary and culture critic and has written numerous books, including *Gates of Eden: American Culture in the Sixties*; *Legends in the Temple: The Transformation of American Action, 1945–1970*; and *Mirror in the Roadway: Literature and the Real World*.

JAMES M. ALBRECHT is an associate professor of English and chair of the English department at Pacific Lutheran University. His areas of concentration are American literature and pragmatism.

BERTRAM D. ASHE has taught in the English department at the College of the Holy Cross. In addition to his work on storytelling, he has written the foreword to the novel *Platitudes*.

H. WILLIAM RICE is department chair and professor of English at Kennesaw State University. He is the author of *Toni Morrison and the American Tradition: A Rhetorical Reading*.

CHRISTOPHER HANLON is an associate professor in the English department at Eastern Illinois University. His writing has appeared in such venues as *New Literary History, American Literary History, College Literature,* and *Pedagogy*.

VALERIE SWEENEY PRINCE teaches in the English department at Hampton University. She has published *Shaping the Sierra*.

TUIRE VALKEAKARI is an assistant professor in the English department at Providence College, Rhode Island. Her essays on American literature have appeared in *Studies in American Fiction, Crossing, Atlantic Literary Review,* and other publications.

ROBERT PENN WARREN, one of the great American poets of the 20th century and the author of the classic novel *All the King's Men*, was also a perceptive critic.

JOSEPH F. TRIMMER is a professor English at Ball State University and the director of the Virginia B. Ball Center for Creative Inquiry.

SANFORD PINSKER is an emeritus professor of English at Franklin and Marshall College. He is the author and editor of many books, including studies of Philip Roth, Cynthia Ozick, Joseph Heller, and J. D. Salinger.

Bibliography

Anderson, Paul Allen. "Ralph Ellison on Lyricism and Swing." *American Literary History* 17, no. 2 (Summer 2005): 280–306.

Arimitsu, Michio. "A Counter-Sign in the Punch Line: The Tragi-Comic Blending of Identities in Ralph Ellison's *Invisible Man*." *Journal of the American Literature Society of Japan* 5 (2006): 54–71.

Baker, Houston A., Jr. "Failed Prophet and Falling Stock: Why Ralph Ellison Was Never Avant-Garde." *Stanford Humanities Review* 7, no. 1 (Summer 1999): 4–11.

———. "To Move without Moving: An Analysis of Creativity and Commerce in Ralph Ellison's Trueblood Episode." In *Close Reading: The Reader*, edited by Frank Lentricchia and Andrew DuBois, pp. 337–65. Durham, N.C.: Duke University Press, 2003.

Beavers, Herman. "Finding Common Ground: Ralph Ellison and James Baldwin." In *The Cambridge Companion to the African American Novel*, edited by Maryemma Graham, pp. 189–202. Cambridge, England: Cambridge University Press, 2004.

Bell, Kevin. *Ashes Taken for Fire: Aesthetic Modernism and the Critique of Identity.* Minneapolis: University of Minnesota Press, 2007.

Blum, Kerstin. "Ralph Ellison and the African American Inferno." In *SORAC Journal of African Studies: Society of Research on African Cultures* 2 (November 2002): 33–42.

Borshuk, Michael. "'So Black, So Blue': Ralph Ellison, Louis Armstrong and the Bebop Aesthetic." *Genre: Forms of Discourse and Culture* 37, no. 2 (Summer 2004): 261–84.

———. *Swinging the Vernacular: Jazz and African American Modernist Literature.* New York: Routledge, 2006.

223

Buchwald, Dagmar. "'Let 'Em Swoller You Till They Vomit or Bust Wide Open': 'Doing the Para-Site' between Chaos and Control in Ralph Ellison's *Invisible Man*." *Amerikastudien/American Studies* 45, no. 1 (2000): 73–90.

Callahan, John F., ed. *Ralph Ellison's* Invisible Man: *A Casebook*. Oxford; New York: Oxford University Press, 2004.

Conti, Brooke. "Ellison's Rinehart and *Invisible Man* and Count Basie's 'Harvard Blues.'" *Notes and Queries* 54 (June 2007): 181–83.

Crouch, Stanley. "Ralph Ellison: Invisible Man and Jazz." *Black Renaissance/Renaissance Noire* 4, nos. 2–3 (Summer 2002): 23–32.

Curtin, Maureen F. *Out of Touch: Skin Tropes and Identities in Woolf, Ellison, Pynchon, and Acker*. New York: Routledge, 2003.

Douglas, Christopher. *Reciting America: Culture and Cliché in Contemporary U.S. Fiction*. Urbana: University of Illinois Press, 2001.

Eichelberger, Julia. *Prophets of Recognition: Ideology and the Individual in Novels by Ralph Ellison, Toni Morrison, Saul Bellow, and Eudora Welty*. Baton Rouge: Louisiana State University Press, 1999.

Ferguson, Roderick A. *Aberrations in Black: Toward a Queer of Color Critique*. Minneapolis: University of Minnesota Press, 2004.

Hakutani, Yoshinobu. *Cross-cultural Visions in African American Modernism: From Spatial Narrative to Jazz Haiku*. Columbus: Ohio State University Press, 2006.

Harris-Lopez, Trudier. *South of Tradition: Essays on African American Literature*. Athens: University of Georgia Press, 2002.

Hill, Michael D., and Lena M. Hill. *Ralph Ellison's* Invisible Man: *A Reference Guide*. Westport, Conn.: Greenwood Press, 2008.

Hobson, Christopher Z. "*Invisible Man* and African American Radicalism in World War II." *African American Review* 39, no. 3 (Fall 2005): 355–76.

Hsu, Hsuan. "Regarding Mimicry: Race and Visual Ethics in *Invisible Man*." *Arizona Quarterly* 59, no. 2 (Summer 2003): 107–40.

Jackson, Lawrence. *Ralph Ellison: Emergence of Genius*. Athens: University of Georgia Press, 2007.

Keresztesi, Rita. *Strangers at Home: American Ethnic Modernism between the World Wars*. Lincoln: University of Nebraska Press, 2005.

Kim, Daniel Y. *Writing Manhood in Black and Yellow: Ralph Ellison, Frank Chin, and the Literary Politics of Identity*. Stanford, Calif.: Stanford University Press, 2005.

Kim, Margaret. "*Invisible Man*, Oral Culture, and Postmodernism." *EurAmerica: A Journal of European and American Studies* 30, no. 1 (March 2000): 1–34.

King, Lovalerie, and Linda F. Selzer, ed. *New Essays on the African American Novel: from Hurston and Ellison to Morrison and Whitehead*. New York: Palgrave Macmillan, 2008.

Larkin, Lesley. "Postwar Liberalism, Close Reading, and 'You': Ralph Ellison's *Invisible Man*." *Lit: Literature Interpretation Theory* 19, no. 3 (July–September 2008): 268–304.

Leak, Jeffrey B. *Racial Myths and Masculinity in African American Literature*. Knoxville: University of Tennessee Press, 2005.

Lee, Kun Jong. "Ellison's *Invisible Man*: Emersonianism Revised (1992)." In *The New Romanticism: A Collection of Critical Essays*, edited by Eberhard Alsen, pp. 177–201. New York, N.Y.: Garland, 2000.

Luter, Matthew. "Dutchman's Signifyin(g) Subway: How Amiri Baraka Takes Ralph Ellison Underground." In *Reading Contemporary African American Drama: Fragments of History, Fragments of Self*, edited by Trudier Harris and Jennifer Larson, pp. 21–38. New York, N.Y.: Peter Lang, 2007.

Miller, D. Quentin. "Ralph Ellison's *Invisible Man*." In *American Writers: Classics, Volume II*, edited by Jay Parini, pp. 145–62. New York, N.Y.: Scribner's, 2004.

Modeste, Jacqelynne. "(Un)Masking Possibilities: Bigger Thomas, Invisible Man, and Scooter." In *Readings of the Particular: The Postcolonial in the Postnational*, edited by Anne Holden Rønning and Lene Johannessen, pp. 229–43. Amsterdam, Netherlands: Rodopi, 2007.

Morel, Lucas, ed. *Ralph Ellison and the Raft of Hope: A Political Companion to Invisible Man*. Lexington: University Press of Kentucky, 2004.

Neighbors, Jim. "Plunging (Outside of) History: Naming and Self-Possession in *Invisible Man*." *African American Review* 36, no. 2 (Summer 2002): 227–42.

Nowlin, Michael, "Ralph Ellison, James Baldwin, and the Liberal Imagination." *Arizona Quarterly* 60, no. 2 (Summer 2004): 117–40.

Porter, Horace A. *Jazz Country: Ralph Ellison in America*. Iowa City: University of Iowa Press, 2001.

Posnock, Ross, ed. *The Cambridge Companion to Ralph Ellison*. Cambridge, England: Cambridge University Press, 2005.

Rampersad, Arnold. *Ralph Ellison: A Biography*. New York: Alfred A. Knopf, 2007.

Raussert, Wilfried. "Jazz, Time, and Narrativity." *Amerikastudien/American Studies* 45, no. 4 (2000): 519–34.

Roberts, Brian. "Reading Ralph Ellison Synthesizing the CP and NAACP: Sympathetic Narrative Strategy, Sympathetic Bodies." *Journal of Narrative Theory* 34, no. 1 (Winter 2004): 88–110.

Shiffman, Mark. "Confessional Ethics in Augustine and Ralph Ellison." In *Augustine and Literature*, edited by Robert P. Kennedy, Kim Paffenroth, and John Doody, pp. 343–62. New York, N.Y.: Lexington; 2006.

Spaulding, A. Timothy. "Embracing the Chaos in Narrative Form: The Bebop Aesthetic and Ralph Ellison's *Invisible Man*." *Callaloo* 27, no. 2 (Spring 2004): 481–501.

Sundquist, Eric J., ed. *Cultural Contexts for Ralph Ellison's* Invisible Man. Boston: Bedford Books of St. Martin's Press, 1995.

Szmanko, Klara. *Invisibility in African American and Asian American Literature: A Comparative Study.* Jefferson, N.C.: McFarland, 2008.

Tabron, Judith L. *Postcolonial Literature from Three Continents: Tutuola, H.D., Ellison, and White.* New York: Peter Lang, 2003.

Thomas, P.L. *Reading, Learning, Teaching Ralph Ellison.* New York, N.Y.: Peter Lang, 2008.

Tracy, Steven C., ed. *A Historical Guide to Ralph Ellison.* Oxford, England: Oxford University Press, 2004.

Valkeakari, Tuire. "Secular Riffs on the Sacred: Religious Reference in *Invisible Man.*" *Crossings: A Counter-Disciplinary Journal* 5–6 (2002–2003): 235–67.

Waligora-Davis, Nicole A. "Riotous Discontent: Ralph Ellison's 'Birth of a Nation.'" *Modern Fiction Studies* 50, no. 2 (Summer 2004): 385–410.

Warren, Kenneth W. *So Black and Blue: Ralph Ellison and the Occasion of Criticism.* Chicago: University of Chicago Press, 2003.

Weinstein, Philip. "Postmodern Intimations: Musing on Invisibility: William Faulkner, Richard Wright, and Ralph Ellison." In *Faulkner and Postmodernism: Faulkner and Yoknapatawpha, 1999,* edited by John N. Duvall and Ann J. Abadie, pp. 19–38. Jackson: University Press of Mississippi, 2002.

Wilcox, Johnnie. "Black Power: Minstrelsy and Electricity in Ralph Ellison's *Invisible Man.*" *Callaloo* 30, no. 4 (Fall 2007): 987–1009.

Acknowledgments

"Tod Clifton: Spiritual and Carnal" by Alan Nadel. From *Invisible Criticism: Ralph Ellison and the American Canon.* ©1988 by the University of Iowa. Reprinted by permission.

"Race Man, Organization Man, *Invisible Man*" by Andrew Hoberek. From *Modern Language Quarterly* 59, no. 1 (March 1998): 99–119. ©1998 by University of Washington. Reprinted by permission of the publisher, Duke University Press.

"Ralph Ellison, Race, and American Culture" by Morris Dickstein. From *Raritan* 18, no. 4 (Spring 1999): 30–50. ©1999 by Raritan. Reprinted by permission.

"Saying Yes and Saying No: Individualist Ethics in Ellison, Burke, and Emerson" by James M. Albrecht. From *Publications of the Modern Language Association of America* 114, no. 1 (January 1999): 46–63. ©1999 by the Modern Language Association of America. Reprinted by permission of the Modern Language Association of America.

"Listening to the Blues: Ralph Ellison's Trueblood Episode in *Invisible Man*" by Bertram D. Ashe. From *From Within Frame: Storytelling in African-American Fiction.* ©2002 by Routledge.

"The Invisible Man in Ralph Ellison's *Invisible Man*" by H. William Rice. From *Ralph Ellison and the Politics of the Novel.* ©2003 by Lexington Books. Reprinted by permission.

"Eloquence and *Invisible Man*" by Christopher Hanlon. From *College Literature* 32, no. 4 (Fall 2005): 74–98. ©2005 by *College Literature*. Reprinted by permission.

"Keep on Moving Don't Stop: *Invisible Man*" by Valerie Sweeney Prince. From *Burnin' Down the House: Home in African American Literature*. ©2005 by Columbia University Press. Reprinted by permission of the publisher.

"Secular Riffs on the Sacred: Ralph Ellison's Mock-Messianic Discourse in *Invisible Man*" by Tuire Valkeakari. From *Religious Idiom and the African American Novel*, 1952–1998. ©2007 by Tuire Valkeakari. Reprinted by permission of the University Press of Florida.

"The Unity of Experience" by Robert Penn Warren. From *Commentary* (May 1965): pp.91-96. © Robert Penn Warren. Reprinted by permission.

"Ralph Ellison's 'Flying Home'" by Joseph F. Trimmer. From *Studies in Short Fiction* 9.2 (Spring 1972): pp.175-182. © Newberry College. Reprinted by permission.

"America, Race, and Ralph Ellison" by Sanford Pinsker. From *Sewanee Review*, Vol. 108, Issue 2 (Spring 2000) © University of the South. Reprinted by permission.

Every effort has been made to contact the owners of copyrighted material and secure copyright permission. Articles appearing in this volume generally appear much as they did in their original publication with few or no editorial changes. In some cases, foreign language text has been removed from the original essay. Those interested in locating the original source will find the information cited above.

Index

Characters in literary works are indexed by first name (if any), followed by the name of the work in parentheses.